# The Struggle for Student Rights

LANDMARK LAW CASES

&

AMERICAN SOCIETY

Peter Charles Hoffer
N. E. H. Hull
*Series Editors*

JOHN W. JOHNSON

# The Struggle for Student Rights

*Tinker v. Des Moines* and the 1960s

UNIVERSITY PRESS OF KANSAS

© 1997 by the University Press of Kansas
All rights reserved

Published by the University Press of Kansas (Lawrence, Kansas 66049), which was organized by the Kansas Board of Regents and is operated and funded by Emporia State University, Fort Hays State University, Kansas State University, Pittsburg State University, the University of Kansas, and Wichita State University

Library of Congress Cataloging-in-Publication Data
Johnson, John W., 1946–
The struggle for student rights : Tinker v. Des Moines and the
1960s / John W. Johnson.
p.   cm. — (Landmark law cases & American society)
Includes bibliographical references and index.
ISBN 0-7006-0866-4 (acid-free paper). — ISBN 0-7006-0867-2 (pbk. : acid-free paper)
1. Tinker, John Frederick—Trials, litigation, etc.   2. Des Moines Independent Community School District—Trials, litigation, etc.
3. Freedom of speech—United States.   4. Students—Legal status, laws, etc.—United States.   5. Vietnamese Conflict, 1961–1975—Protest movements—Iowa—Des Moines.   I. Title.   II. Series.
KF228.T56J64   1997
342.73'085—dc21      97-19621

British Library Cataloguing in Publication Data is available.

Printed in the United States of America

10 9 8 7 6 5 4 3 2

The paper used in this publication meets the minimum requirements of the American National Standard for Permanence of Paper for Printed Library Materials Z39.48-1984.

FOR CHARLOTTE

# CONTENTS

A black armband has long been a symbol of protest or mourning in American history. Especially in the years since World War II, countless individuals have worn dark strips of cloth on their arms to express points of view on such disparate subjects as racial justice, political prisoners abroad, police behavior, women's rights, environmentalism, and, of course, military policy. This book offers an account of the 1965–69 legal clash between a handful of secondary-school students and a metropolitan Iowa school district over the right to wear black armbands on school property to symbolically express concerns about the war in Vietnam. Compared to the stirring civil rights protests in the South during the 1950s and 1960s and the violent antiwar protests on many college campuses between 1964 and 1972, the "armband case"—as it was called in Iowa—seems rather tame. And in many ways it was.

The three students who assumed the role of the named plaintiffs in the armband case were well-scrubbed, thoughtful kids attending public schools in Des Moines, Iowa—hardly a hotbed of protest activity in the 1960s. Before the events related here took place, none of their teachers or school officials would have characterized the three teenagers as troublemakers. Even after the students defied the school administrators' order not to wear armbands to school, the confrontations that occurred were peaceful—although the rhetoric was occasionally hot.

After an initial flurry of activity involving protests, suspensions, and school board meetings in December 1965 and January 1966, the dispute faded from sight. It only occasionally surfaced over the next three years in press reports of legal activity in the federal courts. The final Supreme Court decision in the armband case, *Tinker v. Des Moines Independent Community School District* (*Tinker*), was announced in February 1969. In upholding the Iowa students' right to wear armbands to class, the Court's decision furnished legal justification for a broad range of protests in the high schools and colleges. The *Tinker* decision provided an important step forward for student rights and, at the same time, became one of the landmarks in the American history of freedom of expression. The antiwar movement, which was at flood tide by 1969, was reinforced by the *Tinker* ruling. Thus the quiet undertaking of three young people in a medium-sized city in middle America to be able to wear black fragments of cloth to school had far-reaching consequences.

The legal ruling rendered by Justice Abe Fortas's majority opinion in the *Tinker* case is well known to constitutional lawyers and students of American civil liberties. As with most important court cases, however, a fascinating array of personal detail is not familiar to legal scholars or general readers of newspapers. This book is an attempt to blend details and personalities with legal analysis. In addition, because court cases frequently offer convenient windows through which to observe revealing moments in a nation's overall history, a focus on one such episode in its historical context should be of interest to a wide range of readers on recent American topics. Finally, because a court case has a fairly clear beginning and end, it presents the opportunity for a historian with a preference for narrative history to tell a good story.

# ACKNOWLEDGMENTS

One of the pleasures of engaging in the research and writing of a book such as this is that it presents an author with the opportunity to seek information, advice, and assistance from a myriad of interesting people. Although only an author's name is on the title page, many individuals operate behind the scenes to make it possible for a book finally to appear. I am delighted to have the opportunity here to express my appreciation, inadequate as it may be, for all the help I have received on this project.

My first exposure to the merits of developing detailed case studies of leading U.S. legal disputes came a quarter century ago in graduate history seminars of the late Paul Murphy at the University of Minnesota. After publishing essentially thematic pieces in the 1970s and early 1980s, I finally had the courage to try my hand at a book-length study of a major court case: *Insuring Against Disaster: The Nuclear Industry on Trial* (Macon, GA: Mercer University Press, 1986). The chapters that follow represent my second foray into the Murphy-inspired case study genre.

Any legal case study—even one of historic significance—is, at bottom, the story of individual people. If any of those people are living, it is most beneficial to have their cooperation in writing their story. I had the good fortune to be able to conduct lengthy interviews with many of the leading participants in this Iowa civil liberties controversy as well as a few other Iowans with knowledge of the subject. These individuals are mentioned in numerous places in the chapters that follow and in the Bibliographical Essay at the end of the book. The candid interviews and the files the interviewees shared with me give this study a richness that could not be obtained from the mere "official record" of *Tinker v. Des Moines*. I thank the interviewees for permission to quote from their interviews and to draw from their personal files on the case.

In obtaining records and research materials I was given kind assistance by the following individuals: Cryss Farley of the Iowa Civil Liberties Union; Gerald Peterson of Special Collections in the University of Northern Iowa's Rod Library; George Kampling of the U.S. District Court for the Southern District of Iowa; and David Wigdor of the Manuscript Division of the Library of Congress. I also owe a debt of thanks to Bob Neymeyer, a friend and fellow student of Iowa history, for his help in locating and securing the cooperation of several interviewees.

My colleagues in the Department of History at the University of Northern Iowa (UNI)—whom I am also privileged to have as friends—listened patiently when I talked about this project and, when asked, offered useful advice. I particularly want to thank the following UNI historians: Bob Martin, Chuck Quirk, Tom Ryan, Don Shepardson, and David Walker. Aaron Podolefsky, a well-published anthropologist and creative academic administrator, has been a consistent supporter of my research and writing in his role as dean of the College of Social and Behavioral Sciences at UNI. Scholars from other institutions who provided welcome advice when called upon were Kermit Hall, Mel Urofsky, John Wunder, Linda Kerber, Bill Buss, and the late Joseph Wall.

I was fortunate to have received financial and in-kind support from the University of Northern Iowa at various stages of this project. A UNI "professional development leave" during the first half of 1994 allowed me release-time from teaching and administrative obligations to do a substantial portion of the research on the armband dispute. In addition, two project grants from UNI's Graduate College were also helpful in defraying various research expenses. Several graduate students in the masters program in history at UNI served as research assistants at different stages of this project. Particularly helpful were Sonia Ingles, for her careful transcription of taped interviews and her work on my behalf at the Library of Congress; and Matt Simm, for his research on the events of the 1960s. Vickie Hanson, one of the UNI History Department's fine secretaries, did an excellent job in formatting my computer text and producing handsome copies of the manuscript.

Michael Briggs, editor-in-chief of the University Press of Kansas, provided consistent support, encouragement, and the occasional kick in the pants that authors require from their publishers. I am also indebted to Peter Hoffer, one of Kansas's academic editors for the "Landmark Law Cases and American Society" series, for his trenchant critique of the penultimate draft of my manuscript.

None of these individuals or organizations, of course, can be assigned criticism for any of this book's errors, omissions, or dubious

{ *The Struggle for Student Rights* }

conclusions. As the sole author I must bear and accept the sole responsibility for the book's shortcomings.

My personal debts to friends and family are enormous. First of all, I want to thank Dick Broadie, Bob Sherwood, Lee Luther, Larry Hamilton, and Murray Austin for accompanying me in occasional rounds of golf, thus providing valuable stress-relief from this project and various job-related duties. Secondly, I owe a heavy measure of heartfelt appreciation to my children—Matt, Noah, Barb, Steve, and Chris—for their support and understanding during my time at work on this book.

My greatest personal obligation, however, is to my wife, Charlotte Annie Mull. About the time I began work on this book, Charlotte entered my life. She has enriched it in countless ways since. This book is lovingly dedicated to her.

# CHAPTER I

# Three Iowa Kids

## Genesis of a Gentle Protest

The front page of virtually every newspaper in late 1965 carried at least one story about the Vietnam War. News magazines led their national and international sections with weekly accounts of developments in Vietnam. Television news programs broadcast battle footage in living color and graphic detail. Although President Lyndon Johnson's administration did not yet characterize the fighting in Southeast Asia as a "war," few reporters or critics of presidential policy were as circumspect. The week ending on November 6 brought the highest death toll since the United States had entered the fight four years earlier. During that same week the official American total of soldiers lost to combat in Vietnam passed 1000. By the end of 1965 there would be about 170,000 U.S. soldiers stationed in Vietnam. Clearly this conflict had become a full-fledged war, regardless of the official nomenclature.

In November 1965 about 140 anti–Vietnam War groups staged a "march on Washington," which drew an estimated twenty-five thousand participants. After arriving on the mall, the marchers settled down and listened patiently to speeches near the Washington Monument. This was one of the first of many large-scale protests in the nation's capital during the course of the Vietnam War, but it was hardly the first march on Washington. Throughout American history, Washington has been the destination for various gatherings of protesters. "Coxey's Army" of unemployed industrial workers brought its "petition in boots" to the nation's capital in 1894. World War I veterans journeyed to Washington in 1932 as part of the "Bonus March" to appeal for early payment of promised war pensions. Martin Luther King Jr. led a massive civil rights march on Washington in 1963 that featured his well-remembered "I Have a Dream" speech. And in the fall of 1995, the "Million Man March," inspired by the powerful but inflammatory rhetoric of Louis Farrakhan, took place.

Coordinated by the National Committee for a Sane Nuclear Policy (SANE), the November 1965 march on Washington comprised not so much the vocal draft-card-burning "peaceniks" who were beginning to make news as what *Time* termed "older, quieter protesters." Speakers at the rally urged the United States to make a good-faith effort to settle the war by bringing home some of the American soldiers in South Vietnam and by halting the bombing of North Vietnam. Rather than strident student leaders, the featured speakers at the 1965 antiwar march were Coretta Scott King; long-time Socialist Party standard-bearer Norman Thomas; and the well-known "baby doctor," Benjamin Spock. Compared to the vitriol that would be dispensed by critics of the war later in the 1960s, the fall 1965 protests were almost polite. Typical signs displayed such tepid statements as "War erodes the Great Society" and "Supervised Cease Fire." Several hundred protest "monitors" encouraged the more radical attendees to keep signs hidden that called for American surrender or withdrawal. One of the themes emerging from discussion at the march—an idea being touted by Senator Robert F. Kennedy (Democrat, New York)—was the call for an extension of the planned Christmas truce to allow time for peace negotiations.

Among the thousands attending the march was a small group of Iowans, perhaps no more than fifty. The Iowa contingent included two teenage boys whose beliefs and actions, partly inspired by this march, would eventually lead to a major U.S. Supreme Court decision on freedom of speech and student rights. The teenagers were Christopher Eckhardt and John Tinker. John's sister, Mary Beth Tinker, did not attend the march on Washington, but she would become the third named plaintiff in the case. All three attended Des Moines secondary schools. Christopher Eckhardt was then fifteen and a sophomore at Theodore Roosevelt High School. He was the son of Dr. William Eckhardt, a Des Moines clinical psychologist, and Margaret Eckhardt, then president of the Des Moines chapter of the Women's International League for Peace and Freedom. John was fifteen and a sophomore at North High School; his sister Mary Beth was a thirteen-year-old eighth-grade student at Warren Harding Junior High School. Their parents were the Reverend Leonard Tinker, a Methodist minister who at the time of the armband case was serving as a "peace education secretary" for the American Friends Service Committee (AFSC), and Lorena Jeanne Tinker, who was (and still is) involved in countless liberal causes.

When interviewed in the mid-1990s, the boys and their mothers recalled the energizing effect that the 1965 march on Washington had on the students' commitment to wear the armbands to school to express publicly their strong feelings about the Vietnam War. Two buses, arranged for by the AFSC, the Women's International League for Peace and Freedom, and a number of Iowa peace groups, made the round-trip to Washington for the march. Christopher Eckhardt, John Tinker, and their mothers were on one of the buses. Also on the buses were students from several Iowa colleges and universities, including a few members of a group called Students for a Democratic Society (SDS).

On the trip back home, the passengers on the buses discussed what should be done in Iowa to express their profound disagreement with the war in Vietnam. An Iowa antiwar protest involving black armbands was apparently first suggested at this time, but there is no consensus as to whose idea it was. John Tinker recalls that the idea came from a man with the unlikely name of Herbert Hoover. Hoover was the namesake and eighth cousin of the former U.S. president; he was also a member of the Des Moines Valley Friends, the Quaker meeting that John and his parents regularly attended. Critics of the armband demonstration later alleged that the idea for wearing the black armbands was first raised by a member of SDS. In any case, those who wanted to do something in the way of a symbolic statement against the war agreed to meet at the Eckhardts' home in Des Moines in early December to consider future action.

The meeting was held as planned at the Eckhardts' home on Saturday, December 11, 1965. Margaret Eckhardt remembers twenty-five to thirty people in attendance, including adults as well as high-school and college students. Lorena Tinker described the attendees as members of the small Iowa "peace community" of the mid-1960s. Several were members of a youth organization called Liberal Religious Youth (LRY), associated with the First Unitarian Church of Des Moines. Christopher Eckhardt remembers the meeting lasting several hours, during which time he drifted in and out in order to shovel the snow that had recently fallen.

At some point during the afternoon discussion, a consensus of the group emerged: on Thursday, December 16, the public-school and college students would begin wearing black armbands to classes. Among those interviewed who attended the meeting, all agreed that the wearing of the armbands had two purposes: to mourn all the casualties of the Vietnam War, Southeast Asian as well as American; and to support Senator Robert Kennedy's call for an extension of the anticipated Christmas 1965 truce, which it was hoped would lead to a negotiated end to the war. The three named plaintiffs all emphasized that the first symbolic purpose—mourning the Vietnamese and U.S. casualties of the war—was as important as the call for a truce. The members of the group at the Eckhardts' that weekend agreed that each individual student would decide whether to wear an armband to school; there would be no "party line." The attendees also agreed that it would be a good idea to conduct a fast at some point around the end of the calendar year for the same reasons that the armbands were contemplated.

Leonard Tinker, who came in at the end of the meeting on December 11 to drive his wife home, later stated that there were actually two meetings in which strategy for the wearing of armbands was discussed at the Eckhardt home during the weekend of December 11 and 12, 1965—one on Saturday and one on Sunday. At the Saturday meeting, he maintained, there were mainly adults and college students; those attending the Sunday meeting were generally high-school students who were members of the Unitarian LYR. Others, however, who recall that weekend—John, Mary Beth, and Lorena Tinker, as well as Christopher and Margaret Eckhardt—remember only a single meeting. In addition, the contemporaneous news accounts and later legal materials point to only a single meeting. Regardless of the number of meetings, participants unanimously agree that it was on this weekend that the armband demonstration was planned.

Among the college students attending the December 11 meeting were some members of a local chapter or chapters of SDS, a group that later in the decade became identified with many radical causes. How prominent a role these SDS members played in encouraging the handful of Des Moines secondary-school students to wear armbands to class in mid-December 1965 is, after all these years, not clear. In July 1966 Leonard Tinker recalled that the proposal to wear armbands materialized without a single clear source from the meeting that Saturday.

This group included a few self-described SDS members, but, as he then emphasized, that did not make the decision of his children and others to wear an armband "an SDS proposal." None of the Des Moines secondary-school students who ultimately wore armbands to school were members of SDS, nor were they directed or organized by SDS.

One of the young people attending the December 11 meeting was Ross Peterson, a classmate of Christopher Eckhardt's at Roosevelt and a fellow member of the Unitarian LRY. After the meeting in the Eckhardt home Ross prepared an article for the Roosevelt High School student newspaper, announcing several students' intention to begin wearing black armbands to school on Thursday, December 16, and continue wearing them until the U.S. government acceded to Robert Kennedy's call for a negotiating truce. The article was titled "WE MOURN/ATTENTION STUDENTS!" The complete text reads as follows:

> Some students who are interested in expressing their grief over the deaths of soldiers and civilians in Vietnam will fast on Thursday, December 16th. They will also wear black arm bands starting on that same day. The National Liberation Front (Vietcong) recently proposed a 12-hour truce on Christmas Eve. The United States has not yet replied to their offer. However, Senator Robert Kennedy has suggested that the truce be extended indefinitely pending negotiations. If the United States takes this action, the arm bands will be removed. If it does not, the bands will be worn throughout the holiday season and there will be a second fast on New Year's Day. Students are also encouraged to forgo their usual New Year's Eve activities and meet together to discuss this complex war and possible ways of ending the killing of Vietnamese and Americans. All students interested in saving lives and ending the war in Vietnam are urged to attend.

------

## School Administrators Respond

Ross Peterson showed his draft article to his journalism teacher and newspaper advisor, Donald Haley. The journalism teacher, presumably concerned that there might be problems if students wore black armbands to school, suggested that Ross talk with the principal, Charley Rowley, before he would sanction the publication of the article. Not being able to find Rowley, Ross called Paul Mitchum, the assistant superintendent of the Des Moines schools. On December 13 E. Raymond Peterson, the director of secondary education in the Des Moines schools (and no relation to Ross Peterson), and Rowley spoke with Ross about his draft article. They had what Raymond Peterson characterized as "a very friendly conversation," in which they informed Ross that they would not allow the article to be published. Raymond Peterson acknowledged later that "we did not feel that we had convinced the student that our decision was a just one." In spite of the lack of mention of the armband demonstration in the Roosevelt student paper, word about the armbands circulated around the Des Moines schools, and numerous students considered taking part in the protest.

On Tuesday, December 14, at the direction of Dwight Davis, the superintendent of the Des Moines schools, the principals of five Des Moines senior high schools and E. Raymond Peterson held a hastily called meeting to consider how to deal with the impending protest. Their recommendation, to ban armbands in the secondary schools, was forwarded orally by Peterson to the school district's central office. Peterson would write in a December 29 memorandum to Davis that word of the ban on armbands was "apparently" leaked to the press by a student. The press contacted central administration for comment. Initially school administrators were unwilling to comment, and Peterson's memo notes that "the reporter was asked not to write a story."

The reporter, Jack Magarrell, would not be dissuaded. His short article on the armband prohibition was featured in a brief front-page story in the *Des Moines Register* the following morning—Wednesday, December 15, 1965. Peterson was the only administrator quoted in the article. Peterson maintained that the wearing of black armbands in support of a truce in the Vietnam War would fly in the face of a "general school policy against 'anything that . . . [presents] a disturbing situation within the school.'" "For the good of the school system," Peterson said, "we don't think this should be permitted." Peterson acknowledged that controversial issues could be discussed in class but maintained that "schools are no place for demonstrations." In addition, he chided the students pressing for the right to wear the armbands by saying that they were only interested in publicity. Peterson would later testify in court

{ *The Struggle for Student Rights* }

that the meeting of the five senior high principals on December 14 had come to the same conclusion on the armbands that the school district's central officials—the superintendent, the assistant superintendent, and Peterson himself—had already reached on December 13. Essentially, then, the principals' meeting just rubber-stamped the decision already made by the school district's central administration.

## Second Thoughts?

One high-school student recalls an apparent double standard that emerged from the so-called school district policy against disruptions: "What a joke! Only last year we were all asked to wear black armbands to mourn the loss of school spirit at basketball games. Even a black coffin was marched through the halls! Nobody was afraid of that disrupting the educational process." Mary Beth Tinker also remembers that homecoming buttons, election buttons, and even Iron Crosses were worn without incident from time to time in her school prior to December 1965.

In the wake of the school district's prohibition of armbands and the morning article in the *Register*, Wednesday, December 15 was not exactly a normal day in the Des Moines Independent School District. Mary Beth remembers her math teacher, Richard K. Moberly, spending almost the whole class period talking about student protests. She recalls that he threatened to kick anyone out of his class who protested. She asked him if wearing a black armband would be considered a protest. He responded with an unequivocal "Yes." Also during the day, an announcement was broadcast over the loudspeakers at Roosevelt High School and several other Des Moines secondary schools underlining the administrative decision reported in the morning papers: no black armbands would be permitted. Neither this announcement nor the newspaper story indicated what would be the consequences for students in violation of the policy, but most assumed that it would involve some form of suspension.

There was also the possibility of physical violence. Christopher Eckhardt recalls that the gym teachers at Roosevelt were extremely upset with the possibility of a protest against the war. So, Eckhardt remembers, on December 15, instead of conducting calisthenics to the chant of "Beat East High" or "Beat North High," the gym teachers—especially the coaches—encouraged the students to substitute the phrase "Beat the Vietcong." The football coach, Donald Prior, maintained that the chant "Beat the Vietcong" sprang from the students themselves as a form of "spontaneous combustion." Prior indicated, however, that he saw no reason to stop the chanting because the boys were just "proving their Americanism." Eckhardt argues that the coaches at Roosevelt also made it known that students wearing armbands to class were Communist sympathizers and that they could not be responsible for what might happen to those who demonstrate such a "lack of patriotism." After his gym period, Eckhardt and a friend were confronted by a group of angry students, who threatened them with physical harm if they wore armbands on Thursday: "If you [wear armbands] . . . you'll find our fists in your face and our foot up your ass."

Wednesday evening several of the students who had previously announced their intention to wear armbands met to consider what to do in light of the announced resistance to their contemplated action by the school district administration, as well as by many teachers and fellow students. Some of the students were willing to comply with the newly announced policy. Some were not. When the meeting disbanded it was uncertain how many of the students would elect to defy the district order by wearing armbands to classes the following morning. William Eckhardt recalls Christopher justifying his decision to wear an armband the next day by posing a rhetorical question: "Eichmann only followed orders, didn't he?"

---

## What's in a Name?

Estimates vary as to how many students defied the Des Moines school district administration and wore black armbands to class on December 16 and 17, 1965. The number sixty-six sticks in Christopher Eckhardt's mind. John and Mary Beth Tinker remember the figure as being somewhat smaller, perhaps a couple of dozen. Whatever the number, attention focused on Christopher Eckhardt, John Tinker, and Mary Beth Tinker. These three (along with their fathers as "next friends") would agree to be the named plaintiffs to the suit to test the constitutionality of the school district's ban on armbands. Lawyers approached other students and their parents to become plaintiffs. Ultimately, however, only Christopher Eckhardt, John and Mary Beth Tinker, and their parents agreed to lend their names to the case. The Eckhardts and the Tinkers, already well known in Des Moines for their social activism, were the obvious choices for official plaintiff status in this litigation.

Most stories about the armband case that have appeared in the last thirty years in the press or law journals have focused attention on John or Mary Beth Tinker, not Christopher Eckhardt. There were two Tinkers and one Eckhardt involved in the case, so by a preponderance of surnames the case was officially titled *Tinker v. Des Moines Independent Community School District,* not *Eckhardt v. Des Moines Independent School Community District.* At least that is how Dan Johnston, the Iowa Civil Liberties Union (ICLU) attorney who eventually represented Christopher Eckhardt and the Tinkers in court, explained the nomenclature.

Once the armband dispute officially became the "*Tinker* case," attention flowed toward John and Mary Beth rather than Christopher Eckhardt. The name Tinker was easier to pronounce and spell than Eckhardt, and it lent itself easily to various plays on words (e.g., "Tinkering with Tinker"). Moreover, the Tinker brother-and-sister combination made this a warmhearted family story, further enhanced by the fact that John and Mary Beth's younger siblings, Hope and Paul (elementary-school students in 1965), also wore armbands to school. In addition, Mary Beth was the most photographed of the three plaintiffs. Finally, because the Tinker last name was the one that most people familiar with the case knew about, it was John and Mary Beth who, in later years, were asked to make appearances, accept awards, and talk about the case to sympathetic audiences—not Christopher Eckhardt. These considerations reinforced the name Tinker in the public mind and obscured the name Eckhardt. Partly to redress the balance, Christopher Eckhardt will be profiled first in this retelling of the armband story.

## Christopher Eckhardt

Christopher Eckhardt was fifteen and a sophomore at Des Moines's Theodore Roosevelt High School in 1965–66. At the time of the armband case, Christopher's father was a clinical psychologist and a faculty member at the College of Osteopathic Medicine and Surgery in Des Moines. His mother was the Des Moines chapter president of the Women's International League for Peace and Freedom. His parents were active in the 1960s in the same small Des Moines "peace community" that included Leonard and Lorena Tinker. Through their activities and support for liberal causes, the Eckhardt and Tinker families became well acquainted.

Christopher, as was the case with the Tinker children, was exposed to liberal politics throughout his formative years. His mother recalls Christopher as a young boy attending speeches and meetings with various civil rights advocates whom she brought to Des Moines in her capacity as an officer for the Women's International League for Peace and Freedom. Included among the visitors whom Christopher met were black Georgia politician Julian Bond and John Howard Griffin, the author of *Black Like Me*. Christopher had also accompanied his parents on a number of civil rights marches in the middle 1960s. At the November 1965 antiwar March on Washington he carried a sign that read "Follow the Geneva Courts of 1954." At Roosevelt he helped form what he describes as a "political action discussion group," which brought public figures to school to talk with interested students.

Liberal politics dovetailed with liberal religion for Christopher and his parents. Prior to coming to Iowa, William and Margaret Eckhardt had participated in several different religious groups. For example, they had attended Quaker meetings in North Carolina. In Des Moines, in the mid-1960s, they attended the First Unitarian Church. Christopher was an active member of the LRY arm of the Unitarian Church and later vice president of the Unitarian Youth League. Des Moines LRY members included John Tinker and others who shared Christopher's antiwar sentiments and later came to don black armbands in defiance of school district admonitions.

As a high-school student Christopher was a busy young man. He maintained about a B-plus academic average and was an elected representative to student government. He had previously been the president of two separate school student councils. He was a member of the track team, had won fishing and weight-lifting trophies, and would later be voted "most likely to succeed" in his senior class. He also was voted the student with the cleanest locker. Outside of school he was a Boy Scout and a youth leader at church and had a paper route and a lawn-mowing/snow-shoveling business. His mother describes him as out-going and friendly—and very helpful at home. Dan Johnston, the ICLU attorney who argued the armband case, describes Christopher as a "regular kid."

Young Christopher, however, had a puckish side. During his Roosevelt High years he was a member of what he describes as a social club of about thirty male students called the "All Center Bums." They hung out together after school and on weekends in an apartment they rented in downtown Des Moines. At school assemblies they had their own seating section of the auditorium, where they ritually refused to cheer for the athletic teams or rise to sing the national anthem. Christopher whimsically characterizes the All Center Bums as Des Moines's version of Hell's Angels. At one point in his high-school career (after the district court trial in the armband case), Christopher was denied the opportunity to run for an office in student government because of his membership in the All Center Bums. So he complained to Arthur Davis, a member of the school board who had been sympathetic to the Eckhardts and the Tinkers in the armband dispute. This complaint landed him in the principal's office, where he was confronted by an angry principal and an even angrier representative from the school district office. Christopher listened to some of what they had to say, got mad, and stood up to leave. At that point, he recalls, the school district representative "knocked me back down in the chair and told me I would sit there and I would listen to him and threatened me and told me never to call . . . Arthur Davis again or disturb people again."

---

## John Tinker

Like Christopher Eckhardt, John Tinker was fifteen at the time the armband controversy began. John and his family lived in a working-class area of Des Moines, about seven and one-half miles from the Eckhardts. John attended North High School, not the larger and more affluent Roosevelt High that Christopher attended.

Dan Johnston, the ICLU lawyer, describes John as "ethereal . . . shy and Quakerlike in his personality." As evidence of this, John's mother reports that throughout his childhood John refused to fight with other children. He would not attempt to defend himself or even run away; he would just stand in one place and let angry kids hit him. After one occasion in which he refused to fight, John told his mother, "Mom, I can't stand to see anybody hurt, and I thought if I stood there, maybe he'd change and we could be friends." John was a good young musician, playing the sousaphone in the school band and the violin in the orchestra. He eschewed competitive sports. He did not make top grades, but he demonstrated considerable academic talent on more than one occasion. Lorena Tinker remembers that one year John turned in a science paper so good that the teacher thought his parents had written it.

John's father, Leonard Tinker, was an ordained Methodist minister. But a few years before the armband controversy Leonard Tinker had accepted an appointment as a representative of the AFSC; he continued to work for the AFSC in Iowa, Missouri, and Ohio until his death in 1978. In order to take on this position he was granted a leave of absence from the Methodist Conference. So, although he worked for the Friends in the 1960s and 1970s, he still kept his doctrinal affiliation with the Methodists. John's mother, Lorena Jeanne Tinker, was active in a number of civil rights groups during the fifties and sixties. While the armband dispute was unfolding, she pursued graduate work in psychology at Iowa State University. She completed her Ph.D. in 1969, the same year as the Supreme Court decision in her children's case.

From 1953 to 1957 the Tinkers lived in the small western Iowa town of Atlantic, where Leonard Tinker served as a Methodist minister. The liberal politics espoused by the Tinkers eventually prompted the Methodist bishop to ask them to leave Atlantic. The precipitating event was the Tinkers' public endorsement of the town's one black family's right to use the city swimming pool. In addition, the Tinkers' stature in town was not enhanced by Leonard's being labeled a "pinko" in a McCarthyite brochure that circulated throughout that part of the state.

So the Tinkers were "called" by the Methodist Church to Des Moines. Leonard Tinker's principal duty in his new posting was to lead the fund-raising campaign for a Methodist church building. He was successful, and the Epworth Methodist Church was completed in the early 1960s. During their first five years in Des Moines, the Tinkers continued their support of civil rights and other liberal causes. Once again, however, tension over racial matters caused the Tinkers problems with their congregation. Lorena Tinker was criticized for inviting a black public official to speak to her young-adult class in the parsonage. In addition, when she encouraged other members of this black family to become active in the church, several people in the congregation were upset and complained that "the preacher's wife [was] flaunting this whole race thing." John not only believed in his parents' racial principles, he lived them. For his entire ninth-grade year John took a bus across town to attend school in a more racially mixed area of the city. There he occasionally spent the night with the same black family whom the Tinkers had welcomed into their Methodist church.

The Tinkers and their children were also active in the anti–Vietnam War movement. Leonard Tinker was a devout pacifist who had received a clerical exemption in World War II. When he visited Japan in the 1950s he was horrified by the devastation caused by the two atomic bombs. So when John and his mother went to the November 1965 anti–Vietnam War march in Washington, they were following in a family tradition. As John put it, "Our family was surrounded by the antiwar movement . . . all of the kids were swept up by it."

John attended religious services with his family at the Des Moines Valley Friends Meeting. However, he was also a participant in the LRY arm of Des Moines's First Unitarian Church in 1965–66. In the LRY John, Christopher Eckhardt, and other socially conscious, liberal students discussed the issues of the day. Although allied in the armband case and sharing the same general passion for liberal politics, John and Christopher were not especially close friends. They attended different high schools and, as Eckhardt later recalled, "didn't hang in the same social group." While Eckhardt was in student government and occasionally functioned as a gadfly to the school administration, John was more quiet and introspective. Prior to December 1965 John had never been suspended. In fact John had never been in trouble in school until he put on his narrow black armband.

---

## Mary Beth Tinker

The youngest of the three named plaintiffs, Mary Elizabeth Tinker (generally called either Mary or Mary Beth), was thirteen and an eighth-grade student at Warren Harding Junior High School during the first year of the armband controversy. Although two years younger than Christopher Eckhardt and her brother John, Mary Beth has detailed memories of growing up in a family of social activists. She would testify at the district court trial in the armband case that she first became concerned about politics and peace issues in fourth grade and discussed them almost daily with her parents and siblings from that point on. She recalls that in fourth or fifth grade she wrote a report on the atomic bombing of Japan. The next year she wrote a paper on capital punishment. When asked to reminisce about what she enjoyed doing when she was thirteen, she mentions spending the night at the houses of her girl friends and talking into the wee hours of the morning. Like John she was interested in music, but more in singing than in playing instruments. Her mother remembers her as being popular in school and always making top grades.

The first demonstration Mary Beth remembers participating in concerned fair housing in Des Moines; she was only ten or eleven at the time. Another early memory of Mary Beth's was not understanding why the family had to leave their Methodist parsonage in 1962 when her father took up his assignment with the AFSC. Mary Beth fondly remembers taking trips with her father throughout the Midwest when he served in his capacity as a peace education secretary for the AFSC. She says that her father was like a traveling salesman, only he was selling ideas: "He was giving speeches about peace . . . China and Vietnam mostly. . . . We would go with him and be real proud to be in charge of the literature table." She also recalls her mother telling stories about her volunteering in the South in the early sixties. One story in particular that Mary Beth remembers her mother telling involved civil rights work in Mississippi in 1964. In the course of her activities Lorena Tinker visited the home of an elderly black woman. The woman told her not to sit too close to the window because of the danger of being shot. Then Lorena Tinker was shown a bullet hole near the window from the last time that someone tried to shoot at occupants of the house.

Friends and acquaintances—even Quakers—expressed concern that the Tinkers were starting out their children a bit young in social action. As Lorena Tinker remembers, "People would say to us, 'Why are you taking your children? . . . You're damaging your children or their future.' And we said, 'We don't think we're damaging them. We're committed to certain values, and we want our children to be part of it, and they would jump in the car and go with us willingly.'" John and

Mary Beth confirm their mother's statement. On this point Lorena Tinker tells a fascinating story involving a brief conversation she had with Dr. Martin Luther King Jr. King had been in Des Moines sometime in the mid-1960s to deliver a speech. After the speech he spoke with Lorena Tinker. As a fellow activist and parent, he expressed to her the fears he had about the safety of his children in light of the controversy that seemed to swirl around him. He asked her if, given her local notoriety, she ever worried about her own children's safety. She said, "Of course," and remembers then offering the opinion that if the cause was important enough, certain risks—even to one's own children—were unavoidable. King, she says, sadly agreed. Then he added that because he and his family were Christians they all believed that if they were killed they'd go to heaven. However, he admitted that that didn't keep his children from hiding under the kitchen table if they were scared.

The act of wearing black armbands to school in December 1965, particularly after being expressly forbidden to do so by school authorities, placed Christopher Eckhardt and the Tinker children—as later events would reveal—in some danger. The threat to the Iowa armband wearers was not, of course, on the magnitude of the violence used against civil rights volunteers in Mississippi two summers earlier. But what happened to these three Iowa students and some of their friends when they followed through on their vow to wear armbands still made civil liberties history.

# Two Days in December

## Theodore Roosevelt High School: Thursday Morning

Christopher Eckhardt and a friend were driven to Roosevelt High School on Thursday, December 16, 1965, by Christopher's father, Dr. William Eckhardt. William Eckhardt recalls that Christopher was "fearful and trembling" as he got out of the car. Under his winter coat, Christopher wore a cocoa brown sports jacket with a black armband, about one and one-fourth inches wide, pinned to one of his sleeves. Christopher had arranged to meet Bruce Clark in the school's front lobby that morning. Bruce, a member of the Unitarian LRY who shared many of Christopher's feelings about the war in Vietnam, had also talked about wearing an armband that day. The two of them planned to go to the principal's office before classes started and turn themselves in. As they saw it, they were engaging in an act of civil disobedience. They were intentionally breaking a rule that they believed to be unjust, and they were prepared to accept the punishment to test the rule's fairness and legality.

Christopher arrived at school about eight o'clock, went to his locker, and removed his winter coat. Now his armband became visible to others in the building. On his way to the school's front lobby to meet Bruce Clark, Christopher encountered a student who asked if he realized that there was a rule against wearing an armband. Christopher replied that he was aware of the rule and explained the reason he was breaking it. He recalls then being confronted by the captain of the football team, who attempted to rip the armband off his jacket. Christopher remembers telling this "big character . . . [who] later went on to play semipro football" to take his hands off him because he was on his way to the principal's office to turn himself in. The football player left Christopher with words to the effect that he had better take the armband off in the principal's office or he would come looking for him. As Christopher continued to walk to the principal's office he met Bruce Clark. Christopher remembers Bruce wearing a dark suit, not a black armband. Together they went into the administrative office suite and asked to see the principal, Dr. Charles Rowley. But they were told that they would be seeing Donald Blackman, vice principal of Roosevelt, instead. The two boys sat in Blackman's outer office for about forty-five minutes. While they waited, students they knew came by the glass-enclosed office and taunted them with such remarks as "You're dead."

Finally Blackman ushered Christopher into his office. Bruce had left by then, perhaps going back to class. Blackman asked which teacher had sent Christopher to the office. Christopher replied that no one had ordered him to report to the office; he said he had come voluntarily to turn himself in because he knew that by wearing a black armband he was violating the recently established school-district rule. Blackman asked whether any school official had ordered Christopher to remove the armband. He said, "No." So Blackman said, "Oh, well, I'm asking you at this time to remove your armband." Christopher refused to remove the armband and stated that he believed he had a constitutional right to wear it to school.

Christopher and Blackman talked for several more minutes. In spite of Blackman's repeated demands to remove the armband, Christopher refused. About this time Velma Cross, the girls' advisor at Roosevelt, came in. Blackman explained the situation to her, and she attempted to convince Christopher to remove the armband by saying that a suspension would look bad on his school record. She told him that he was "too young to have opinions" and that "colleges didn't accept protesters so if . . . [he] planned to go to college that . . . [he'd] better take it off." She also told him that if he was suspended he could look for another high school to attend because they didn't want him back at Roosevelt.

At about this point, Christopher recalls that Blackman told him that the "senior boys were not going to like what I was doing" and then he asked him if he "was looking for a busted nose." In retrospect, Christopher believes that the "busted nose" comment could have had a double or even a triple meaning. It could have been a threat that Blackman himself would hit Christopher; it could have been a prediction that fellow students might attack him once they found out about the armband incident; or it could simply have meant that a suspension would look like a broken nose on Christopher's school record. Whatever the meaning of this statement, Christopher felt intimidated and started to cry. Blackman talked to Christopher for several minutes, apparently attempting to find out his motivation for wearing the armband. Ultimately, however, he told Christopher that the point of the protest was not important. What was important was that Christopher was a student breaking a school rule and would be punished. He also agreed with Velma Cross's assertion that failure to take off the armband would lead to a suspension and place a blemish on Christopher's academic record.

When it became clear that Christopher was not going to follow the order to remove the armband, Blackman called Christopher's mother. Margaret Eckhardt was aware that Christopher had worn the armband that morning and that he intended to turn himself in before classes began. So she was expecting a call from the administration. Blackman told her that Christopher would be suspended if he did not remove the offending piece of cloth, and he tried to convince her to persuade her son to comply with his order. She responded, "I think he has every right to wear the armband, and I will not ask him to take it off." In reply Blackman said, "In that case, we'll have to suspend him." And Margaret Eckhardt said, "So be it." After hearing that Christopher would be suspended and sent home, Margaret Eckhardt called her older son, who lived not far from Roosevelt, and asked him to meet Christopher at school and make sure that he arrived home safely. Christopher and his brother reached home without incident, with Christopher carrying the suspension notice that Blackman had handed him.

In the following morning's *Des Moines Register,* Vice Principal Blackman was quoted as saying that Christopher Eckhardt was the only Roosevelt High School student—at least as far as he knew—who had worn a black armband on Thursday and that he was also the only high school student suspended in connection with this matter. Blackman also stated that there was "no commotion or disturbance at the school in conjunction with the arm band wearing." Although it didn't cause any "commotion or disturbance," Don Scales, a Roosevelt High sophomore in 1965–66, remembered an incident that occurred at the school on the same day that Christopher Eckhardt wore his armband. As he was walking into his fourth-period gym class, Scales noticed that two coaches, Al Comito and Donald Prior, were standing by the locker-room door—something they seldom did. He had the feeling they were checking to see if any students coming to their class were wearing armbands. Confirming his suspicion, as class began, Scales remembered Prior demanding to know if there were "any armband finks" in the group. Most, if not all, of the students yelled back, "No!" Then, according to Scales, the coaches told them to chant "Beat the Vietcong" as they performed calisthenics.

---

## Warren Harding Junior High School:
## Thursday Afternoon

Mary Beth Tinker decided after the meeting at the Eckhardts' home on Wednesday evening that she would wear an armband the next day to her eighth-grade classes at Harding Junior High. She would later testify at the district court trial that she was not encouraged to wear the armband by anyone else, even by her parents. Her mother confirms this, emphasizing that the Tinker children generally shared their parents' liberal beliefs but that she and her husband did not go out of their way to encourage them in any particular courses of action—including the wearing of armbands.

Mary Beth walked to school on the morning of December 16 with an armband on the sleeve of her sweater. Unlike Christopher Eckhardt, she did not go immediately to the principal's office to turn herself in for performing an act of civil disobedience. She just went to classes as usual. She remembers several students asking her the purpose of the armband during the morning. She explained that she was wearing it to mourn casualties of the war in Vietnam and to support a Christmas truce. None of the students with whom she spoke seemed upset or angry. Mary Beth had the impression that most of them just did not have strong feelings about the war. A few suggested that she might get in trouble if she didn't take it off. A couple of teachers looked at it closely but didn't say anything to her. During her science class late in the morning Mary Beth circulated a petition, ultimately signed by a handful of classmates, saying that students should have the right to wear armbands or crucifixes. At lunch she was teased by a table of boys, who jokingly said that they wanted black armbands for Christmas. In other words, the armband was noticed, but it probably caused no more disruption than an unusual piece of jewelry or article of clothing.

Her armband did not draw serious attention from anyone in an official capacity at Harding until Mary Beth's afternoon math class—the class in which the teacher had spent most of the period the previous day excoriating student protesters. Shortly after Mary Beth arrived in this class and seated herself, the math teacher, Richard Moberly, handed her a pass and told her to go immediately to the main office. Mary Beth picked up her books and went to the main office and asked to see the girls' advisor, Vera Tarmann. However, Tarmann wasn't there, so Mary Beth met instead with Leo E. Willadsen, the vice principal. He asked her why she had come to the office. School passes had a space to indicate the reason the student was being sent to the office, but this pass was blank. Mary Beth told him she wasn't sure but that she assumed it had to do with the fact that she was wearing a black armband. He told her to take it off and she could go back to class. So she complied. At the time she did not know, as she later put it, "about protesting and Supreme Court cases." After removing the armband she was allowed to return to class. A few minutes after she had settled back into math class, Vera Tarmann entered the classroom and informed the teacher that she needed to talk to Mary Beth Tinker in her office. So off Mary Beth went again to the office. In her office Tarmann told Mary Beth that she understood and respected her point of view because she herself had Quaker ancestors who had been pacifists. However, she said, Mary Beth had violated a school-district rule and she, in her capacity as a school-district employee, had no choice but to suspend her. So she handed Mary Beth the suspension notice and sent her home.

In the 1960s suspension notices in the Des Moines schools were mailed to parents. But, to avoid delays through the mails on this occasion—it was, after all, the Christmas season—Vera Tarmann sent the notice home with Mary Beth. Suspension notices provided a space for the parents' signatures before a suspended student could be reinstated. Suspension from the Des Moines schools carried with it grade penalties for work missed during the suspension and several hours of detention (supervised time spent after school). The story in the *Des Moines Register* the following morning noted that Mary Beth Tinker, a Harding eighth grader, had been sent home for wearing a black armband. The story quoted Chester Pratt, the Harding principal, saying that Mary Beth's armband had not caused any disruption but that "she was sent home in line with the ban on armbands announced earlier by school officials."

---

## The Eckhardt Home: Thursday Evening

In the wake of the suspensions of Christopher Eckhardt and Mary Beth Tinker earlier that day, Leonard Tinker called a meeting for that evening, to be held at William and Margaret Eckhardt's home. The purpose was to consider how to respond to the two suspensions and whether other students should begin wearing armbands and thus risk their own suspensions. About twenty-five people, mainly Des Moines secondary school students and their parents, attended the meeting. In contrast to the meeting the previous weekend, few college students attended on December 16. At the end of the meeting a person identified only as a "spokesman" for the attendees said that the group wished to go on record "express[ing] deep concern" that the two suspended students had been "deprived of an important opportunity to participate in this form of expression."

Prior to the evening meeting, one of the Roosevelt High School students active in the LRY—either Ross Peterson or Bruce Clark—phoned Ora Niffenegger, president of the board of the Des Moines Independent Community School District. The student appealed to Niffenegger to call an emergency meeting of the school board to discuss the right to wear armbands. Niffenegger informed his caller that the matter "wasn't important enough to require a special board meeting" and that the issue could be presented at the next regularly scheduled board meeting, Tuesday, December 21. At that time the students would have "the same right as anyone else to speak."

One of the reasons that most of the students at the meeting at the Eckhardt home wanted a special board meeting was that waiting even a few days for the December 21 regularly scheduled board meeting would push the issue too close to the Christmas holidays, scheduled to begin Thursday, December 23, to constitute a meaningful protest. If the board reversed the school principals' December 15 decision banning armbands, that would give protest-minded students only one school day to wear the armbands before the Christmas holiday. School Board President Niffenegger referred to the two suspensions as disciplinary measures to be handled by the schools. He said that he "fully supported the school administrators in the matter." As an individual, he said, he did not countenance the wearing of armbands because such action presented a "disturbing influence" that had no place in an educational institution. He also declared that American citizens should support the course of action that the country's leaders had established in Southeast Asia.

One of the students at the Thursday evening meeting at the Eckhardt home was John Tinker. Unlike his younger sister Mary Beth, John had decided not to wear a black armband to school on Thursday. Hence he was very interested in the discussion that took place that evening about whether additional students should wear armbands the next day and probably risk suspensions. John had elected not to wear an armband on the first day of the protest because he felt that the school administration should be given a chance to reverse the ban on armbands before any symbolic protest began. John did not want a confrontation with authority if there was any possibility of avoiding it. He wanted to talk over the varying views of the Vietnam War held by students and school administrators, with an eye toward working out differences. This squared with his Quaker philosophy. However, when Niffenegger told the students that it was a "trivial" matter and could be brought up, if the students really felt the need, at the next regularly scheduled school board meeting, that convinced John to wear an armband to school on Friday.

## North High School: Friday Morning

As usual, John Tinker was running late on Friday. He lived about fifteen blocks from North High and ended up dashing most of the way, arriving about half past seven. He had dressed in an uncharacteristically formal fashion: white shirt, tie, dark slacks, and a dark suit coat.

He was rushing so much that he did not have time to attach the black armband he had decided to wear. But he kept it in a pocket, planning to pin it to his sleeve when he had the time. He attended orchestra practice before school, and just slipped into his homeroom desk seconds before the bell rang to begin the school day. After his homeroom class he went into a boys' restroom and attempted to affix the armband. A friend from his homeroom saw that John was having difficulty pinning on the armband, so he assisted him. Together they eventually succeeded in getting the armband attached to his jacket.

John wore the armband to morning classes without much comment or incident. If his teachers saw it, they said nothing. During his first period drama class a few students asked him why he was wearing it, and he explained his reasons. He recalls feeling "kind of . . . self-conscious." Some students disagreed with his position on the war, but he recalls very few students challenging his right to wear the armband. There was no discussion of the armband in second-period math class.

John's last morning class was gym. Right before the gym period began a few of John's friends warned him that he might get in trouble if he didn't take off the armband. Near the end of that period, just after he had changed out of his gym uniform and was putting on his street clothes, it occurred to him that the reason that so few people had appeared to notice his armband was because it did not contrast sufficiently with his dark suit coat. Having realized that his armband's message was being obscured, John left off his suit coat and pinned the black strip of cloth to his white shirt.

In the boy's locker room after gym class he met with his first real hostility of the day. Some students, not close friends, made what John later described as "not . . . very friendly remarks" over a course of three or four minutes. After gym class he went to lunch. At lunch the armband was quite visible. Students reacted in various ways: some warned him that he was going to be suspended like his sister and the "kid from Roosevelt"; others made insulting remarks; and a few students even encouraged him. He also recalls that there was discussion around his lunch table about whether wearing the armband was right or wrong. John participated in the discussion. He would later testify in district court that he "welcomed questions at school" about the armband because one of his reasons for wearing it was to spark concern about the war.

In contrast to Christopher Eckhardt's threatening contacts with members of the football team over his black armband, John Tinker experienced support for his right to wear an armband from at least one football player at North High. While John was in the school cafeteria on Friday this member of the football team told the students who were harassing John over his armband to "just leave him alone." As he put it, "Everyone has a right to his own opinion."

About the time his lunch period ended, someone from the clerical staff in the main office noticed John's armband and carried the news to the administration that North High had an armband wearer. North High Principal Donald M. Wetter had previously advised his faculty and staff to refer to his office any student wearing a black armband. John Tinker turned out to be the only North High student sent to his office over this issue. To the best of his knowledge, no other North student displayed a black armband in December 1965.

As he walked into his first afternoon class, John's English teacher told him that he was wanted in the principal's office. Before he went to the office he made a quick phone call home. His father had told him to call home "if anything went wrong or I got in trouble." John remembers telling his father that he had been called to the principal's office and that he would probably be coming home soon. After hanging up the phone John went to the principal's office. John had previously had no problems with Principal Wetter; and on this day John's dealings with his high school administration were relatively non-confrontational. No one threatened him with a busted nose, and there was no talk about likely physical attacks from upper-class students. John describes Wetter as being critical of his position but "respectful of me."

Wetter noticed the black armband as soon as John walked into his office. He asked John if he was aware of the recently instituted policy on armbands. John indicated that he was. Then Wetter asked him to remove the armband and return to class. If he did not comply, John was told, his parents would be called to take him from school and he would not be allowed to return to classes until he removed the armband or the policy was changed. Wetter and John talked for a few minutes about what John was trying to accomplish by wearing the armband.

John said that he and others were wearing armbands to express their sympathy for the deaths and casualties in the Vietnam War and to declare their support for an extension of the Christmas truce. John recalls Wetter then relating some of his experiences in World War II and reminding him of the importance of patriotism. He said he understood John's desire to mourn those who died in combat, but he suggested that a more appropriate form of mourning would be for John to participate in a Veterans' Day or Memorial Day ceremony. In the context of this discussion, he advised John that he was making a "big mistake" by wearing an armband and that it would reflect badly on his record if he was disciplined for violating a school-district policy. John said that he would not take off the armband and that he was prepared to accept the consequences of this refusal.

Wetter asked John if he was going to inform the press of his being asked to leave school because of his armband. John remembers Wetter raising the point in the form more of a statement than a question: "Well, I suppose you're going to call the newspaper." John told Wetter he did not intend to do so. He also reminded Wetter that it was the school board, not the students or their parents, that had first alerted the press to the controversy earlier in the week by releasing its statement banning armbands.

Then Wetter asked John for his phone number and tried to call John's father. As he was hanging up after receiving no answer, his secretary informed him that Leonard Tinker had just arrived in the outer office. John's father came in and talked with the principal for several minutes. John stayed to hear the conversation. Wetter explained the substance of the school district's armband policy to John's father. He emphasized that, in light of the banning of armbands from school property, John would not be allowed to attend school so long as he insisted on wearing an armband. Unlike Christopher Eckhardt and John's sister, Mary Beth, John was not formally suspended. The principal told Leonard Tinker that John would be welcomed back to the school as long as he did not wear an armband. Moreover, Wetter indicated that John would suffer no adverse consequences in respect to his grades, and he said would do everything in his capacity as principal to protect John's personal safety in the face of any antagonism from other students at North. At that point John and his father left North High and went home.

## Other Venues: Thursday and Friday

The two youngest Tinker children, Hope and Paul, wore black armbands to their elementary school at the end of the crucial week in
December. Hope was eleven and in fifth grade; Paul was eight and in
first grade. They attended Des Moines's James Madison Elementary
School. Lorena Tinker remembers Hope coming down to breakfast that
Thursday or Friday with an armband (actually more of an "arm rib-
bon") on her sleeve. She recalls her husband saying, "Oh, Hope, not
you, too." Hope replied, "Dad, I grieve for those children in Vietnam.
Is it wrong for me to show that I'm grieving? Isn't that what a black
armband is all about?" Her father responded, "Okay, honey. But they're
going to say, 'There go the Tinkers again.'"

Actually the youngest Tinker children had fewer problems with their
elementary school over the armbands than did John and Mary Beth with
their secondary schools. For one thing, there was no official prohibition against armbands in the elementary schools. Lorena Tinker emphasizes that school officials "didn't dream that elementary kids would
wear them." In addition, the teachers in the elementary schools seemed
more willing to view the wearing of an armband as an occasion for learning rather than as a threat to school discipline. For example, when a
couple of the young boys in Hope's class said that she was unpatriotic
for wearing an armband, Mrs. Tinker recalls that the teacher, Linda
Ordway, said, "Hope is very patriotic. She has a cause to believe in,
and that's why she's wearing that armband." Paul had a similarly positive experience with his elementary teacher. On the first day he came
to school with an armband, his teacher spent about half an hour talking to his class about the purpose of freedom of expression.

Ironically, one man who remembers taunting Hope about her black
armband, as a boy in elementary school thirty years ago, is now a liberal activist and attorney in Waterloo, Iowa. Today Dan Holm, Hope's
former classmate at Madison Elementary School, occasionally in his
general practice defends the civil liberties and civil rights of clients
against the government. Holm remembers Hope as one of the most
intelligent and thoughtful of his elementary school friends. He also
applauds their teacher for smoothing over their differences and for
using Hope's armband as a vehicle for learning rather than a threat to

the school's routine. Lorena Tinker believes that the Des Moines elementary teachers, besides being creative educators, were not as afraid of professional consequences over the armband issue as were secondary-school teachers and administrators.

Ultimately, only five Des Moines secondary-school students were singled out for discipline for wearing armbands in December 1965: Christopher Eckhardt, John and Mary Beth Tinker, Roosevelt sophomore Christine Singer, and Roosevelt senior Bruce Clark.

By Friday the armband controversy had moved beyond the schools. Craig Sawyer, an assistant professor at Des Moines's Drake Law School, announced that, at the request of the ICLU, he would represent the suspended students at the hearing before the school board the following week. Sawyer's involvement arose from the Tinkers' and Eckhardts' request to the ICLU to look into the legality of the school district's prohibition on armbands.

In conjunction with Craig Sawyer's announcement, the ICLU board of directors issued the following statement:

> In connection with the present prohibition against the wearing of black arm bands in the Des Moines Public Schools, the Iowa Civil Liberties union expresses regret that students have been suspended for using what is otherwise a permissible means of expression. While the Iowa Civil Liberties Union recognizes the interests of the school in protecting the educational atmosphere of the school, a complete prohibition of such activity is unfortunate. It is hoped that the School Board will review the action of the school administration and in so doing fully recognize and protect the students' right to freely express themselves, even though the subject matter is controversial or concerns an unpopular point of view.

When asked to comment on the ICLU press release, Des Moines School Superintendent Dwight Davis said that the school district's prohibition of black armbands was not designed to thwart free expression by students. He acknowledged that "there should be an opportunity to discuss controversial issues in school. Our question is how far a school should be involved in demonstrations." He later added that district officials were concerned that such a protest might have "a disruptive influence at school." This was, of course, the very point advanced by the five principals earlier in the week when they announced the armband prohibition. Davis was also quoted as saying, "It's not that we don't think these students should have views and be willing to stand up for them. . . . You have to draw the line somewhere." School Board President Ora Niffenegger drew his own line quite clearly. He stated on Friday that he was "absolutely opposed to this type of demonstration within the confines of the school." With positions in the armband controversy crystallizing, the next theater of action promised to be the school board meeting on the afternoon of Tuesday, December 21.

# CHAPTER 3

# Not Your Typical
# School Board Meetings

School board meetings in Midwestern cities usually do not generate front-page headlines, even in local newspapers. But the meetings of the board of education of the Des Moines Independent Community School District in December 1965 and January 1966 were exceptions to the rule. At these meetings, the parents of the handful of students who had worn black armbands to class earlier in December and had been disciplined for their actions were given the opportunity to raise objections to school district policy on the wearing of armbands. The meetings were well-attended, acrimonious, and widely covered in the media. Ultimately the parents of the students most involved, the Eckhardts and the Tinkers, would fail to move a majority of the board; but they would succeed in attracting attention to the important principle of political speech involved in the dispute and thus lay the foundation for a legal challenge to the school district policy on armbands.

## Anticipating the First Board Meeting

On Saturday, December 18 —three days before the school board meeting on the armbands—Ora Niffenegger, president of the board, received a letter supporting the ban on armbands, signed by the Reverend Joseph W. Arnett, pastor of the Bethel Bible Church, and elders and deacons of the church. The letter expressed these church officials' "deep appreciation for your firm stand in discouraging the use of public school facilities and school time for 'black arm band' and other demonstrations." In a page-one story on Monday, December 20, the *Des Moines Register* reported several further developments in the armband controversy. The story referred at length to a meeting of parents and students supporting the armband protest that had been held over the weekend at the headquarters of the AFSC. It also mentioned the allegation that some Roosevelt coaches had encouraged students to chant "Beat the Vietcong" during calisthenics. Finally, the story noted that Ross Peterson and a few other unnamed students who had worn armbands to class reported being harassed, "slugged," and even kicked by critical classmates.

December 1965 newspapers also carried reports of one of the first ground battles involving American troops in the Vietnam War. It had been fought in a place called the Ia Drang Valley in mid-November. Although casualty figures were not immediately available, American forces took an incredible pounding. Many years later, an ABC news documentary reported that 155 Americans lost their lives in this battle; perhaps as many as 1000 North Vietnamese soldiers were killed. The news of this brutal battle shared the headlines in the Des Moines papers with the armband story during the last two weeks of 1965.

The December 20 newspaper story also quoted Drake law professor Craig Sawyer to the effect that he expected the board of education to uphold the ban on armbands at the meeting the next afternoon. He said, "I doubt that the school board realizes they have to follow the constitution." Although Sawyer expected that the armband prohibition would ultimately have to be tested in court, he recognized that no legal challenge to school policy on armbands could be mounted until the board had officially had the opportunity to vote on the ban.

One woman attending the weekend meeting at the Friends Meeting House claimed that two school board members, Arthur Davis and the Reverend L. Robert Keck, had told her in telephone conversations that they supported students' rights to wear armbands and that they would oppose any school board action to uphold the ban on armbands and the suspension of students defying the ban. In another development at that weekend meeting, a proposal from Iowa State University's SDS chapter to picket the board of education's offices was defeated. Attendees feared that picketing in advance of the board meeting would alienate parents. The consensus of the meeting was that it would be premature to initiate any picketing until the school board was given the opportunity to overturn the armband suspensions. Additional discussion addressed the hypothetical question of whether the board should be picketed if the five suspended students were not reinstated, but no decision was made. In the few days leading up to the board meeting, Christopher Eckhardt's mother, Margaret Eckhardt, received a number of anonymous telephone calls. In one, a sarcastic voice asked her, "How do you join the Communist Party?" Another unidentified speaker informed her, "You're looking for trouble, and you're going to get it." Clearly the battle lines had being drawn.

---

## The December School Board Meeting

On Tuesday afternoon, December 21, one day before the beginning of the school district's Christmas holiday, about two hundred people packed the board meeting room in the Des Moines Technical High School building. William Eckhardt later wrote that this was an impressive turnout to address an issue the board president had termed "unimportant." A typical school board meeting generally drew about twenty people from the community. In gaveling the meeting to order, board president Niffenegger expressed the wish that more school board meetings would be as well attended. Whatever business the board had previously intended to transact at this meeting was displaced by the armband dispute. Margaret Eckhardt, who characterizes the atmosphere as "highly charged," remembers the local affiliate of CBS television covering the meeting. Outside the school building a handful of pickets carried signs with messages like "Why Conformist Education?"; "Freedom Begins at Home"; and "Freedom Means Free Speech." Most of those picketing were members of SDS chapters at Iowa universities; they were operating in defiance of the vote against premature picketing taken at the Friends Meeting House a few days earlier.

During the two-hour meeting, scores of residents of the school district and many board members expressed their opinions about students' right to wear armbands to school. The following morning the *Des Moines Register* made the school board meeting its lead story, under the large-point type headline: "200 ATTEND BAN ON ARM BANDS." That day's paper contained a number of related stories and pictures concerning the school board meeting and the armband dispute.

Near the beginning of the meeting, school district superintendent Dwight Davis reminded the audience that the wearing of black armbands was originally prohibited by a unanimous vote of Des Moines high school principals at a meeting the previous week. The school administrators took this action, he maintained, because they believed that the wearing of armbands presented a "potentially disturbing element in our schools."

Craig Sawyer took a leading role in the ensuing discussion by challenging the legality of the school district ban on armbands. He argued that the hastily instituted school policy violated the U.S. Constitution's injunction against laws restricting the freedom of expression. He therefore demanded that the school district policy be rescinded and that the suspended students be readmitted to classes without penalty. School board member George Caudill questioned Sawyer's broad support of freedom of expression, asking him if he would also support a student's right to wear a Nazi swastika armband. The combative Sawyer responded quickly, "Yes, and the Jewish Star of David and the Cross of the Catholic Church and an arm band saying 'Down with the School Board.'"

Scores of comments from the audience reflected a split in the Des Moines community. For example, Merle Emerson, identifying himself as a World War II veteran, expressed strong opposition to the student right to wear armbands. He said that schools need discipline, just as does the military. He suggested that the wearing of symbols of protest in opposition to school policy was insubordination, which must be dealt with swiftly and sternly by the authorities, just as the military deals swiftly and sternly with its discipline problems. Robert Hamilton, executive secretary of the Des Moines Education Association, declared that his organization of teachers and administrators "urges the board to rely upon and concur with the judgment of the school administrators."

On the other side of the issue, several Des Moines residents favored what they believed to be the legal right of students to express themselves symbolically. For example, George Telford, who identified himself as an associate professor of social science at Drake, stated that he was at the meeting "to protest against a violation of the spirit and letter of the Constitution of the United States." A few speakers expressed philosophical or educational reasons for objecting to the prohibition on armbands. Curtis Page, a Drake English professor, pleaded that school administrators should demonstrate confidence in students by allowing them to express their ideas in various forms. As he put it: "Any search for the truth is, by its very nature, unsettling."

The *Register* reported that a number of secondary-school students spoke at the meeting. Some expressed support for the administration's ban on armbands; others championed students' right to wear armbands and urged a rescinding of the prohibition. Ron Cohen, the seventeen-year-old president of the Roosevelt student council, said that he believed that wearing armbands and the trouble that it stirred up were "detrimental to education." By contrast, Bruce Clark, one of the Roosevelt students suspended for wearing an armband, pointed out that several Des Moines secondary-school students had worn black armbands in the past for such diverse purposes as to memorialize Negro children killed in a Southern church bombing and to mourn the "death of school spirit." In neither case was there a noticeable disruption of the educational process.

The question of whether the armbands were disruptive generated a great deal of comment at the meeting. Craig Sawyer contended that the Des Moines schools might be less disrupted by black pieces of cloth on the sleeves of students than by the words on some of the buttons that city students had worn to school in the past without sanction. He reported that two such legends were "Down with Pants" and "Go Riders" (Riders being the nickname of Roosevelt's athletic teams). Sawyer was challenged on this point by Gordon McCollum, president-elect of the Roosevelt student council, who said that wearing a black armband was indeed disruptive, akin to wearing a "Go Riders" button in the halls of a rival school such as East High. Even if the armbands did provoke strong feelings, Frank Singer (father of suspended student Christine Singer) maintained, the threat of violence constituted a "poor reason" for banning peaceable demonstrations.

The Eckhardt and Tinker families—parents and children alike—attended the meeting. Lorena Tinker told the board and the audience that she and her husband had not raised John and Mary Beth to be defiant but that they certainly supported their children's right to express their views on governmental policy in the fashion that they had chosen. Mary Beth told a reporter after the meeting that she would stay away from school until the prohibition on armbands was lifted. A picture in the *Register* of December 22 shows Mary Beth and her mother in the audience at the board meeting. Both have somber expressions, and Mary Beth is wearing her black armband. William Eckhardt and Leonard Tinker also spoke to reporters after the meeting. William

Eckhardt maintained that his son's right to wear an armband at school was "too important an issue to be dropped. I have a feeling that we are being told we have freedom, but we are not to use it." Leonard Tinker pointed out that his children and the other Des Moines students who had concerns about the Vietnam War resorted to acts of civil disobedience only after their attempts to work through "ordinary channels" had been rejected. He perhaps had in mind the censoring of a student-newspaper article that criticized American policy in Vietnam. At the meeting itself, Craig Sawyer made a similar point: several students had attempted to petition the school board on the armband question but had their petitions confiscated. Sawyer concluded that the Eckhardts and the Tinkers "have attempted as fairly as they can to go through the proper procedures to settle the matter promptly and the board has refused."

To be fair to the school board, it had not conceived the policy prohibiting armbands. The high school principals and the director of secondary education had crafted it without consultation with the board. The first opportunity that the board had to deal with the armband issue came at the meeting on Tuesday afternoon. Ora Niffenegger was the only board member who publicly acknowledged having conversations with school administrators about the armband issue prior to December 21. To make exactly that point, Arthur Davis, another one of the board members, used the occasion of the afternoon's board meeting to publicly criticize school district superintendent Dwight Davis (no relation) for not consulting the board on the armband issue. Board member Davis stressed that the issue of whether or not to permit students to wear armbands was a policy matter that should have prompted administrative consultation with the board.

In a separate story in the December 22 issue of the *Register,* the clash between the two Davises was featured. Besides criticizing Dwight Davis for failure to consult the board on the armband issue, Arthur Davis also charged that the administration listened too closely to the voices of Don Prior, Roosevelt's head football coach, and Al Comito, the school's head basketball coach. Sparked by reports that the coaches were leading calisthenics to the chant of "Beat the Vietcong," board member Davis claimed that for "every controversy that the school board is involved in, there is discussion of it in the Roosevelt High School gym class." Prior, Comito, and Superintendent Davis refused to comment on Arthur Davis's charges. But Miles Brown, an officer in the Des Moines Federation of Teachers, said that he objected strongly to criticism of the two coaches at a public meeting at which neither man was present to defend himself.

Discussion by board members themselves at the December 21 meeting indicated that they were as split as members of the audience on the issue of the armband prohibition. The seven members of the board were Niffenegger, an attorney and former college administrator; Arthur Davis, also an attorney; the Reverend L. Robert Keck, pastor of a local Methodist church; Mary Grefe, a housewife and former teacher; Dr. George Caudill, a children's physician; John Haydon, district manager of an electric-shaver company; and Merle Schlampp, a retired junior-high-school principal. Caudill and Schlampp spoke out strongly in favor of the ban; Davis's and Keck's comments clearly indicated opposition to it.

Caudill and Schlampp seemed persuaded by the administrators' contention that the wearing of armbands posed a threat to order and discipline. Caudill submitted that he did not oppose discussion of controversial subjects in class. He said, however, that he drew the line at demonstrations: "Regardless of the type of demonstration, it will be disruptive to some degree." Schlampp echoed the need for school administrators to maintain control. He said that students and parents objecting to the ban on armbands should have asked the board to reverse the administration policy but observed the ban while the appeal was pending.

Robert Keck said that he understood there to be two main arguments in support of the prohibition of armbands: to avoid a disruption of the normal educational program and to protect armband wearers from threats and violence from students who disagreed with them. As to the first reason, Keck said that he did not see any real difference between students wearing black strips of cloth or political campaign buttons. Any controversy caused by either action, he stated, might have positive educational results. In his words, "Controversy is at the heart of education and the disturbance of set thinking is the catalyst." As for the latter reason, Keck said essentially that the potential of violence from the "ruffian element" in the high schools should not thwart the students' right to express political views. A ban on armbands for this reason amounted to punishing victims. Arthur Davis declared himself in favor of the legal right of the armband-wearing students to express their political views by the symbolic means they selected. To him, the wearing of an armband presented "a clear issue of an individual's constitutional right of free expression." Nevertheless, he conceded that he questioned the wisdom behind the students' behavior, saying that "my personal view is that the banners of the Vietnamese war should not be brought to the classroom." He also added that the whole matter might have been resolved without fanfare and headlines if the school administrators had consulted with the board prior to adopting a position on the wearing of armbands. According to Davis, the principals and the school superintendent had "hidden behind timid policies" and "handled . . . [the situation] just as the Army would have handled it."

Finally, after two hours of heated discussion, board member Haydon made a motion to postpone a decision on the armband issue, pending further study, until the January 1966 meeting of the board. ICLU lawyer Craig Sawyer objected strongly to the delaying tactics, shouting at the assembled Board, "Take a stand, that's what you're here for!" In spite of Sawyer's outburst, the board went ahead and voted on the motion to postpone. Four members (Haydon, Schlampp, Caudill, and Niffenegger) cast votes in favor of the motion to delay; three (Davis, Grefe, and Keck) voted against it. Not surprisingly, the board members endorsing the delay were those who had spoken at the meeting in support of the continuance of the ban on armbands. Two of board members voting against a postponement (Davis and Keck) had spoken in favor of the students' right to wear armbands; the other vote against postponement was cast by Mary Grefe, who did not indicate at that meeting how she felt about the prohibition on armbands. Thus the meeting ended with nothing resolved and with the passions of students, parents, and Des Moines residents further agitated.

―――――

## Between the Meetings

The suspended students and their families were frustrated by the school board's action to delay ruling on the armband issue. William Eckhardt recalls that Craig Sawyer immediately tried to obtain an injunction to lift the ban on armbands at least until the school board rendered a definitive ruling on the matter. But the judge that the ICLU approached refused to grant such a court order because there was only a single school day left before the onset of the Christmas holidays.

Mary Beth Tinker remembers that the students involved in the symbolic protest in the Des Moines schools on December 16 and 17 had agreed to wear their armbands only until New Year's Eve or a truce in the Vietnam War was declared. So when the headlines in virtually every American newspaper on the morning of Thursday, December 23, 1965, screamed that the U.S. government had declared a thirty-hour "Christmas truce" in the war, it appeared as if the Iowa armband wearers had had their prayers answered. A brief front-page story in the *Register* that day quoted Margaret Eckhardt to the effect that "she was sure the arm bands would be removed during the truce period." But she also indicated that some individual students and adults might well put their armbands back on their sleeves after the end of the truce and wear them until New Year's Eve.

Also on December 23, the *New York Times* carried a long article on the Des Moines armband controversy. In a byline report from a midwestern correspondent, the *Times* gave a summary of the events in the controversy through the December 21 school board meeting. The *Times* article, with the subtitle "Antiwar Arm Bands Bring Suspensions," offered essentially no information that had not already appeared in the *Register* and other Iowa newspapers. But the very fact that the august *New York Times* ran such a story signified a modest national interest in the Iowa controversy.

During the Christmas holidays, while many Americans wondered if the truce would have any long-term effects, the families involved in the armband protest were the object of a great deal of attention. Although most of the written notes and telephone calls received by the Eckhardts and Tinkers supported of the positions taken by their children, there were a number of mean-spirited messages directed at the two families. William Eckhardt recalled one anonymous note that read, "Go back to Russia if you like communism so much." Mary Beth Tinker remembered red paint being thrown at her house. The Tinkers also received a phone call on Christmas Eve threatening that their home would be bombed before morning.

On the evening of December 23, the parents and friends of the students suspended in the armband incident met for five and one-half hours. Included at this gathering were members of the Women's International League for Peace and Freedom, members of local chapters of SDS, and other students from various Iowa colleges and universities. On Christmas Eve, Margaret Eckhardt typed a two-page statement summarizing some of things talked about and agreed to at the meeting the previous day. She wrote that the group chose not to blame individual board members or any other specific persons for the suspension of the five students; instead they laid the responsibility for the denial of freedom of expression in this situation at the door of the American educational system because of its emphasis on conformity and order as opposed to individuality and creativity. Margaret Eckhardt mentioned in her statement that members of the city's peace community had dispatched telegrams to U.S. President Lyndon Johnson and the presidents of North and South Vietnam, thanking them for agreeing to the Christmas truce and encouraging them to extend the truce indefinitely. Those attending the meeting also discussed, without apparent consensus, whether the students should return to school in January wearing armbands if the truce was not extended. Margaret Eckhardt's Christmas Eve statement also indicated that the affected students and parents were considering taking the matter to court if they did not see their position supported by the board at its January meeting. Finally, there was a great deal of talk at the meeting about how the Vietnam War was compromising the vigor of the "War on Poverty" and the civil rights movement.

Christmas was celebrated on a Saturday in 1965. The following Monday, Ora Niffenegger and Leonard Tinker appeared on the "People's Press Conference" on Des Moines television station KRNT-TV. In the course of their comments, Niffenegger and Tinker agreed that it was appropriate to discuss the Vietnam War in secondary-school classrooms, but they parted company on whether schools should be the sites for symbolic protests such as the wearing of armbands. For Niffenegger, classroom discussion was preferable to protests because it was "organized and controlled." Tinker disagreed: "How much control can you have and still have a democratic country?" On the television program Niffenegger offered a basis for prohibiting the armbands that had previously not been suggested. According to Niffenegger, there was a "group of students . . . organizing to counter the armband thing and this would have led to chaos." To this statement Tinker responded, "If the school authorities can't handle this situation, I would have to question whether the administration is doing its job." When challenged by the television program moderator as to why he supported his children in defying the school prohibition on armbands, Tinker declared, "When your children do things that are right, you have to support them."

On Wednesday, December 29, the big international news was that American B-52 bombing raids against Vietnam, which had been suspended during the Christmas truce, had recommenced. On the same page of the *Des Moines Register* that reported the resumption of the bombing, there was an article pertaining to an interview conducted the previous day with Niffenegger. In his statements to the press, Niffenegger qualified his previously articulated position on the armband protest. While the school board president's intention may have been to appear conciliatory, several of his comments added fuel to the fire.

Niffenegger stated that he was under the impression that the armbands Christopher Eckhardt, the Tinker children, and others wore on December 16 and 17 were intended as a protest against American foreign policy in Vietnam. However, he indicated that he now accepted the fact that the students' motivation was to mourn casualties in Vietnam and support a battlefield truce in the war. In his view, either the armband wearers' purposes had shifted or the original purposes had not been clearly reported. The school board president claimed that he had no problem with students wearing armbands as symbols of mourning. Thus, he admitted that the original prohibition on the wearing of armbands might have been "a mistake." However, to the extent that the armbands were worn to display criticism of U.S. governmental policy, he stated that they should have no place in the Des Moines schools. As he put it, "I think we should support our leaders." Several times in the interview Niffenegger indicated that the school administrators who instituted the ban on armbands had to make a "snap decision" once they had been informed that some students would be wearing black armbands to class. Even if the original prohibition had been based on an incorrect understanding of what the pieces of cloth symbolized, Niffenegger declared that the ban on armbands was still a duly promulgated district rule that should have been obeyed. Niffenegger argued that because the principals and the superintendent were worried about this symbolic protest leading to large antiwar demonstrations on school property, their decision to ban black armbands was prudent. Several times Niffenegger came back to his conviction that the halls and classrooms of public school buildings were not appropriate forums for demonstrations. At one point he stated, "If our students can flout the rule now existing, which prohibits the wearing of armbands, and at the same time be praised by their parents and some self-appointed leaders for breaking the rule, what then would prohibit a group of students from staging other demonstrations?" He also said, "We must have law and order. If we don't we have chaos."

Niffenegger followed this with a statement that particularly angered the Eckhardts and the Tinkers: "It is disturbing to many folks in our community—and it certainly is to me—that the armband demonstration takes place against a background of radical and extremist groups, including American Friends Service Committee, Women's International League for Peace and Freedom, and Students for a Democratic Society." The article went on to point out that Leonard Tinker was the peace education director for the AFSC and that Margaret Eckhardt was the president of the Des Moines chapter of the Women's International League for Peace and Freedom. Although the Eckhardts and the Tinkers participated in meetings with SDS, they took exception to Niffenegger's linking of the pacifist AFSC and Women's International League for Peace and Freedom with the more radical student group.

William Eckhardt composed a four-page statement responding to the December 29 *Register* article and the views expressed by Niffenegger on the intentions of the armband wearers. Eckhardt may have sent his statement to the local media or directly to the school board, although it did not appear anywhere in the media in its entirety. Contradicting the board president's statement, Eckhardt's document stressed that the purpose of the armband protest had not shifted. From the beginning, the armband wearers had two unwavering purposes: to mourn the dead and wounded in Vietnam and to support an open-ended truce in the war. Eckhardt indicated that the press had reported this dual purpose correctly and, therefore, Niffenegger knew or should have known the group's intentions—if only from reading the newspapers. In addition, Eckhardt saw a problem in Niffengger's logic: if the original prohibition on the armbands was a mistake, as the board president had since acknowledged, why was he prepared to vote in favor of continuing the ban? To Eckhardt, Niffenegger's position sug-

{ *The Struggle for Student Rights* }

gested that citizens of a democracy should bow to authority in all instances—even when that authority was founded on mistaken facts or assumptions. The Eckhardt statement challenged the board president on another point. Niffenegger had alleged that the armband protest threatened violence and disorder on school property. But Eckhardt noted that the minor acts of violence or intimidation that took place on December 16 and 17 were initiated by students objecting to the wearing of armbands. He asked whether students should bear the blame for being attacked while exercising their rights.

## A Secret Meeting?

On the final day of 1965, all seven members of the Des Moines Independent Community School Board, the superintendent of the system, and board attorney Allan A. Herrick had lunch in a private room at the Hotel Savery in Des Moines. Two days later, a front-page story in the *Des Moines Register* accused the board of conducting a "secret meeting," in violation of the board's ten-year-old policy that required public meetings for the conduct of all district business, except that involving personnel issues. Whether the luncheon discussion—which took place over a period of three and a half hours—constituted an official meeting in the legal sense was a matter of contention. However, a picture published in the *Register* showed a closed room door at the Hotel Savery with a sign outside it that read "D.M. School Board Meeting."

Board members quoted in the *Register* story indicated that the luncheon was called to allow the board to speak with Allan Herrick (usually referred to as "Judge Herrick"), the board's attorney, about an advisory opinion that he had drafted concerning the legality of the district's recent suspension of students for wearing black armbands. School board member Mary Grefe said that the discussion was useful because it permitted board members to query Herrick directly and in private on the nuances of his advisory opinion rather than receiving his statement in the mail and having to phone him later for clarifications. Although the armband-wearing students had indicated earlier that they would discard their armbands after Christmas, Grefe was not certain whether they would keep their word. She indicated that the board wanted to have a general policy on protests and demonstrations in place in the event any other such situations presented themselves.

Exactly what advice did Allan Herrick offer to the board at the extended luncheon? The gist of Herrick's counsel to the board was summarized in a memorandum that the school board lawyer drafted. Portions of the memorandum were later released to the press. The memorandum argued that school administrators had a legal right to ban armbands from classrooms and halls. The memo noted that at the time the prohibition was announced (December 14, 1965), school administrators were under the impression that the black armbands were to be worn as a symbol of protest against the war in Vietnam. Only later, Herrick's memo states, did the administration become aware that the armbands were also to be worn for the purpose of mourning the victims of the war. Insofar as the objective of the symbolic action was one of protest against the war, Herrick's memo contended that the displaying of black armbands was analogous to the carrying of anti-war placards, which "would obviously result in disturbances and a breakdown of school discipline." Therefore, he concluded that the ban on armbands "clearly fell within the classification of conduct which may properly be prohibited by rules of the administration."

According to several board members, as useful as was Allan Herrick's advice, there was no vote at the December 31 luncheon on whether or not to uphold the ban on armbands. The next public meeting of the board was scheduled for Monday evening, January 3, 1966. Mary Grefe indicated that the armband controversy would be discussed at that meeting and that the board would cast a formal, public vote on the legality and/or wisdom of the prohibition of this symbolic means of protest in the public schools. In a later interview with a news reporter, Grefe maintained that the reason the December 31 luncheon/discussion took place in private was that she and other members of the board did not want to be embarrassed publicly by not being able to respond knowledgeably to questions regarding the law on the rights of students and the obligations of school administrations. Board member Robert Keck had a different reason for why the board on this occasion decided not to conduct its business in public. He said that the personnel status of two coaches, Al Comito and Dan Prior, might have come up and that would best be determined by confidential deliberations. These coaches were the same two whom Arthur Davis had criticized at the board meeting on December 21.

Whatever the reason for the Savery Hotel luncheon, the *Register* story that appeared on January 2, 1966, correctly predicted the alignment of the board members on the armband question. The official vote on whether or not to continue the prohibition of armbands in the city schools would not be announced until the scheduled public meeting on the evening of January 3. In predicting that five board members (Niffenegger, Schlampp, Haydon, Caudill, and Grefe) would vote to uphold the armband prohibition and that two (Davis and Keck) would dissent, did James Flansburg, the *Register* reporter, just guess correctly? Or did he have a source at the Savery luncheon/meeting on December 31 who relayed to him the terms of the discussion and the alignments of the board members? Either interpretation fits the facts, but there is no compelling evidence favoring one view over the other.

On January 2, Ora Niffenegger provided a further explanation of the nature and purpose of the December 31 luncheon. He explained that the Savery session "was not secret in the sense of cloak and dagger." Then he added, "It's true, of course, the press wasn't invited." According to Niffenegger, discussion at the Savery luncheon included references to specific individuals—coaches, students, and parents. He maintained that a candid exchange about individuals was best done in private. He further said that concerns about the activities of the coaches in question would be investigated by the superintendent, Dwight Davis.

A few days later, an officer in the local chapter of the League of Women Voters addressed the propriety of the so-called secret meeting of the board in a letter to Niffenegger, which included this passage: "The League of Women Voters of Des Moines has studied for many years . . . the issue of open meetings . . . , arriving at the position that meetings of all governmental bodies, except those for discussion of personnel and sites, should be open to the public. Thus, it is with deep concern that the League read of the recent closed meeting of the Board of Education." In reply to this letter, Niffenegger said that he "assumed full responsibility" for the meeting of the board in question. He added, "I apologize to no one for that meeting. As often as necessary, whenever a sensitive and delicate matter is to be discussed pertaining to individuals and personnel, I will attend such a meeting."

William Eckhardt remembered celebrating New Year's Eve at home, discussing peace and freedom with his family. Later the Eckhardts attended a midnight peace service at the First Unitarian Church of Des Moines. He recalled the minister preaching from the text "A little child shall lead them." For some in the church, this lesson had particular relevance to the efforts of the armband-wearing Des Moines teenagers. The Eckhardts celebrated New Year's Day with the Tinkers. Together they wrote a letter to the school board, which stated that a "democratic demonstration can only contribute toward a democratic educational process rather than disrupt it." The letter also strongly advised the school board to formulate a policy permitting non-violent free expression in the city's schools, pursuant to the spirit of the First and Fourteenth Amendments to the U.S. Constitution. Copies of the Eckhardt/Tinker letter were sent to Governor Harold Hughes, asking him to direct the state attorney general to take steps to ensure that free expression was protected by all state agencies, including the public schools. William Eckhardt recalled that the governor responded in a letter a few weeks later, saying that he had indeed referred the free-speech matter in the black-armband case to the attorney general. Eventually the attorney general wrote to the Eckhardts and Tinkers, indicating that they would probably need to retain a lawyer if they wished to follow up on their concerns.

Shortly after the reports on the school board luncheon/discussion at the Hotel Savery, Margaret Eckhardt announced to the press that her son and perhaps other students would continue to wear armbands to mourn the casualties of the Vietnam War. She also indicated that "others will do so [wear armbands] to mourn the death of freedom in the public schools." In her statement she did, however, express hope that the Des Moines School Board at the upcoming open meeting on January 3, 1966, would rescind the prohibition on armbands and vote to "bring freedom back to life."

On the eve of the January 3 school board meeting, Ora Niffenegger publicly criticized the New Year's Day letter that he had received from the Eckhardts and the Tinkers. In the letter, the two families had characterized the wearing of black armbands as "a special instance of the freedom of peaceful thought, feeling or opinion." Niffenegger objected to the use of the word "peaceful," arguing that the wearing of armbands violated the privacy of others, who were asked to "turn their heads" and pay attention to the armband wearers. Niffenegger promised that visitors to the January 3 board meeting would have an opportunity to express their views before the board members voted on whether to uphold the ban.

The school board meeting was scheduled for the evening of the first school day of the new calendar year. Of the five students suspended for wearing armbands in December, two attended classes the first day after the Christmas holiday and three did not. Christine Singer, a Roosevelt sophomore, and Bruce Clark, a Roosevelt senior, elected to return to classes without their armbands. But the three Des Moines students who would eventually become litigants in the court challenge to school district policy—Christopher Eckhardt, John Tinker, and Mary Beth Tinker—all chose to stay away for at least one more day, in hopes that the school board would reverse the administration's prohibition of armbands.

---

## The Second (Public) School Board Meeting

The long-awaited school board meeting on Monday, January 3, offered few surprises. As predicted by *Des Moines Register* reporter James Flansburg, the board members split 5–2 to uphold the administrative ban on the wearing of armbands in Des Moines schools. Voting in support of a motion to continue the ban were board president Niffenegger and board members Caudill, Grefe, Haydon, and Schlampp. Davis and Keck voted in the negative. The meeting generated a banner headline—"BAN ON ARM BANDS UPHELD"—in the next day's *Des Moines Register*. As with the December 1965 meeting, the article reported that the school board meeting room was packed to overflowing. As promised by the board president, members of the audience were given the opportunity to express their feelings on the issue. Although a few in attendance spoke in support of the school district position, most of the audience commentary was in opposition to the administrative ban on armbands. For example, Glenna Johnson, identified in the press as "a national director" of the Women's International League for Peace and Freedom, spoke in support of students' right to wear armbands because there are "periods in history when an individual's only course may be to refuse to comply with government actions which violate the individual's conscience." Louise Noun, chairman of the ICLU, submitted for the record of the meeting a lengthy statement, written by a volunteer ICLU attorney, that implored the board to reverse the administrative ruling on armbands and tolerate "students' freedom to identify themselves with ideas and causes, at least when done, as here, by means of unobtrusive symbols." Noun did not get a chance to speak until near the end of the meeting, and then she was cut off after a sentence or two because of lack of time.

Just as they did at the previous meeting, the Eckhardts and Tinkers spoke from the audience. William Eckhardt read a prepared statement that challenged those on the board and in the audience who maintained that the students should have observed the administration policy on armbands because good citizenship requires obeying rules. Eckhardt stated that bowing without question to authority was a principle "so greatly admired in Nazi Germany." He said that the armbands "started out to symbolize peace against war, but because of the reaction against them, they have taken on the further meaning of freedom against authority." Christopher Eckhardt also spoke from the audience. In the course of his remarks he asserted, "The administrators put a ban on the armbands because they believed it would cause a disturbance in the schools. Well, by now you ought to know that the armbands caused no such disturbance in the schools, although the ban itself has caused quite a disturbance in the community." He continued, "The whole trouble would never have been caused had the principals let us wear the armbands." Leonard Tinker emphasized that he and his family felt great anguish over the war in Vietnam, a war that he called "a tragedy of history." He maintained that the board should vote to overturn the ban on armbands and protect the right of his children "to act out the anguish we feel as a family." Of the people speaking from the audience at the board meeting on January 3, according to William Eckhardt's recollection, ten spoke in favor of the students' right to wear armbands and only two spoke against their position.

Interspersed among comments from members of the audience at the meeting were a few statements and observations by board members themselves. In general, however, board members were less vocal in this meeting than had been the case at the December 21 hearing. It was clear that the board had collectively dug in its heels. Of the seven board members, only Mary Grefe had switched her vote between the two public meetings. The other members of the board maintained the positions that they had staked out at the earlier meeting.

# CHAPTER 4

# Growing Controversy in Des Moines

After the meeting on January 3, 1966, William Eckhardt recalled, many of the supporters of the armband wearers' cause made their way to his home. There they pondered the obvious question: "What next?" Few of those in attendance were inclined to drop the issue. Some of the students wanted to return to school wearing armbands, but that strategy was eventually rejected. William Eckhardt recalled that it was the counsel of several "civil liberties lawyers" at his home that night that ultimately pointed the direction that the armband controversy would henceforth take. Two of these civil liberties lawyers were Craig Sawyer, the first ICLU spokesperson for the armband-wearing students, and Val Schoenthal, the attorney who drafted the statement that Louise Noun attempted to read at the board meeting on January 3.

The ICLU attorneys advised the students to return to school without armbands. The attorneys suggested that if they still wanted to express their concern for the victims of the Vietnam War, they wear black clothing. But they should not further antagonize school administrators or board members by staying away from school or by wearing the prohibited armbands. The students, whom William Eckhardt described as "emotionally involved," were commended by the attorneys for "performing a miracle in this town" by challenging "more people [to] think seriously about civil liberties now than ever before." Although the armband-wearing students may have lost a skirmish before the school board, the civil liberties lawyers pointed out that Christopher Eckhardt and John and Mary Beth Tinker already occupied the high ground in the important court of public opinion. To stay away from school or to attempt to return to school flaunting armbands, the attorneys warned, would undercut the public support that existed for the suspended students' cause.

Attorneys and nonattorneys involved in the struggle for civil liberties maintain that educating the public about the value of civil liberties may be as important as winning court cases for clients whose constitutional rights have been infringed by government actions. The media coverage of the Des Moines armband controversy in the winter of 1965–66 was extensive. By the estimates of William Eckhardt and the civil liberties attorneys at his home on January 3, twenty-two articles and thirty-five pictures on the armband controversy had already appeared in the morning *Des Moines Register* and its affiliated afternoon paper, the *Des Moines Tribune*. The local radio and television stations had also covered the dispute extensively. Finally, they noted that the controversy had been featured in a long article in the *New York Times* and a segment on the CBS evening news. This coverage led to (or would soon lead to) a number of editorials in the *Register* and other Iowa papers.

Newspaper editorials and letters to the editor offer good windows into public opinion on many issues. Between mid-December 1965 and the end of January 1966 the *Register* and the *Tribune* published several editorials on the armband controversy. Similarly, local radio and television stations aired a number of their own opinion pieces on the matter. The two Des Moines newspapers also carried several opinion columns that dealt with the issue, and approximately fifty letters to the editor on the armband matter appeared in the Des Moines press. The varied press commentary and readers' responses defy easy summary, but a sampling can reveal their flavor.

## Editorials and Commentary

The first editorial on the armband controversy in a Des Moines newspaper appeared in the *Tribune* on Saturday, December 18, 1965. The editorial took essentially a middle-of-the-road position: it commended school officials for disciplining students who violated the armband prohibition, but it questioned the school administrators' contention that a few strips of black cloth were disruptive of the educational process. The editorial concluded, "A vital function of schools is teaching respect for rights of expression of opinion and the values to be derived from the free clash of ideas. We wish school officials had been more willing to show their faith in these principles and less fearful of the possible result of a few students wearing black arm bands to school."

The *Des Moines Register*'s first editorial on the armband affair was published on December 23, two days after the first board meeting. It observed that the attempt by the city's school administration to avoid disruption by banning armbands had resulted "as often happens in attempts to suppress free expression . . . in blowing up the trouble." The *Register* editorial criticized the extreme positions on both sides articulated at the board meeting on December 21, hoped that tempers would cool over the Christmas holidays, and expressed faith in the board to arrive at a "sound policy" to permit free expression and still avoid disruptions to the educational process. Following the January 3 board meeting the *Register* again editorialized on the armband issue. In a piece titled "Mistakes in Arm Band Affair," the *Register* was balanced in assigning blame for the controversy: administrators were wrong for a hastily conceived policy to ban the armbands; armband-wearing students and their parents should not have "taken the law into their own hands" by determining which school rules they would obey and which ones they would flout; and the board was at fault for upholding a ban on symbolic expression that, if carried to its logical extension, would suppress student utterances on any controversial topic.

The *Register*'s liberal columnist, Donald Kaul, addressed the armband controversy in a tongue-in-cheek style in a piece published shortly after the school board's vote to postpone on December 21. Kaul referred to individuals on the board as being members in good standing of a mythical organization known as the "Society for the Blunting of Controversial Issues" (S.B.C.I.). According to Kaul, "one of the bylaws of the S.B.C.I. [is] that a member never makes a decision on anything the first crack out of the box. Why I've seen members take three tries to get through a revolving door." S.B.C.I. members (such as the four-person majority on the school board), he alleged, practice procrastination because it gives a problem every chance to go away. Would the school board grant students the right to wear armbands if the Vietnam War ended before the next school board meeting? In that unlikely case, Kaul stated, "they'd certainly take it under advisement."

On January 10 the *Register* published the statement that board member Mary Grefe had presented at the contentious school board meet-

{ *The Struggle for Student Rights* }

ing a week earlier. Grefe declared that the question that determined her vote to affirm the administration's armband prohibition was "Who is to administer the schools in Des Moines?" Was it to be decided, she queried, "by students themselves under the spurious label of free speech, or . . . by a small group of parents and college students who wish to use the public schools as a vehicle for promoting their ideas and convictions?" Answering these rhetorical questions in the negative, she submitted instead that it was the responsibility of the district administration "to develop and enforce regulations applicable to the conduct of all students in school." Perhaps in response to Grefe's statement, the *Iowa State Daily* editorialized in late January 1966 that by the time the board had met for the first time on the armband issue in December, the rationale for the prohibition had shifted from the concern about disruption to "the old 'who's in charge here, anyway?' approach." The editorialist acknowledged that there was never any question that the administration and the board were in charge, but it suggested that there may be "some question about the program being administered when it is 'disrupted' by free expression."

## Vox Populi

The letters to the editor on the armband controversy in the Des Moines newspapers present a complex tapestry of opinion in the Hawkeye State.

Those favoring the ban on armbands generally stressed one of two themes: (1) that school discipline was undercut by the students who violated the prohibition on armbands; (2) that the students who wore the armbands were not really exercising sincere freedom of speech but were merely vehicles for the antiwar beliefs of their parents and a small minority of radicals.

The discipline argument was powerfully advanced in a letter written by Des Moines resident Melvin Hall, published on January 1, 1966. In his letter Hall claimed that permission to allow students concerned about the war in Vietnam to wear armbands would logically commit school officials to a policy of tolerating the brandishing of even more controversial symbols—such as Nazi armbands or Ku Klux Klan regalia. "If they [students] have this right, then let's forget about using our schools for learning and make them halls for demonstrators." Anything would be permitted, he continued, bizarre clothing as well as politically controversial symbols. He concluded, "If there were no law and order in our schools, they would be in a chaotic state. It is chaos that some of the arm band-wearing people want."

The claim that the suspended students were exploited by their left-leaning parents was mentioned in about half a dozen letters. A typical expression of this viewpoint was a January 15 letter from Rolf Heiberg of Des Moines. He began with a series of questions: "Do the writers of the arm-band letters really believe the children involved arrived at their own decision to wear the bands? Do they believe the children had access to and had the intellectual maturity to understand the significance of the complicated Viet Nam problem? Is it not more reasonable to suppose they were being used by their parents to publicize and foster the parents' opinions?" Later in his letter he urged adults to seek the remedy of the ballot box for weaknesses that they perceived in American foreign policy rather than by "fixing arm-bands on their children's clothing to wear to school."

Given the general support for U.S. policy in Southeast Asia by the majority of Americans in the middle 1960s, it is not surprising that several letter writers, because of their animus toward war protesters, agreed with the school board position banning armbands. A foreman at the Firestone Tire & Rubber Co. declared, "I'm for the school board all the way. I'm against these demonstrations, all of them that are against United States policies. I feel this is my government and I have to be for it. I've been in service myself and most of these phonies haven't been and probably won't go." Mrs. Ed Foulkes, who wrote several letters to the editor critical of the armband wearers during December and January, had this to say in one of her epistles: "[T]he 'peace mongers' with their lousy demonstrations are behaving in a very unpeaceful manner. . . . [T]heir behavior is non-violent, but it incites violence in others. So, though their hands do not hold the sword, they are just as guilty as the hands that held it."

About two-thirds of those addressing the armband controversy in letters to the Des Moines newspapers in late 1965 and early 1966 supported the right of Christopher Eckhardt and the Tinkers to wear armbands to school. At some point in most of the letters favoring the students there was language about the importance of tolerating free expression of unpopular views in a democracy. The classic free-speech position was articulated by a writer from Ankeny, Iowa, in a *Register* letter published on January 8: "Our nation was built on ... freedom of speech ... the right to speak one's mind, to express free opinion, to be an American. ... Do the American people have a right to care what happens to those who die in their behalf? The Des Moines Public School Board answered ... [this question] by denying sympathetic Americans the right to again say, 'That they shall not die in vain.'" A writer from Iowa City made a similar point in a letter published in the *Register* the following day: "[T]he real issue is the right of dissent. ... Will we defend the right of even the most loathsome individual to convince the people of the rightness of his views, or will we defend only those whose protest is ineffective or whose views reflect those of the majority?"

One of the most eloquent arguments in favor of the student right to wear armbands to school came from the pen of a U.S. Marine, who noted in the first paragraph of his letter that he was then in the process of being discharged from the military for a disability. Lance Corporal Harry M. Corry wrote, "I am appalled at what I consider not only an infringement upon the civil liberties of U.S. citizens but also at the seeming lack of concern for my friends and fellow Marines who are fighting and dying in Viet Nam for this very cause. To me this is not just a great injustice but the height of hypocrisy. Why defend a society that cannot even allow its citizens to honor the very people who keep it free?"

Several of the writers to Des Moines newspapers, in the two months during which the armband affair was most prominently in the news, identified themselves as high-school or college students. The student writers believed that they had a clear stake in the controversy, and, not surprisingly, they saw the issue of free expression as paramount. David Dillon, a Grinnell College student and Roosevelt High alumnus, maintained, "Although open discussion may exist in the classroom, forbidding arm bands brings about censorship on an all-campus level. ... To the extent that this free dialogue is curbed, the high school becomes an intellectual desert, a realm of strained social competition and group conformity." A graduate student in history at the University of Iowa wrote that "the refusal to permit the wearing of these arm bands seems to be another manifestation of a rather grim, anti-democratic spirit present in our land today. ... When dissension is repressed, when sincere (though perhaps unattractive) persons questioning our foreign policy are viewed with suspicion and dislike, then we as a nation have lost more than the opportunity to hear the other side (so necessary for a comprehension of the truth). We have also lost the very soul of freedom." On December 22 the *Register* published a letter from David Litwack, president of Drake University's Student-Faculty Council, announcing that the assembly he represented had just passed a resolution citing the Des Moines School Board's ban on armbands as a "breach of academic freedom."

A handful of letter writers critical of the school board position characterized the armband affair as a missed educational opportunity. A good example of this position was a letter from Glenn E. Riddle, Jr. that appeared in the December 27, 1965, issue of the *Register*. Riddell wrote, "Citizens of Des Moines are indebted to the handful of high school students who have created a situation fraught with possibilities of great educational value. ... It is regrettable that the school administration did not seize the occasion of the wearing of black arm bands as an excellent opportunity to teach principles of respect for diversity basic to our democracy. These authorities apparently feel it safe to talk about these principles in the classroom but unsafe to practice them there."

Several letter writers pointed out what they saw as hypocrisy in the school board's prohibition of antiwar armbands, given the fact that symbols of popular causes (including armbands) had been tolerated for years in the Des Moines schools. In a letter published on New Year's Day, 1966, an Indianola writer took board president Niffenegger to task for saying that the armbands would have been tolerated if they had been intended solely to be worn in sympathy for casualties of the Vietnam War, but because there was an element of criticism of the war effort behind the donning of black strips of cloth, the school board felt justified in prohibiting the armbands. This, the Indianola writer maintained, suggested that the school board held to a double standard: freedom to express an opinion symbolically "is possible only so long as it supports a particular point of view."

A number of letter writers challenged the school board's contention that the armbands presented a disruptive influence in the Des Moines schools. Indicative of this position was a December 27 letter from Ethel Kisner of Des Moines. She stated, "It was charged that students wearing black arm bands were disruptive. How disruptive? Did they try to start fights and arguments? Did they shout rabble-rousing shouts? No, it was the other way around. The arm bands inspired other students to troublesome behavior."

One letter sympathetic to the positions taken by the armband-wearing students chided board president Niffenegger for the statement he had made in late December characterizing the Quakers, the AFSC, and the Women's International League for Peace and Freedom as "radical extremist groups." Richard A. Morton of Mount Vernon, Iowa, wrote, "The American Friends Service Committee has earned acclaim and respect for its decades of assistance to people all over the world. . . . "[T]he A.F.S.C. is about as extremist and controversial as the Campfire Girls."

Throughout December 1965 and January 1966 the Eckhardt and Tinker families closely followed news accounts and letters to the editor concerning the controversy. William Eckhardt even felt moved on January 9 to write a letter to the editors of the *Register* and the *Tribune*, applauding them for "their complete and accurate reporting of the armband issue." In his letter, published on January 13, he declared, "[T]he local and national media deserve much credit for seeing through the smoke screen laid by the local school authorities who, unfortunately, were almost blind to the democratic values at stake in this controversy." Eckhardt made an effort at the very end of his letter to link nonviolence in world affairs and peaceable protest at home. He wrote, "If we really want to make the world safe for democracy, we should turn toward more non-violent methods in the execution of our foreign policy, and practice democracy as much as possible in the execution of our domestic policy." In the abbreviated version of the letter published by the *Register,* the final clause of Eckhardt's last sentence was excised.

## Whither the Students?

When the board voted to uphold the prohibition on armbands, Christopher Eckhardt and the Tinker children were upset. But rather than defy the school administration by putting back on their armbands, they followed the advice of the ICLU attorneys at the post–board meeting at the Eckhardt home and returned to school the following day without the armbands. However, all three wore black articles of clothing that day and for some time afterwards. Mary Beth recalls that her brother John wore *only* black until the end of the school year in June. When asked for his reaction to the students' black attire, board president Niffenegger reportedly said, "Well, I guess we'll have to let them keep their clothes on."

Over the second half of the 1965–66 school year Christopher Eckhardt and John and Mary Beth Tinker were the focus of a great deal of attention. Some classmates and members of the community expressed hostility, but many conveyed grudging respect. Mary Beth recalls that, although most classmates did not agree with her stand, the majority still were willing to accept the fact that she had the right to wear an armband if she chose to do so. She remembers "some bitterness and name calling . . . [but] on the whole, the reactions of our classmates were quite good. Most supported us." John had less positive memories of the second half of the school year. Because he persisted in wearing black long after the other students returned to normal student attire, he was a constant object of attention. Although several students and teachers defended his right to dress and express himself as he chose, many students and a few teachers used words to his face like "Communist . . . traitor or . . . coward." John also recalls a particularly nasty incident in the school swimming pool: he was aggressively dunked and held under water by a classmate who punctuated his actions with an expression of dislike for John's politics. The swimming teacher who saw it all stood by and took no action. Lorena Tinker also remembers that John, for no apparent reason, received a D in band that spring and was not allowed to march in the band's Memorial Day parade. She emphasizes that this "really hurt him because he loved . . . music and . . . was an excellent musician."

Christopher Eckhardt's memories of early 1966 are more detailed than John's and Mary Beth's. Christopher also kept a file of many of the letters and postcards on the armband affair that he and his family received in early 1966; they provide corroboration for his recollections. Finally, Christopher has also retained copies of the letters and accounts that he himself wrote at the time. His experiences illustrate the risks and rewards that accrue to someone who takes an unpopular stand.

Christopher's father, William Eckhardt, remembers Christopher saying on January 4, 1966, "We went back to school, not because we believed the school board was right, but because the school board had the might." Once in school Christopher found that his status among his classmates had actually climbed from the previous semester. He became more of a leader in his social group, the All Center Bums. Even the gym teachers, who had previously tolerated (or perhaps instigated) the "Beat the Vietcong" chanting, treated him well. He recalls them inviting him to lead the class in calisthenics on several occasions in the January to June 1966 semester. When asked to account for the turn-around in the gym teachers' attitude, Christopher maintains that it was because they were worried about being named in court actions that the Eckhardts and the Tinkers were then contemplating.

Christopher recalls a couple of occasions during the early months of 1966 when he was hassled for his role in the armband affair. In one instance a drunk called him a "Communist," and in another a student playing in an informal football game yelled as Christopher walked by, "Hey, peace boy, why don't you come play football with us?" Never-theless, Christopher does not remember being punched or threatened by students in the remainder of his time at Roosevelt.

Christopher and his family did receive a considerable amount of hate mail in 1966 and 1967—much of it anonymous. For example, one letter, addressed to Christopher's parents, contained a typed statement on the danger of Communist subversion of America's youth allegedly perpetrated by left-leaning educators. At points in this letter where "educators" or "professors" were mentioned, the anonymous sender had added the phrase "& parents." In the upper-right-hand corner of this letter is written this message: "The shoe is becoming tighter & tighter for you Eckhardt." A postcard addressed to the Eckhardts read in part, "It seems that someone needs to psychoanalysis you two parents for what you are putting your children thru. . . . I'd do a lot of thinking about this . . . because it looks like your going to have a Harvey Lee Oswald on your hands . . . Also, if your wife doesn't like this country then she can always go back to England and Germany . . . But it gauls all of us that stupes like you do this to the kids and they get the blame

... We think the community would be a better place for all concerned if people like you would move out." Another postcard was addressed to "Herr Doctor Wilhelm E. Eckhardt" and "Frau Margt. Eckhardt."

In 1967 the Eckhardts moved to Oakville, Ontario (a suburb of Toronto), because William Eckhardt accepted a job in the newly founded Canadian Peace Research Institute. Some of the hate mail followed the Eckhardts to their new address. One postcard queried, "At the meetings of that COMMUNIST front, THE POLITICAL ACTION INSTITUTE, do your lecturers speak to you in RUSSIAN or CHINESE?" Another anonymous correspondent asked, "What's the matter, Dr. Eckhardt, did golf get too boring?—you had to take up TREASON, too." The fact that Christopher was living on his own in Des Moines and the Eckhardts were hundreds of miles away in Canada was a matter of concern to some writers. One cautioned, "Canada will soon get wise to U.S. Defectors. Better take the boy along or he will have a hard time ere the Men from Viet Nam get home. They will eliminate the protestors and the domicile at Lane-wood [the Eckhardt's former address in Des Moines] will have a nice coat of YELLOW."

Not all of the mail Christopher Eckhardt received in early 1966 was condemnatory. In January he received a flattering letter from a Princeton, New Jersey, rabbi who identified himself as a former student in the Des Moines public schools. The rabbi's letter read in part, "I was filled with admiration for your sensitivity. It ... requires a great deal to identify ... with the suffering of one's 'enemies'. .... I was [also] inspired by your courage. It is not easy, in these times, to affirm basic human values in the face of that powerful combination of nation-state idolatry and increasingly mechanical, remote, non-human, and unfeeling instruments of human destruction. At any level, and especially within one's own immediate community, it takes great courage to challenge prevailing slogans and ideologies." The letter ended, "Bravo for you, your parents, and all who have supported you!"

Christopher Eckhardt spent a great deal of time in early 1966 putting his thoughts about the armband controversy on paper. For example, he wrote a letter to President Lyndon Johnson on January 5. His letter captures both the idealism and the anger that he was feeling in the immediate aftermath of his brush with authority. He wrote, "Dear President Johnson, How goes it with you? I'm sure you are busy with the Viet Nam war. Do you really believe all this killing is necessary to insure Democracy? You do not have to worry about this letter because I am only fifteen, and that makes me a non-voter." He continued, "Escalation of the war can serve no useful purpose, besides the lose [sic] of all the people, it will also take away from important matters here in the U.S. We should try to practice Love and Peace not Hate and Fear. Why Don't you try harder to get this war over with so more people would learn more about Peace and Love and less about hate and fear." Christopher also tried his hand at a longer written account of the armband affair, apparently for a school assignment. In an essay dated January 20, 1966, he engaged in a bit of counterfactual analysis: "May we all be thankful God has not turned the situation around and, instead of us killing all the Vietnamese, and Vietcong, having the Vietcong bombing our homes, our children, our parents, and our brothers and sisters."

Christopher Eckhardt's most poignant expression of feeling on the armband controversy was a piece of rhymed verse composed in late 1966 or early 1967. It was written to fulfill the terms of an English assignment that asked students to produce a parody of a piece of literature. Christopher chose "Mary Had a Little Lamb" as his literary foil and titled his parody "Harold Had a Black Arm Band." This is the poem in its entirety:

> Harold had a black arm band,
>   As black as black could be.
> Everywhere that Harold went,
>   That band was there to see.
> He wore it to his school one day,
>   Which was against the rule.
> It made the teachers jump and shout
>   To see it there at school.
> They said, "My boy, that band must go,
>   But you may gladly stay."
> Harold would not take it off,
>   Nor let this issue lay.
> Harold missed a week of school,
>   Suspended for the sin
> Of wanting war to end at last
>   And peace to usher in.

Harold finally went to court,
   His rights were what he sought.
That children also might be free
   Is that for which he fought.
He lost that case, but not in vain,
   For much was brought to light.
As Harold stuck by his beliefs,
   And still thinks he was right!

Chris received an A on his parody.

---

## The ICLU and the School Board

The board of directors of the ICLU first discussed the armband issue at a meeting on December 17, 1965. Craig Sawyer reported to the board on the meeting at the Friends' House the previous evening and the suspension of Mary Beth Tinker earlier that day. The ICLU board prepared a moderate statement "regret[ing] that students have been suspended for using what is otherwise a permissible means of expression." The statement also asked the school board to review the action of the Des Moines administrators and "recognize and protect the students' right to freely express themselves, even though the subject matter is controversial or concerns an unpopular point of view." The statement was released to the press and was quoted in several of the news stories on the armband affair.

Although the ICLU Board did not meet again until January 19, it was by no means idle. Val Shoenthal, the ICLU board's vice chair, prepared a three-page single-spaced statement supporting the rights of the armband-wearing students for Louise Noun, the ICLU board chair, to deliver at the January 3 board meeting. Although Noun was cut off after only a sentence or two because of time constraints, her entire statement was published in the *Register* on January 5. This ICLU statement, like the earlier one, was moderate in tone. It noted that the wearing of black strips of cloth by a handful of students was about "as minimal and innocuous a form of expression as could have occurred." Nevertheless the right to make such a symbolic statement was important in principle and did not warrant the administration's prohibition.

{ *The Struggle for Student Rights* }

The statement noted that the "demonstrators" were completely peaceful and "if provocative, they invited only cerebral or emotional responses" and that their demonstrations were accomplished "without . . . creating a clear and present danger to the educational environment or processes." The statement closed with a plea to the board: "We hope and respectfully urge that you accept this chance to turn what began as a problem into an opportunity for the recognition and demonstration of the strength, vitality and success of our American Way based on 'speaking out,' respecting the rights of others to disagree (and even to be 'wrong') and, finally, to make up our own minds."

At its meeting on January 19 the ICLU board heard a report from Sawyer regarding a brief that he had just filed in federal court supporting Stephen Smith, an Iowa student who had been indicted for allegedly burning his draft registration card. Several of the board members saw a similarity between Smith's symbolic speech and that of the armband-wearing Des Moines students. The minutes of the meeting indicate that Val Schoenthal, the ICLU's "legal committee chairman," pointed out that "there was no precedent on the wearing of any symbols." The minutes also indicate Schoenthal's contention that the armband case was stronger than the draft-card-burning case because it presented a "definite First Amendment issue that should have a court test." The board referred the armband matter to the "legal committee" to determine what action to pursue.

Craig Sawyer did not attend the January 3 school board meeting, in which the board members voted 5–2 to uphold the prohibition on armbands. Louise Noun remembers that the ICLU board asked Sawyer to stay away from the January school board meeting because he had "rubbed [people] the wrong way" at the December meeting. In her 1990 autobiography, *Journey to Autonomy: A Memoir,* Noun characterized Sawyer as "volatile and abrasive." Sawyer may not have attended the January board meeting, but that did not stop him from commenting on what transpired. In an interview with a *Register* reporter shortly after the meeting had adjourned, Sawyer asserted that the Eckhardts and the Tinkers were "extremely disappointed" in the school board ruling and were "not going to forget this issue." He announced that a formal legal action against the Des Moines Independent Community School District by the families of the suspended students was "under consideration." Sawyer then faded from the scene and another young Iowa attorney, Dan Johnston, became identified with the arm-band case.

A recent graduate of the Drake University Law School, Johnston was born in 1938 in Montezuma, Iowa. During his youth he lived with his parents in Wichita, Kansas, and various central Iowa towns, eventually graduating from high school in Toledo, Iowa. As Johnston later stated in a newspaper interview, "My parents were poor and moved around a lot." He attended Iowa State University for two years on an ROTC scholarship and then attended Westmar College in Le Mars, Iowa, from which he received a baccalaureate degree in 1960. After graduation Johnston served for a year as the vice president of the U.S. National Student Association (NSA). In his capacity as an officer of NSA he toured the country, working with the student governments that were constituent members of NSA. During his senior year at Westmar Johnston made his way to New York City. There he met William Stringfellow, an activist New York attorney, philosopher, and author of a strident 1960s book, *My People Is the Enemy*. Accompanying Stringfellow through the streets of Harlem kindled Johnston's social conscience and sparked a desire to attend law school and pursue a career as an activist attorney. After his stint with NSA, Johnston moved to Des Moines in order to seek a law degree at Drake University. He graduated from Drake in 1964 and shortly thereafter was admitted to the Iowa bar. Johnston began his legal practice as a partner of Norman Jesse in a two-person Des Moines office. Their firm handled a number of civil liberties cases, some of them on behalf of the ICLU.

Even before completing law school, Johnston had been attending meetings of the board of the ICLU. When it became clear that the Eckhardts and the Tinkers wanted to take their dispute with the Des Moines School Board to court, Johnston seemed the logical choice. He was already acquainted with the case through discussions with Sawyer and the ICLU board; he was committed to the civil liberties issues that the two families hoped to test in court; and he had negotiating and organizational skills that Sawyer lacked. One drawback was Johnston's minimal legal experience. But even that could be construed positively: it meant that he was also inexpensive. Louise Noun and her brother Joseph Rosenfield agreed to pay Johnston's fee. Noun and Johnston recall that this amounted to no more than a few hundred dollars. The other expenses in the case—clerical services and filing fees—were borne by the ICLU itself. The ICLU would announce in March—at the time Johnston filed its complaint in federal court—that it was seeking additional donations specifically to defray the expenses in the armband case.

Although Dan Johnston would be the most visible advocate for the Eckhardts and the Tinkers in the months and years to come, behind-the-scenes support from the ICLU board was critical. The ICLU today, just as in the 1960s, is an affiliate of the national body, the American Civil Liberties Union (ACLU). The ACLU's literature indicates that the affiliates "operate autonomously day to day, making their own decisions about which cases to take and which issues to emphasize." The ACLU was founded in 1920 and has grown to become the nation's leading advocate of individual rights, that is, those liberties enunciated by the Bill of Rights to the U.S. Constitution or by state bills of rights. ACLU attorneys regularly argue more cases before the U.S. Supreme Court than any organization except for the federal Department of Justice. Besides taking court cases involving civil liberties, the ACLU and its affiliates also work to support legislation favorable to civil liberties and participate in public education on the Bill of Rights and personal freedoms. The armband affair presented an opportunity for the ICLU to advance two of the three goals of the national organization: litigation and public education.

The ICLU, like most ACLU affiliates, has some attorneys as members. But the strength of the organization—in numbers, time commitments, and contributions—comes from its nonlawyers. The most active of the ICLU nonlawyers in the armband controversy was Louise Rosenfield Noun. Louise Rosenfield was born into a wealthy Des Moines family in 1908. Except for her education and occasional travel, she has lived in Iowa's capital city ever since. She graduated in the 1920s from Roosevelt High School, the same school Christopher Eckhardt attended in the 1960s. She received a baccalaureate degree from nearby Grinnell College in 1929 and a few years later received a master of arts degree in art history and museum management from Radcliffe College/Harvard University. Back in Des Moines, in the early 1930s she married Maurice Noun, a dermatologist. By her own account she spent most of the 1930s and 1940s as a society matron. Gradually she gained confidence in her abilities and began devoting time to public service. Noun's first civic notoriety came with the Des Moines League of

Women Voters. As president of the League she received a "distinguished citizen" award in 1956 from the National Conference of Government for her efforts in bringing the council-manager form of government to Des Moines. In the early 1960s, when the city's League of Women Voters failed to support her efforts to address segregation in housing, Noun decided "it was time to go over to the [Iowa] Civil Liberties Union." Despite her timid demeanor, Noun quickly took a leadership role in the ICLU, becoming its board chair in 1964 and serving in one leadership capacity or another for the group throughout the 1960s and into the 1970s.

In recalling her role in the armband case, Noun maintains that she was just one of many ICLU members seeking vindication for the First Amendment rights of Christopher Eckhardt and the Tinker children. She says that her name figured prominently in many of the newspaper stories only because she was the board chair and the ICLU press releases—usually prepared by others—went out under her name. In her 1990 autobiography, Noun remembers her leadership with the ICLU Board involved mainly "raising money, recruiting members, searching out people to head committees, organizing local chapters, and in general seeing that the organization ran as smoothly and effectively as possible." Despite Noun's unwillingness to take credit for the activities and recognition of the ICLU, it was on her watch that the ICLU's income grew from about five thousand dollars in 1965 to more than twenty thousand dollars in 1972; in the same period the organization's membership more than doubled.

During the early weeks of 1966—while the Eckhardts, the Tinkers, the ICLU, and Dan Johnston were deciding whether to seek a court test of students' right to wear armbands—administrators and board members for the Des Moines Independent Community School District kept a low profile. They did not issue press releases and seldom responded to reporters' questions. If a complaint was to be filed against the school district for its prohibition on armbands, the attorney who would assume the leading role in response would be Allan Herrick, whose Des Moines law firm of Herrick, Langdon, Sandblom & Belin had provided legal representation for the schools for a number of years. Herrick took his retainer as the school district counsel so seriously that he routinely attended school board meetings. It was Herrick who participated in the so-called secret meeting with the board and Superintendent Dwight Davis on December 31, 1965, for which Herrick prepared a memorandum advising the board that it was on firm legal grounds in banning armbands in the schools. His principal argument was that the armbands were a "disrupting influence" that could undermine the order and discipline necessary to operate a public school system. The armbands, he said, might even provoke violent encounters—something the school district had every right to take measures to prevent.

One of Herrick's former law clerks in the mid-1960s, Edgar H. Bittle, remembers Herrick as being incensed by left-wing protesters. Herrick was distressed by the recent March on Washington and other antiwar protests that were making headlines in 1965 and 1966. He did not want to see such turmoil hit his home town of Des Moines. Herrick was a veteran of the First World War. He had served on the Iowa district court in the 1930s but was defeated in the Roosevelt landslide of 1936. Because of his time on the state bench he was often addressed as "Judge" Herrick. Herrick was a no-nonsense conservative Republican. Associates and opponents always knew where he stood on an issue. He was also a leader of the First Methodist Church in Des Moines. Bittle has speculated that Herrick might have had a particular antagonism toward Leonard Tinker because Tinker took a leave of absence from the Methodist Church to spearhead peace education activities with the AFSC.

Herrick was a vigorous man who practiced law into his nineties, arriving at his office about six or half past on most mornings. At the time of the armband case, he was in his late sixties and still regularly playing handball. Bittle remembers Herrick as a tough taskmaster but a good mentor—much like the Professor Kingsfield character in the novel and later television series *The Paper Chase*. If the armband affair went to court, Herrick—the conservative attorney for the school district—would provide quite a contrast to the students' attorney, Dan Johnston—the disciple of William Stringfellow and former NSA vice president.

# CHAPTER 5

# Lawyers' Preparations

The Iowa armband case provides an example of a truism in recent American legal history: the law's procedural gears grind much more slowly than the events that set them in motion. The incidents in the dispute between the Eckhardt and Tinker families and the Des Moines Independent Community School District occurred between mid-December 1965 and early January 1966—a period of less than three weeks. By contrast, the legal resolution of the dispute—from the initiation of a complaint with the federal district court in early 1966 to the final decision by the U.S. Supreme Court in February 1969—took almost three years.

Whether the Eckhardt and Tinker families would take the Des Moines Independent Community School District to court over the right to wear armbands to class was never really in doubt. Within just a few days of when the Des Moines students were disciplined for wearing armbands, the ICLU had begun preparing the Eckhardt and Tinker families for a judicial test of the right of symbolic expression under the First Amendment. The ICLU had agreed to provide some financial support for the Eckhardts and Tinkers, and it had initiated an appeal to its membership for Dan Johnston's fees as the attorney for the children. The only thing that would have prevented a filing in court would have been a school board reversal of the administrative ban on armbands. So once the board decided on January 3, 1966, to uphold the prohibition on armbands, the die was cast.

# Opening Legal Volleys

Shortly after the January 1966 school board meeting, ICLU attorney Dan Johnston began putting together the suit against the school district. On March 14, on behalf of Christopher Eckhardt and the Tinker children and their fathers as "next friends," he filed with the clerk of the U.S. District Court of the Southern District of Iowa a formal "complaint" against the Des Moines Independent Community School District, the board of directors of the district, and several named school district officials. The named defendants included the seven members of the school board, Superintendent Dwight Davis, the principals, vice principals, advisors, and a few teachers in the Des Moines secondary schools. There were twenty-three named defendants in all.

The complaint in *Tinker v. Des Moines Independent Community School District* was only eight pages long—quite short as legal documents run. It began by stating the basis for the claim, a section of the statutory laws of the United States—Title 42, U.S. Code, section 1983. This law was enacted almost a century earlier for a far different purpose than the one to which it was put in this litigation. It was originally part of the Civil Rights Act of 1871, passed by the Republican-dominated Congress in the Reconstruction Era to deal with the actions of the Ku Klux Klan and other white paramilitary groups bent on violence against the newly freed African-Americans and their supporters in the former Confederate States. This law exposed state agencies or persons acting under the auspices of state law to various penalties for violating the legal rights of individuals. The relevant section of this law, in the compilation of the U.S. Code in effect in 1966, read:

> Every person who, under the color of any statute, ordinance, regulation, custom, or usage, of any state or territory, subjects, or causes to be subjected, any citizen or the United States or other person within the jurisdiction thereof to the deprivation of any rights, privileges, or immunities secured by the Constitution and laws, shall be liable to the party injured in an action at law, suit in equity, or other proper proceedings for redress.

Dan Johnston's complaint included the names of the plaintiffs and the fact that they were citizens of the United States and residing in the territory covered by the Federal District Court of the Southern District of Iowa. It noted that the three students were minors and were duly enrolled in the defendant school system. It then listed the names of the defendant groups and individuals and stipulated that the school district was organized pursuant to Iowa law and that the named defendants were duly appointed or elected officials of the school district.

About midway through the document Johnston began a short recitation of the facts at issue. He pointed out that the three plaintiff students had decided to wear black armbands to school to "mourn the fatal casualties of all combatants . . . in the warfare then and now existing in South-east Asia commonly called 'The Viet Nam War'" and in support of "the proposal of United States Senator Robert F. Kennedy that a cessation of warfare or truce proposed for Christmas Day, 1965, be extended indefinitely." He then took two and one-half pages to recite the events of December 14 through 17, 1965. Finally Johnston posited the necessary jurisdictional statement that justified bringing this matter to federal court. He alleged that Christopher Eckhardt and the Tinker children were "lawfully and peacefully engaged in the exercise of the right of free speech secured for them by Amendments One and Fourteen of the United States Constitution" and that, by depriving the plaintiffs of their right to free speech, the defendants were in violation of these amendments and section 1983 of Title 42 of the U.S. Code.

The remedy Johnston requested was a "permanent injunction" against the defendants, that is, a court order compelling the school district to lift the ban on black armbands and to readmit Christopher Eckhardt and the Tinker children to their respective schools without penalty. Johnston also asked the district court to assess the judicial costs of the action, plus the nominal sum of one dollar, to the defendants. The reason that Johnston asked for one dollar in nominal damages, he later stated, was because he was concerned about the passage of time eroding his case. Between the filing of his complaint and the time the case was heard in court, it was possible that one or more of the armband-wearing students might have graduated or have no longer wished to wear an armband. Thus, in order to keep the case from being declared "moot"—when the issues in the original controversy have ceased to exist—he inserted the nominal damage count for the "injuries" that had been sustained previously by the three students.

Two days after Johnston's complaint was filed, the *Des Moines Register* carried a front-page story by Jack Magarrell, the reporter who had written the first newspaper stories about the armband case. His story summarized the complaint and incorporated some additional information contained in an ICLU press release. Among other things, his story mentioned that Superintendent Dwight Davis had alerted members of the school board and other school officials to the possibility that federal marshalls would soon be serving them with copies of Johnston's complaint. In fact, in mid-April the clerk of court's procedural record of the case notes that copies of the complaint were successfully served by federal marshalls upon the board members and the other named defendants.

On April 29 Allan Herrick filed the defendant's three-page "answer." It began by alleging that the complaint "fails to state a claim against defendants upon which relief can be granted." Then it proceeded to a point-by-point response to each paragraph in the plaintiffs' complaint, as required by the Federal Rules of Civil Procedure. The answer challenged much of the detailed factual narrative of the armband incident offered by Johnston, particularly regarding the announced motivation of the plaintiffs for wearing the armbands. Near the end of its answer the defendants provided a short statement of the argument that would henceforth be their consistent legal position in the dispute, namely that "the wearing of said armbands was done in direct violation of the reasonable rules for the regulation of conduct of students . . . and to permit continued violation of said rules and regulations threatened a breakdown in the discipline and orderly conduct of classes in said respective schools." Herrick concluded the answer by insisting that the complaint should be dismissed and that costs should be assessed to the plaintiffs. A copy of the answer was sent to Johnston.

At about the time that the Des Moines school year was ending, without fanfare or media attention, Judge Roy L. Stephenson handed down an order to the attorneys in the armband dispute calling for a pretrial conference for May 31. Judge Stephenson assigned himself as the judge to conduct the pretrial conference and, if necessary, the trial itself. Pretrial conferences are the norm in federal cases. Under Rule 16 of the Federal Rules of Civil Procedure, they permit the trial judge to work with the contending attorneys to stipulate points of agreement, highlight points of difference, and generally move to and through a trial in as efficient a manner as possible. Stephenson's order for a pretrial conference commanded that the attorneys should complete their "discovery proceedings" (the sharing of documents, exhibits, and witness lists) before the conference on May 31. It also dictated that Herrick and Johnston should meet promptly to determine which facts in the dispute were not in contention and which factual issues remain in dispute "with the view of avoiding all non-essential proof at trial." The order also requested that the attorneys "discuss and explore such avenues of settlement as may fairly and honorably resolve any or all issues between the parties."

Given the strong feelings on both sides, it is not surprising that the attorneys were not able to settle the dispute informally. Hence, the pretrial conference took place as scheduled on the last day of May 1966. At that time Johnston and Herrick presented their jointly agreed-to stipulations. In the single-page document they concurred in the following points of fact: (1) that sometime prior to December 16, 1965, the Des Moines principals and director of secondary education met in their official capacities and decided to prohibit the wearing of black armbands while in school; (2) that this prohibition was duly announced to students and school personnel; and (3) that on December 16 Christopher Eckhardt and Mary Beth Tinker wore black armbands during school and were told by school district employees to leave school and not to return unless and until they removed their armbands. The stipulations made no mention that John Tinker was sent home, but not officially suspended, for wearing an armband on December 17.

For the pretrial conference, Dan Johnston submitted not only a list of potential witnesses—Christopher Eckhardt, John and Mary Beth Tinker, and several school district personnel—but also brief summaries of their likely testimony at a trial. At the pretrial conference, Stephenson reviewed the stipulations of facts of both parties. He noted, for the record, that the plaintiffs had filed their list of witnesses but that the defendants had not done so. He agreed to let the school district have until July 1 to provide the plaintiffs with its list of witnesses, and he directed that the school district should make its witnesses available during the first two weeks of July if the plaintiffs' attorney wished to "depose" them (conduct transcribed interviews under oath). He then ordered a nonjury trial before him to begin on July 25, 1966. He set aside two days for the trial but stated that he hoped it could be completed

{ *The Struggle for Student Rights* }

in one. Stephenson directed that each side prepare a trial brief and submit it to him by July 21. He gave each attorney ten days to file objections to any of his orders. As duly ordered, Herrick filed the defendants' list of witnesses a few days before the July 1 deadline. Perhaps for tactical purposes, Herrick's list contained the name of every one of the twenty-three individually identified defendants as potential witnesses. To depose and prepare to cross-examine all these officials would have added significantly to Johnston's burden as he prepared for trial. As it turned out, the defendants would only call one of the named defendants to testify at the trial.

During the month of July the school district attorneys took depositions of four of the plaintiffs' potential witnesses at the trial: Christopher Eckhardt, John Tinker, Mary Beth Tinker, and Leonard Tinker. Based on the questions posed by Allan Herrick at the depositions of his witnesses, Johnston believes that the defendants were operating under two slightly different theories as to why the students wore black armbands in December 1965: either their actions were part of a Communist plot through the SDS connection, or their parents had put them up to it to advance a radical protest agenda. Johnston remembers being so angry at Allan Herrick's questioning of Leonard Tinker that he threatened to halt the deposition of his client. Johnston felt that Herrick was "impugning that Leonard was somehow a Communist."

## The Trial Briefs

Critics of the legal system often point out that a lawyer's brief—a written legal argument—is usually anything but brief. However, the briefs for the plaintiffs and the defendants in the district court trial in *Tinker v. Des Moines Independent Community School District* were, respectively, only thirteen and twenty-two legal-sized pages long. The defendants' brief, written by Allan Herrick and his associate Philip C. Lovrien, was filed with the clerk of the district court on July 21, 1966. The plaintiffs' brief, written by Dan Johnston, arrived in the clerk's office the following day. The purpose of trial briefs in a nonjury district court trial is to alert the federal judge to the salient factual and legal issues in the case as seen by attorneys from both sides. These briefs would be of particular importance after the trial when the judge would have the opportunity to study them in light of the oral testimony offered in his court.

After presenting a three-page statement of the facts in the case, Johnston's brief for the plaintiffs advanced what he felt to be the four issues of fact and law awaiting adjudication in the pending trial: (1) whether the plaintiffs' wearing of black armbands constituted privileged freedom of expression; (2) whether the school officials who suspended the students were acting in the course of their official duties; (3) whether the meeting of the secondary-school administrators at which the prohibition on armbands was formulated constituted a "prior restraint" upon free expression; and (4) whether the interest of avoiding disturbances in the schools justified a limitation of the students' rights to free expression.

On page seven of his brief, Johnston argued that the relevant federal statute, Title 42, U.S. Code, section 1983, provides a civil remedy for persons denied rights under the U.S. Constitution resulting from the misuse of power by state officials. He cited federal case law in support of this point. He then argued that a public school board is a proper defendant in an action such as this because the normal defense of government officials from litigation—the principle of "governmental immunity"—applies only to actions for substantial monetary awards, not the injunctive relief and nominal damages sought in this case and available under section 1983. The last piece of preliminary legal groundwork to be laid was to confirm that the defendant school officials possessed the authority under state law to suspend students for violation of school rules. This was easily accomplished by referring to provisions of the Code of Iowa that clothed school officials with various disciplinary powers. Finally the ICLU attorney was ready to address the important constitutional issues.

Johnston maintained that the opinions of Christopher Eckhardt and the Tinkers on the conduct of the War in Viet Nam "enjoyed a privilege established by Amendment One of the U.S. Constitution as ' . . . freedom of speech, . . . or the right of the people to peaceably asemble [sic], and to petition the Government for a redress of grievances.'" Lorena Jeanne Tinker, the mother of John and Mary Beth Tinker, recalled that in 1966 her children were upset because it seemed that Johnston and the ICLU were unduly emphasizing the student rights and political protest component underlying the wearing of the armbands. This recollection was confirmed in interviews with John and Mary Beth Tinker. According to the Tinkers, the armband-wearing students regarded the mourning of the casualties of the war to be as important a motivation for their symbolic act as their calling for an extension of the Christmas truce. They were briefly angry at Johnston and the ICLU for seeming to leave that justification out of the legal analysis. John even recalled thinking at the time, "Civil liberties don't mean much if you continue to kill people every day." However, John, Mary Beth, and Lorena Tinker later came to realize that—from a tactical lawyer's perspective—Johnston was correct in stressing the political-speech/student-rights element of the armband protest.

Johnston then argued that the due process clause of the Fourteenth Amendment to the U.S. Constitution—that "No State shall . . . deprive any person of life, liberty or property, without due process of law"— applied the same standards of protection to individuals confronted by state law as does the First Amendment to individuals in the face of federal governmental encroachment. To use the parlance of constitutional scholars and judges, the Fourteenth Amendment "incorporated" the relevant provisions of the First Amendment. Thus, federal *and* state units of government are constitutionally bound to take note of an individual's right of free expression.

But is a symbolic expression such as wearing a black armband worthy of the same protection as actual speech or the written word? Johnston's brief cited three famous U.S. Supreme Court cases that placed symbolic speech under the umbrella of the First Amendment. In *Stromberg v. California* (1931), the Court found that displaying a Communist-inspired red flag was protected speech. In 1940, in *Thornhill v. State of Alabama,* the Court determined that labor-union picketing fell under the coverage of the First Amendment's freedom of expression clause. And in *West Virginia State Board of Education v. Barnette* (1943), the Court held that the custom of Jehovah's Witnesses *not* to salute the flag was also protected speech under the First Amendment.

Johnston acknowledged that freedom of expression could be restricted in cases involving public safety. However, he stated that "suppression of the privilege of free expression cannot be made a substitute for the duty of public officials to maintain order." Furthermore, he noted that, pursuant to decisions of the U.S. Supreme Court, state authorities have a duty to make "all reasonable efforts to protect a speaker without curtailing his freedom of expression." He cited a U.S. Circuit Court of Appeals case from Iowa, *Sellers v. Johnson*, in support of the proposition that a state can suppress speech only if that speech poses a *substantial* threat to public order. The *Sellers* case concerned a religious sect in Lacona, Iowa, that wished to use a public park for a meeting place. The sect had been threatened by violence if it held its meetings, and the city decided to ban their religious meetings because of the prospect of violence. However, the appeals court upheld the right of the sect to meet, despite threats of disturbances from hostile members of the community. Based on this decision and others, Johnston argued that it was the duty of the school district to prove that the threat to public safety presented by black armbands in the Des Moines schools was more than merely "trivial" or "conjectural." Furthermore, he emphasized that any "prior restraints"—such as the Des Moines school district's prohibition on armbands before any armbands had even appeared—could be constitutionally authorized only in the most extreme circumstances. The court cases he cited, particularly *Near v. Minnesota* (1931), established a "heavy presumption against . . . constitutional validity" of any prior restraint.

The plaintiffs' brief ended by pointing out that, as much as the Des Moines school district would like to contend that the wearing of armbands conflicted with the business of public education, there was good reason to believe that the type of free expression practiced by Christopher Eckhardt and the Tinkers was perfectly consonant with what schools should be encouraging, namely independent thought and academic freedom. Johnston documented this point with a long quotation from a 1955 speech by a well-known academic administrator and critic of traditional education, Robert Maynard Hutchins, lamenting that the "Cold War mentality" of the 1950s too often unjustly linked criticism with disloyalty. Johnston apparently wished to leave Judge Stephenson with the impression that the armband protest was not merely a distracting episode to be tolerated but that the students involved in this gentle display of conviction were just putting into practice the free expression that they had learned about in civics and history classes.

The defendants' trial brief began with about a two-page recitation of the facts. The brief also repeated the defendants' claim that the original complaint did not state a claim upon which relief could be granted.

Herrick and Lovrien then enumerated the three issues that they saw as critical in the case: (1) did the defendants deprive the plaintiff students of rights of free speech protected by the First and Fourteenth Amendments?; (2) does governmental immunity insulate some or all of the defendants?; and (3) is the school district as a corporate body insulated from liability under Title 42, U.S. Code, section 1983?

The first issue was the most weighty, and the defendants' discussion of it occupied most of their brief. The position of the school district attorneys was that the First and Fourteenth Amendments do not confer absolute rights on individuals who wish to express themselves through symbolic speech. Such expression must be balanced against "legitimate government and public interest." As a result, the administrators' prohibition of black armbands fell within the duties of the administrators to "operate and maintain an orderly and disciplined school." In support of this position, Herrick and Lovrien devoted about fourteen pages (over 60 percent of their brief) to a close analysis of several U.S. Supreme Court, lower federal court, and state appellate court cases. In the course of its case analysis, the defendants articulated and strongly endorsed the famous "balancing test" of the First Amendment in this fashion: "[T]he value to the public of the exercise of free expression of ideas is weighed against the value to the public of the regulation and prohibition of limitation of free speech, which the regulation may achieve." The first case discussed in the brief was *Cox v. New Hampshire* (1941), in which the U.S. Supreme Court upheld a conviction of Jehovah's Witnesses for violating a state law that prohibited a public parade without a license. One passage from the opinion in *Cox* was highlighted by the defendants: "Civil liberties as guaranteed by the Constitution, imply the existence of an organized society maintaining public order without which liberty itself would be lost in the excesses of unrestrained abuses."

Although the plaintiffs' brief did not raise the issue of speech being tolerated by society so long as it does not pose a "clear and present danger," the defendants' brief noted that this commonly mentioned standard is not the appropriate one to apply in cases concerning the actions of administrative bodies designed "to protect or promote some substantial public policy." The brief supported this contention with a page-and-a-half quotation from Chief Justice Harold Vinson in *American Communication Association v. Douds* (1950), a case in which the Court upheld a federal law requiring that labor-union officials sign an affidavit stating that they were not members of the Communist Party.

The defendants' brief illustrated how the U.S. Supreme Court had employed the balancing test in several other leading decisions: *Kovacs v. Cooper* (1949), upholding the constitutionality of a New Jersey statute banning sound trucks; *Konigsberg v. State Bar of California* (1961), upholding a state professional association's denial of membership to an applicant refusing to swear that he was not a member of the Communist Party; and *United Public Workers v. Mitchell* (1947), upholding the constitutionality of the Hatch Act, the federal law prohibiting federal employees from engaging in political activity.

Another case cited in the defendants' trial brief that came in for discussion was a 1960 federal court decision from the state of South Carolina, *Byrd v. Gary*. In that case secondary-level students were expelled for attempting to organize a boycott of the school cafeteria. Prior to the expulsion, the students had been warned by school officials that such a boycott would not be tolerated. In that case the district court acknowledged that school officials had "discretionary powers" to curb the potential disruption of a boycott even though there existed "elements of free speech" in the plaintiffs' claim.

Following the extensive case analysis, the Herrick/Lovrien document noted that, in all the cases discussed to that point in the brief, the courts had weighed freedom of expression against other governmental interests. They proposed to engage in the same kind of weighing in this case. The plaintiffs in *Tinker* sought to persuade other students (and perhaps teachers) of their objections to the Viet Nam War through the symbolic display of their concern—the wearing of black armbands. The school district attorneys, however, felt that their clients' position was no different, in principle, from that of the South Carolina school district confronted by students carrying placards. The Des Moines school officials had no problem with classroom discussion of controversial issues, but in their judgment wearing black armbands made it very difficult "to maintain a scholarly atmosphere conducive to educating pupils in a disciplined environment."

At this point the school district attorneys presented an argument earlier enunciated by board president Niffenegger, namely that pupils in a school are a "captive audience" who, if the plaintiffs had their way, would be forced to witness and endure a "continuous demonstration" of black armbands throughout the school day. Permitting armbands to be worn at school, the defendants argued, would be analogous to allowing students to audibly voice their beliefs about the Viet Nam War at any time and in any classroom, regardless of the subject matter. Public schools, Herrick and Lovrien maintained, "are not supported by . . . taxpayers as a forum for pupils, or teachers, or parents of pupils to promote their own points of view on any and all subjects." To stray from established curricula in a secondary school would lead to "nothing but chaos and confusion."

The defendants argued further that school officials must possess the authority to make "reasonable rules and regulations governing the conduct of pupils under their supervision." They cited the following language in a recent Iowa Supreme Court case to support this proposition:

> The court should hesitate to interfere with the regularly constituted school authorities in the management of the scholars placed under their charge. It was plainly intended that the management of school affairs should be left to the discretion of . . . [school officials and the school board] and not to the courts, and we ought not to interfere with the exercise of discretion on the part of the school board as to what is a reasonable and necessary rule, except in a plain case of exceeding the power conferred.

Given the strong feelings about the Vietnam War that prevailed among students and teachers in late 1965, school officials had reason to believe that disruptive behavior could take place if symbols of protest against the war were permitted into the schools. Even if, as the plaintiffs alleged, there were no serious problems when a few dozen students wore armbands on December 16 and 17, 1965, that does not prove that school authorities were unreasonable in believing that disruptions were a possibility.

The second issue, addressed very briefly by Herrick and Lovrien, was whether school authorities, in the exercise of official discretionary functions, are immune from a suit for damages. Although the damages sought by the plaintiffs were nominal and would be difficult to establish, the defendants' attorneys felt it important to contest this claim on principle. In support of their conviction that school officials were covered by the precept of governmental immunity from suits under Title 42, U.S. Code, section 1983, the defendants cited a number of recent federal cases and one U.S. Supreme Court decision. The salient language in one of the cited decisions is as follows:

> The approach of granting immunity to government officials for discretionary acts done within the scope of their authority seems a proper one. Without the presence of a particularly discriminatory intent they have no liability in any event.... [W]e will not inquire subjectively—into their state of mind—where they are exercising a discretionary function.

In concluding their analysis of this point, the defendants' attorneys submitted that exposing school officials to suits for damages under federal legislation whenever they formulate or seek to enforce a policy would have a chilling effect on good school administration.

The third issue—whether Title 42, U.S. Code, section 1983, authorizes an action against a corporate body, such as a school district—the defendants dispensed within a paragraph. They cited the majority opinion of Justice William O. Douglas in the Supreme Court case of *Monroe v. Pape* (1961), to the effect that section 1983 applies only to persons and does not establish a cause of action against a municipality. Therefore the defendants argued that the suit should be dismissed against the Des Moines Independent Community School District.

The second and third issues addressed in the defendants' brief occupied only four pages. One reason for the limited coverage, as the Herrick and Lovrien brief freely acknowledged, was the defendants' attorneys' belief that the plaintiffs would not prevail on the constitutional issue of free speech.

In a short conclusion to their brief, the defendants submitted that the school administration's December 1965 prohibition on the wearing of armbands was a "simple exercise of the necessary discretion vested in the school authorities." If that policy resulted in any denial of free expression, it was slight when balanced against the public interest of avoiding disruptions in the Des Moines schools. The defendants, therefore, urged dismissing the plaintiff's petition and assessing them the costs of the litigation.

With the submission of the trial briefs by Johnston and Herrick, all of the preliminary skirmishing in *Tinker v. Des Moines Independent Community School District* had been completed. The parties were now ready for the trial before Judge Stephenson.

# CHAPTER 6

# Armbands on Trial

During the week of the district court trial in the Iowa black-armband case, most of the news on the Vietnam War was distressing. As the U.S. bombing of North Vietnam escalated, Hanoi officials announced that American pilots shot down would be treated as war criminals. By mid-year the U.S. had lost three hundred planes in the air war, while the third week in July alone brought 737 American casualties on the ground. As the Johnson administration maintained that the North Vietnamese were being worn down due to "steady gains" by Americans in the war, the headline in the *Des Moines Register* on July 25 was simply "A Lot of Dead Marines."

## The Judge

On Monday, July 25, 1966, Des Moines received about a quarter inch of rain. With the mercury reaching eighty-eight degrees Fahrenheit, it was a hot, humid day in the heartland. At half past nine that morning, in the Des Moines Federal Court Building, Judge Roy L. Stephenson, chief judge of the Southern District of Iowa for the U.S. District Court, greeted the attorneys for the contending parties in Civil Case Number 7-1810-C-1, a nonjury trial titled *John F. Tinker, et al. v. Des Moines Independent Community School District, et al.* In attendance, besides the lawyers and witnesses, were members of the Eckhardt and Tinker families and various individuals from the Des Moines "peace community."

Both parties had agreed on a nonjury trial in this civil (that is, not criminal) case. For a case such as this—involving more legal than factual issues—attorneys usually prefer a hearing before an experienced trial judge over the uncertainties and delays inherent in a trial before a jury. Hence the focus of attention of the attorneys and the witnesses on this day would be on the judge. Judge Stephenson, forty-nine years old at the time he presided over the *Tinker* case, had been appointed to the federal bench in Iowa in 1960 by President Dwight Eisenhower. Prior to his judicial tenure he had been an attorney and Republican Party stalwart in Des Moines. And prior to that he had been a high-ranking army officer, serving in World War II and receiving both the Bronze Star and the Silver Star.

Edgar Bittle, who had just finished his second year of law school at the University of Michigan and was serving as a law clerk for Allan Herrick, had the opportunity to observe Judge Stephenson closely at the trial. He remembers Stephenson as having a gruff manner but handling the hearing in a serious, even-handed fashion. As he put it, "you didn't have any idea what he [Stephenson] was thinking about the case." Dan Johnston, the attorney for the students disciplined for wearing black armbands to school, was trying his first case before Stephenson. Like Bittle, Johnston remembers Stephenson as being a firm jurist who "ran a very professional courtroom." Johnston would later get to know Stephenson fairly well because, during the turbulent days of the late 1960s and early 1970s, he tried a number of draft cases in Stephenson's court. Johnston believes that, given his military background, Stephenson found it very difficult to sympathize with any form of war protest— even the silent wearing of black armbands. Nevertheless, Johnston acknowledges that during the trial Stephenson "was always very polite to my witnesses, always polite to me."

<hr>

## John Tinker's Testimony

After exchanging good mornings with the judge, the attorneys indicated that they were ready to proceed. Judge Stephenson complimented both sides on their excellent briefs and offered the attorneys the opportunity to present opening statements. Both declined. As the plaintiffs' attorney, Dan Johnston presented his witnesses first.

The leadoff witness for the plaintiffs was John Frederick Tinker. After stating his name, address, age, school attending, year in school, and father's name and occupation, John described the events of December 1965 that led to the litigation. He next explained the reasons that he, his sister, and Christopher Eckhardt had for wearing black armbands to school. Then Johnston asked John to describe what happened when he wore the armband to North High on Friday, December 17. With Johnston's prompting, John recounted his entire day—from his orchestra practice before school, through several periods in which the armband did not stand out clearly over his dark jacket and was noticed only by a few students, until he finally took off his jacket and the black armband on the white shirt attracted the attention of teachers and school administrators. John testified that his classmates' response to the armband had been mixed: some agreed with his display, some told him that he would get in trouble for it, some made "not . . . very friendly remarks," and some made "smart remarks." To Johnston's inquiry as to whether anyone threatened him or hit him, John replied: "Not as I can remember. I don't believe so, no."

John testified that it was not until after lunch on December 17 that he was sent to the administrative office because of his armband. He described his meeting with principal Donald Wetter, noting that when asked to remove his armband he refused. As a consequence he was sent home. He testified that he had not been suspended and that Wetter told him that he would be readmitted to school without penalty when he removed the offending piece of black cloth. John concluded his testimony by indicating that he had never before been sent home from school, except for being ill. He also said that if he returned to school in the fall of 1966, he would like to have the opportunity to wear an armband to express a particular belief.

Philip Lovrien—whom Dan Johnston recalls getting along with much more easily than with Allan Herrick—conducted the cross-examination of John Tinker for the defendants. It lasted almost as long as his direct testimony. Lovrien was most interested in eliciting from John the identity of the person or persons who convinced him to wear his armband on December 17. In response, John indicated that he talked about many things with his parents and his friends, but that the decision to wear an armband was his alone. Lovrien seemed unconvinced. He asked John where he obtained the. cloth for the armband. John replied that he found it around the house. Lovrien then wanted to know who bought it and when. John said that he assumed his mother had purchased it but "probably" a long time prior to the armband incident. Lovrien then wanted to know whether John had participated in other demonstrations, and if so, whether his parents had participated in them also. John replied in the affirmative to both questions. Lovrien also was interested in who called the meeting the evening before John decided to wear his armband to school. John said he didn't remember. In recalling this whole line of questioning years later, John said he believed that the defendants' attorneys were attempting to cast the parents as the "instigators" of the whole incident but that Lovrien and Herrick "underestimate[d] the ability of [us] kids to see what's going on."

Lovrien also questioned John for several minutes about why he didn't wear the armband on the first agreed-on day of the demonstration. John repeated his direct testimony: he did not want to take an extreme step without first attempting to discuss the matter with school administrators. However, when board president Ora Niffenegger said that the armband issue was "trivial," John decided to take his stand. He told the defendants' attorney that the issue involved was not trivial to him and that he understood that by wearing the armband to North High, he was intentionally violating announced school policy. Lovrien probed John only slightly regarding whether the armbands were disruptive to the normal activities of his school. John stressed, just as he had in direct testimony, that he did hear both complimentary and uncomplimentary remarks about his armband, but that after a football player told everyone essentially to "lay off," the smart remarks ceased. The defendants' attorney, perhaps realizing that he would have better results demonstrating through other witnesses that the armbands were disruptive, abruptly terminated this line of questioning.

On redirect examination, Johnston had John emphasize that the personal conviction behind his decision to wear an armband was far from trivial. John stated, "I morally think it's wrong, and when people are getting killed, I guess that's important to me." Johnston also attempted to allow John to testify again that he came to his decision to wear an armband of his own volition. In the face of repeated objections from Lovrien, Johnston was able to elicit from John that the decision to display an armband "was not a view imposed on me. It was my own view. I like to think that I thought it out myself." Again over Lovrien's objections, John testified that his father had even been against the wearing of the armband in the first place. Finally Johnston was able to extract from John the information that none of the uncomplimentary remarks that had been occasioned by his armband had required the intervention of a teacher or school administrator. On recross-examination Lovrien succeeded in getting John to admit that during lunch, when most of the uncomplimentary remarks about the armband were made to him, he was not aware of any teachers or school staff who had heard the exchanges. At that point Lovrien and Johnston indicated that they had no further questions of John Tinker, and Judge Stephenson declared a fifteen-minute recess.

----

## Mary Beth Tinker's Testimony

Johnston's next witness, Mary Elizabeth Tinker, explained the reasons why she decided to wear an armband to school on Thursday, December 16, 1965. With Johnston's prompting, she also discussed her views on current issues and her experiences in protest demonstrations prior to December 1965. She indicated that wearing the armband to school had been her decision and that she had definitely not been talked into it by either of her parents. She also testified that she had found the cloth for the armband herself and had cut and affixed it to her sweater without help or encouragement.

Johnston then led her through a recounting of the events on the day in question. She testified that few students noticed or commented on her armband during the morning. At lunch she remembered that "a table of boys ... [made] some smart remarks." She characterized it as teasing. Mary Beth indicated that teasing was common between tables in the cafeteria. In any case, if any teachers or staff noticed what was taking place they did not feel it serious enough to intervene. Mary Beth then testified that she was asked to go to the school office during her mathematics class, about one o'clock. She related the events of her meeting with Leo Willadsen, Harding's vice principal, that Willadsen told her that all she had to do was take off her armband and she could go back to class. Mary Beth testified that she removed the armband and went back to class. Years later she confessed that she did not, back in 1965, fully comprehend what was involved in an act of civil disobedience. In any case she was nervous and decided to comply with the order of a person in authority.

She testified that she had been back in her math class for only a few minutes when Vera Tarmann, the girls' advisor, came in to the classroom and asked her to accompany her back to the main office. Although

Mary Beth had removed the armband when Willadsen asked her to do so, when she reached the main office for the second time in fifteen minutes, she still received a suspension notice. Mary Beth testified that she was given the suspension notice in person to take home to her parents. In concluding his examination of Mary Beth, Johnston asked her if now—eight months after the incident—she would still want to wear an armband to school. Mary Beth said she would want this right and, if the Vietnam War continued, would want to have the opportunity to exercise it.

In Lovrien's cross-examination, he elicited from Mary Beth an acknowledgment that she had discussed the wearing of armbands with her parents prior to December 16, 1965. She also acknowledged that several Tinker children had worn armbands to the Des Moines public schools on December 16 and/or 17. Then Lovrien and Mary Beth engaged in a tense exchange about who bought the cloth for her armband. He reminded the witness that she had testified in her deposition that her mother, Lorena Jeanne Tinker, had purchased the material for the armband on or about December 15, when it had been determined that one or more of the Tinker children would be wearing black armbands to school that week. However, in court at this time, Mary Beth insisted that her mother had purchased the material long before December 15, 1965, and thus that the black cloth had been around the house for a good deal of time. Having made his point that Mary Beth had given two slightly different versions of the origins of the Tinker children's armbands, Lovrien moved to another line of questions.

Lovrien asked Mary Beth if she remembered Richard Moberly's statements about protests and protesters on December 15. After some verbal sparring with the defendants' attorney, she said she did. He then asked her to remind the judge what warning Moberly, her math teacher, had issued. According to Mary Beth, Moberly said that a student who wore a black armband to school "would be kicked out of his class." On redirect examination, Dan Johnston allowed Mary Beth to clarify that Moberly initiated the discussion about protests that was held in his mathematics class on December 15. There was no recross-examination.

## Christopher Eckhardt's Testimony

In some ways, Christopher Paul Eckhardt was the key witness for both sides in the trial. From the plaintiffs' point of view, Eckhardt was able to articulate the principle of civil disobedience more clearly than either of the Tinker children. From the defendants' perspective, Christopher's experience on the day he wore the armband suggested that disruptive incidents did occur as a direct result of his actions. Thus Christopher's time on the witness stand was the longest and most contentious of any at the trial.

Johnston began his questioning by asking Christopher how he learned of the contemplated armband demonstration. He testified that there had been a meeting at his parents' house on December 11, 1965, to express concerns about the Vietnam War and discuss what actions people in the Iowa peace community might take. At the meeting were several adults, a number of college students, and a few high-school students. Since Christopher was shoveling snow during most of the time that the meeting was taking place, he heard about the armband strategy only after the fact. He testified that "it sounded like a nice thing to do."

Johnston then asked Christopher about his familiarity with the controversial issues of the day. He indicated that he regularly talked about international politics and civil rights in the LRY group of Des Moines's First Unitarian Church and that he had participated in a number of demonstrations for "civil rights, race, peace, and things of that sort." He also acknowledged that he talked regularly with his parents about war, peace, and social issues. Christopher testified that he decided on December 15 that he would wear a black armband to school the following day. He stated emphatically that his parents had neither tried to persuade him to wear the armband nor tried to dissuade him from wearing it.

Then Johnston asked Christopher to recount the incidents on December 16. He testified that he wore a black armband, clearly visible over a brown sports jacket, to school that day. After arriving at school, he went to the main office to "turn himself in." He informed the court that he was aware of the school district's ban on armbands, that he had intentionally violated this policy, and that he had fully expected to be suspended for his actions. He would later recall, "I was doing civil disobedience. That was my game plan."

Christopher next described his long wait in the Roosevelt administrative office and the taunting he received from fellow students who were passing by where he sat. He also testified as to his exchanges with vice principal Donald Blackman and the girls' advisor, Velma Cross. In the context of this testimony he recounted the cryptic "busted nose" story. Christopher testified that when he refused to remove his armband, Blackman called his mother. Christopher was then sent home and told that a suspension notice would be mailed to his parents shortly.

Johnston asked his witness if he had had any discussion with Blackman that morning about his reasons for wearing the armband. Christopher replied that he thought they did and that he had expressed his reasons for doing so. After fending off several objections from the defendants' attorneys, Christopher testified that Cross had indicated at some point in their conversation that he was "too young and immature to have too many views." She also told him that if he was suspended he would probably have "to look for a new school." In addition, he testified that either Blackman or Cross told him that the armband incident would lead to "lots of bad publicity for the school." Finally Johnston asked Christopher if he had changed his mind since December 1965 regarding "this business about the war in Viet Nam." Eckhardt answered, "No." Nor, he added, would there likely be any changes in his views in the near future if the U.S. government continued its escalation of the war. Since his feelings about the war had not changed since December 1965, he submitted that he would like to have the right to wear an armband on return to school in the fall of 1966.

Philip Lovrien's cross-examination began with an exchange involving matters mentioned in both Christopher's just-completed direct testimony and his deposition taken by the defendants' attorneys earlier in the month. The testimony at issue was the conversation involving Blackman, Cross, and Christopher in the Roosevelt administrative offices on December 16. Johnston objected to the admissibility of the deposition into evidence. But the judge overruled the objection and allowed the admission of the deposition. With the deposition and subsequent testimony, Lovrien was able to establish that Christopher was allowed to return to classes at Roosevelt after the Christmas holidays and that he did not flunk any of his fall semester classes. Then Lovrien moved on to other issues.

Lovrien also asked Christopher to recall the December 11 afternoon when the armband demonstration was discussed at his home. Christopher said that he was outside most of the time shoveling snow. Lovrien asked him if he could remember who attended. Christopher said he was "pretty sure" both his parents were there as well as Roosevelt students Bruce Clark and Ross Peterson. Lovrien then asked Christopher about the November 1965 march in Washington that he attended with his mother. He wanted to know what Christopher did at that march; he replied that he carried a placard and listened to speeches. Over Johnston's objection he asked Christopher who organized the march in Washington. When Christopher was finally allowed to answer he said he did not know which persons or groups organized it.

Then Lovrien began to probe into Christopher's reasons for wearing the black armband to school on December 16. He asked him if he wore the armband as a matter of protest of the war in Viet Nam. Christopher responded with the by now well-known justification of all the Des Moines armband wearers, that "it was to mourn the dead in Viet Nam and to hope for a Christmas truce." Lovrien wondered if Christopher would consider the armbands worn to school on December 16 and 17 to be part of a demonstration. Christopher rejoined, "Oh, let's see—if you want to call it a demonstration—it wasn't much of a demonstration." Lovrien asked him if the armbands were meant to influence public opinion. Christopher agreed that they were.

Lovrien then attempted to obtain a sense of the degree of organization of the December armband demonstration. He wanted to know if there was a group or society that sponsored it. Christopher replied that students were expected to decide as individuals whether or not they would wear armbands on the designated days. As this point Lovrien introduced into evidence, without objection, a copy of a statement written by Ross Peterson, titled "WE MOURN/ATTENTION STUDENTS!" that was read at the Des Moines First Unitarian Church on December 12 and mimeographed and handed out at Roosevelt on December 13 and 14. This was the same document that the Roosevelt High School administration did not permit to be published in the student newspaper the week of December 13 to 17.

Christopher testified that he agreed with the sentiments in the essay. At this point, Judge Stephenson called a recess for lunch.

At about a quarter of two the court session resumed, with Philip Lovrien continuing his cross-examination of Christopher. He began by posing questions about Christopher's personal participation in protest demonstrations. Christopher indicated that he had taken part in a handful of civil rights and anti–Vietnam War demonstrations, in only some of which had he been joined by his parents. Then the subject switched to a meeting at the Eckhardt home on December 16, late on the afternoon of the day that Christopher had been suspended from Roosevelt High for failure to remove his armband. The defendants' attorney wanted to know who had attended the meeting. Christopher indicated that several students from Roosevelt and other Des Moines schools attended. He was, however, uncertain as to all of the names. He also testified as to some of the details of the meeting at the Des Moines headquarters of the Iowa chapter of the AFSC on the evening of the same busy day. According to Christopher's recollection, this meeting was called by either Leonard Tinker or Christopher's father, William Eckhardt. Christopher recalled that the attendance at that meeting was about twenty, including his family, members of the Tinker family, several Roosevelt students, and Craig Sawyer.

On redirect examination, Johnston asked Christopher when he finally went back to school and under what circumstances. Christopher testified that he did not return to school until January 4, 1966, the day after the January school board meeting at which the board had voted to uphold the administration's ban on armbands in the schools. Johnston completed his questioning of Christopher by asking if he felt that wearing the armband to school back in December 1965 hurt him in any way. Christopher responded in the negative. Then, for whatever reason, Johnston inquired whether Christopher played baseball. Christopher responded "now and then." Johnston asked him if wearing the armband hurt his pitching arm. Christopher said, "No." On that strange note, the testimony of Christopher Eckhardt ended.

## Testimony of School District Witnesses

The remaining seven witnesses at the trial on July 25 were employees or representatives of the Des Moines Independent Community School District. The plaintiffs' attorney, Dan Johnston, summoned the first six of these to testify under rule 43 of the Federal Rules of Civil Procedure as "adverse witnesses." In conducting the direct examination of adverse witnesses, an attorney is permitted to ask what are called "leading questions"—questions that instruct a witness how to answer or put into his/her mouth words to be echoed back. Except for this exception, the Federal Rules of Civil Procedure permit leading questions of witnesses only on cross-examination.

The first adverse witness the plaintiffs called was Donald Wetter, the principal of North High School. He testified that on December 15, 1966, he had instructed the teachers at North High to send any student wearing an armband to see him in his office. He also testified that this instruction was based on the policy adopted by the Des Moines secondary principals and the director of secondary education at a meeting on December 14. He said that his encounter with John Tinker, resulting in John being sent home, occurred on December 17. Finally he testified that, to the best of his knowledge, no student at North High had worn an armband to school prior to December 17. The cross-examination of Wetter was conducted by Allan Herrick. Although Herrick was the lead attorney for the defendants' team, this was the first time in the trial that he had taken an active role in questioning a witness. Herrick asked Wetter to tell him what took place when John Tinker came to his office on December 17. In his testimony, Wetter emphasized that John was not formally suspended, furthermore that he would be welcome to return to school at any time without his armband, that he would not have his grades lowered as a result of this incident, and that Wetter would do everything in his power as principal of North High School "to protect his [John's] rights, including his personal welfare." Then Wetter testified that he suggested to John that his concern about casualties in the war in Vietnam could better be demonstrated by participating in Veterans' Day or Memorial Day activities than in wearing an armband to class in December. On redirect examination Johnston elicited from Wetter that John Tinker had not come before him for any disciplinary problems prior to December 17, 1965.

The plaintiffs called Donald Blackman, the vice principal of Roosevelt High, as the next witness. Blackman testified regarding his encounter with Christopher Eckhardt on December 16. Blackman indicated that, in issuing the suspension of Christopher, he was acting in his official capacity to enforce the school district's prohibition of armbands that had been duly enacted at a meeting of administrators on December 14. On cross-examination by Philip Lovrien, Blackman said that he had talked with Christopher "quite thoroughly" at the time about his reasons for wearing the armband. Blackman went on to say that regardless of Christopher's motivation for making this symbolic statement, he was still violating a school district policy; for that reason, he informed Christopher that he would be suspended. On redirect examination, Johnston asked Blackman if students at Roosevelt ever wear religious symbols or political campaign buttons to class. Blackman answered, "I suppose. I haven't really been paying any attention." He was then asked if the Des Moines schools or Roosevelt High in particular had any policies against students wearing religious symbols or political campaign buttons at school. Blackman testified that, to the best of his knowledge, the prohibition on armbands had been the first official prohibition of the wearing of any symbols in the Des Moines school system.

Johnston's next witness was Leo Willadsen, the vice principal of Warren Harding Junior High. Willadsen testified that Mary Beth Tinker had been sent to his office on the afternoon of December 16, 1965, because she appeared to be violating the recently devised policy against wearing an armband in school. At the time he asked Mary Beth for the armband, and she gave it to him. Then he testified that he informed Mary Beth that she would not be able to return to class until the girls' advisor, Vera Tarmann, talked with her. On this point Willadsen's testimony conflicted with Mary Beth's, who remembered returning to class briefly and only after that being summoned to speak with Tarmann. In any case, Willadsen learned later in the day that Mary Beth had been suspended by Tarmann. The defendants' attorneys did not cross-examine Willadsen.

The next witness, appropriately, was Vera Tarmann, the girls' advisor at Warren Harding Junior High. Like the three previous school district employees called to testify by the plaintiffs' attorney, she was an adverse witness. Tarmann testified that she was at lunch on December 16 when she was informed that Mary Beth was wearing a black armband. She also learned that Mary Beth had been sent back to class after a short meeting in the office with Willadsen. After Tarmann completed lunch she found Mary Beth in her math class and asked her to come with her back to the school's main office. She testified that she and Mary Beth talked for a while; she also indicated that Willadsen had later given her Mary Beth's armband and that she was keeping it "in my office, in my right-hand upper drawer." Johnston asked Tarmann if she suspended Mary Beth. She replied, "Well, I will not use the word 'suspension.' Mary Elizabeth was not what we would call actually suspended. . . . Mary Elizabeth was sent home that afternoon, and I called her mother to tell her that she would be sent home until I had an opportunity to talk to her parents." She then said that she talked to Leonard and Lorena Tinker in her office the following morning, indicating to them that Mary Beth could return to school at any time provided she did not wear an armband. She mentioned that she was not aware of any other students wearing black armbands in mid-December 1965 or at any other time. She stated further that she was not aware of students at Harding Junior High wearing other political or religious symbols, nor did she know of any school district rules against the wearing of such tokens. Finally she testified that she had discussed her actions concerning Mary Beth Tinker's armband "informally" with her superiors and that there had been no criticism or revocation of her disposition of the matter. Herrick waived cross-examination of Tarmann, and she was excused.

After a ten-minute recess, Johnston said that he had just two more witnesses to examine before the plaintiffs could rest their case. He predicted that the examination of these witnesses would be "quite short." Johnston may have been indulging here in a bit of gamesmanship, because his final two witnesses were dealt with in anything but a perfunctory fashion.

Johnston's penultimate witness was E. Raymond Peterson, director of secondary education for the Des Moines schools. Peterson was called to testify regarding the decision to ban armbands from the Des Moines schools. In response to Johnston's questions, he said that he convened a meeting of the five senior-high principals in the Des

Moines system on December 14. He testified that he called the meeting at the direction of the superintendent and the assistant superintendent of the system for the purpose of deciding what to do about
the possibility of armbands being worn to school later that week as part
of a demonstration. He confirmed that it was at that meeting that the
policy against the wearing of armbands was devised and then recommended by him to the superintendent, Dwight Davis. Peterson also
testified that he and Davis had agreed prior to his meeting with principals on December 14 that banning armbands would be advisable. The
implication of his testimony was that the principals in their meeting
on December 14 were just endorsing a course of action that was already
set in motion by districtwide administrators.

In response to Johnston's questions, Peterson indicated that the
policy against armbands was not put in writing at the time but was later
covered by a broad written policy on student conduct adopted by the
school board. Peterson stated that the policy directed that a student
wearing an armband to school would be asked by school administrators to remove it. If the student refused, the parents would be contacted
and asked to persuade their son or daughter to remove the armband.
If the student still refused, he/she would be sent home "until such time
that the black armband should be removed or that the Board of Education should reverse the . . . policy." Johnston also asked Peterson
whether there were any school district regulations regarding political
or religious insignia prior to December 1965. Peterson didn't answer
the question directly, indicating that "it is not necessary that everything be written out word for word as such," but that principals and
other administrators must have discretion to act as they think best.
Finally Johnston asked Peterson if the policy instituted on December
14 was directed "solely at the students whom you had heard were going
to wear black armbands to support their views on the Viet Nam war?"
Peterson responded that the policy was not directed at any particular
students but "at the principle of the demonstration." Johnston persisted,
asking the witness, "Was the regulation as it was promulgated specifically related to the wearing of black armbands?" Peterson replied:
"It was at this time, this particular meeting, yes."

Herrick conducted the cross-examination of Peterson. He began by
asking the witness if the policy regarding the armbands as reported in
the *Des Moines Register* and *Des Moines Tribune* on December 15, 1965,

was correctly stated. Peterson acknowledged that it was a correct statement of the policy. Herrick then introduced a photocopy of the *Register* article referred to in his question as a defendants' exhibit. Johnston objected to the article as an exhibit because it was not "the best evidence of whatever it is offered . . . to prove." Judge Stephenson, without explicitly overruling Johnston's objection, indicated that it was his understanding that the exhibit was only offered as a statement of what appeared in the press, which the witness verified to be accurate. So he admitted it into evidence for that purpose. Johnston acquiesced.

Then Herrick requested the introduction of two more defendants' exhibits, neither of which Johnston contested. The first of these was titled "Proposed Policy for Secondary Principals Regarding Student Conduct," dated December 23, 1965. The second was a memorandum from Peterson to superintendent Davis concerning "Events Leading up to Banning of Arm Bands," dated December 29, 1965. The policy statement consisted of four brief typed paragraphs and covered about half a page. It never referred to armbands specifically but talked in general terms about "conduct by teachers or students which tend to disrupt the orderly conduct of the everyday educational program of the school, or which are considered by school administrators as likely to do so." The statement also indicated that these policies were consistent with the provisions of the legal Code of Iowa, which authorized the suspension or other disciplining of students for "conduct detrimental to the best interest of the school."

The other defense exhibit, the Peterson memorandum, provided an interesting addendum to his testimony. It began by asserting that the news media in December 1965 indicated that the original purpose of the armband demonstration had been to protest U.S. policy in Vietnam. Only later, he stated, was the purpose changed to "mourning all the dead" and applying pressure for a Christmas truce. Peterson's assertion as to the media's understanding of the purpose of the armband protest was at odds with the testimony offered earlier in the trial by Christopher Eckhardt and John and Mary Beth Tinker and with a close reading of the stories in the mid-December Des Moines papers.

Peterson next noted in his memorandum that the school district's concern about an armband demonstration was occasioned by a draft of an article that Ross Peterson, a Roosevelt High senior, wished to have published in the school newspaper. This article encouraged students concerned about casualties in the Vietnam War and the extension of the Christmas truce to wear black armbands to school beginning on December 16. Raymond Peterson reported that Paul Mitchum, the assistant superintendent, met with the student on Monday, December 13, and asked him "to hold up on this article until someone could talk to him." The talk about whether this article would or would not be published led to the December 14 meeting of Raymond Peterson and the five Des Moines senior-high principals. Out of that meeting came the recommendation to the school district to ban armbands. Shortly after the principals' meeting, still on December 14, Raymond Peterson and Charles Rowley (the Roosevelt principal) met with Ross Peterson about his article. Raymond Peterson reported in the memo that "it was a very friendly conversation, although we did not feel that we had convinced the student that our decision was a just one." Whatever were Ross Peterson's feelings, the article was not published.

The Peterson memo next noted that an announcement was made to students in the Des Moines schools that armbands would not be permitted. Then follows an intriguing statement: "[O]ne of the students apparently contacted the newspaper. The reporter then contacted the school administrators for information. The reporter was asked not to write a story." The reporter, Jack Magarrell, persisted and wrote what would be the first story on the armband incident, appearing in the *Register* on December 15. The Peterson memo also acknowledged that the secondary principals met again on December 23, two days after the first school board meeting on the armband issue, and recommended maintaining the prohibition of armbands. The memo reported that several reasons were given for the principals' recommendation to continue the ban. Among the reasons cited were the following: (1) that mourning the dead in past or current wars was best done on Veterans' Day or Memorial Day; (2) that permitting black armbands might open the door to the display of other symbols, including Nazi insignia; (3) that students who had friends or family members who had died in Vietnam might become angry at students wearing black armbands and that that "might evolve into something . . . difficult to control"; (4) that public school students are captive audiences who "should not be forced to view the demonstrations of a few"; and (5) that the original decision to prohibit armbands was consistent with "standard procedure" for dealing with "inappropriate . . . actions."

Once the various documents had been admitted into evidence, Herrick proceeded quickly to end his cross-examination of Peterson. His final question was whether the Des Moines schools have "a general rule of policy so far as demonstrations in the class room is concerned." Peterson replied, "It's understood among the principals that anything which interrupts the general educational procedure of the school may be excluded by the principals in the building itself." Johnston had no questions on redirect examination, and Peterson was excused.

The plaintiffs' final witness was Ora Niffenegger, the president of the school board. Johnston began by asking Niffenegger when the matter of the disciplining of the students for wearing black armbands first came to his attention. Niffenegger answered that it was on December 16. Johnston then asked him if and when the school board considered upholding the administrative ban on armbands. Niffenegger explained that the matter had been delayed at a board meeting on December 21 but was voted on and endorsed at a board meeting on January 3, 1966.

Herrick began the cross-examination by asking the witness to provide more detail on the circumstances of his knowledge of the armband affair. Niffenegger mentioned receiving phone calls on the afternoon and evening of December 16 from Ross Peterson and Bruce Clark (both identifying themselves as Roosevelt students) and from two women whose names he did not recall. In response to his callers' requests to schedule an emergency board meeting to deal with the armband issue, Niffenegger explained that certain "formalities" and legal procedures—including adequate notice and a prepared agenda—had to be followed to convene a board meeting. However, he told them that the matter could come up at the next regularly scheduled board meeting on Tuesday, December 21, and that they were free to be present then and state their views. To his callers on December 16, Niffenegger said he maintained that the armband demonstration was "the wrong way out," suggesting that policy in Vietnam "should be handled at the ballot box and not in the halls of our public schools." Finally, Herrick asked the school board president if there were any demonstrations at the board meetings in December and January. Niffenegger indicated that the board room was filled on both occasions, that a few signs were visible, and that "on several occasions it was . . . touch and go as far as maintaining order." Niffenegger indicated that some of the individuals "demonstrating" at the board meeting may have come from outside the city. After Herrick completed his cross-examination of Niffenegger, Johnston indicated that he had no questions for the witness on redirect examination. Then Johnston rested the plaintiffs' case.

The only witness called by defendants' attorney Allan Herrick was Richard K. Moberly, Mary Beth Tinker's mathematics teacher at Harding Junior High. Herrick wanted first to know about his conversation with the students in his class on December 15. Moberly testified that the article about the pending armband demonstration in the *Register* that morning had prompted him to say something about the subject in Mary Beth's math class. He described this class as "an exceptional group . . . with sharp minds," and he indicated that he sometimes found it educational to discuss subjects other than mathematics with such a good group of students. This, apparently, was one of those occasions. He testified that as much as thirty minutes was spent that day talking about demonstrations. They started talking about students wearing black armbands but moved on to discussing other types of demonstrations. He indicated that he expressed strongly his view that he would tolerate no demonstrations—except regarding mathematics—in his class.

On cross-examination by Johnston, Moberly said that he had no indication that Mary Beth Tinker might be one of the students wearing an armband the day after he strongly denounced demonstrations to her class. Moberly then admitted that he might have permitted the discussion on December 15 to continue too long: he indicated that this was because, as a teacher, he was torn between trying to teach the content and skills of his subject and still being open to student questions and concerns about a variety of subjects. Asked by Johnston if Mary Beth Tinker was a good student, he replied that she was a "very good student . . . with or without an arm band."

Then Johnston shifted the questioning to the issue of whether other political or religious symbols were worn at Harding Junior High. Moberly indicated that such symbols had, so far, been kept to a minimum at his school. Johnston asked him if a student wearing a button with a picture of Senator Barry Goldwater or President Lyndon Johnson on it would disrupt his class. He responded, "I hope not." Johnston asked him if wearing a button with a picture of President Johnson on it would be a violation of the school district ban on armbands. Moberly indicated that if such a situation ever presented itself he would need to "ask my superiors for an interpretation." Johnston queried Moberly on whether symbols of the German Third Reich, such as the Iron Cross, were included under the school district ban on armbands. Moberly said that he did not think so but that he found Nazi symbols highly objectionable. He allowed that he had seen Iron Crosses around Harding Junior High in the months since Mary Beth was suspended for wearing her black armband, but that he did not believe the Nazi symbols disrupted class. He also testified that, as far as he knew, no students wearing Iron Crosses had been suspended at his school. At this point the witness was excused and Lovrien announced that the defendants rested. Johnston indicated that the plaintiffs had no rebuttal witnesses. The court was adjourned at 3:40 P.M.

## The Trial Ends

The following morning's *Des Moines Register* not only offered a brief account of the development of the case, but also provided highlights from the testimony at the trial. The story quoted John Tinker's justification for wearing a black armband to school on December 17: "When people are getting killed it's important to me." It cited Christopher Eckhardt's contention that the U.S. government has been more interested in escalating the war in Vietnam than in trying to make peace. And it quoted Mary Beth Tinker's response to the question of whether she would wear an armband again: "I'm not sure if I would wear one or not, but I'd like to be able to." The *Register* story on July 26 also referred to the testimony offered by school district officials. It mentioned that Dan Johnston, the attorney for the students, had questioned several administrators about the fact that students were sent home for black armbands worn in mourning for casualties in Vietnam but were allowed to wear religious symbols and political buttons without sanction.

Although the testimony was completed and the exhibits were submitted on Monday, there were still the lawyers' closing arguments, which began at half past nine the morning of Tuesday, July 26. Regrettably there is no transcribed record of these arguments in the district court records of *Tinker v. Des Moines Independent Community School District*, and memories of what was said thirty years ago are understandably fuzzy. The "best available evidence"—to use a lawyer's term—for the closing arguments in the Iowa black-armband case is provided by the Des Moines newspapers of July 27, 1966.

According to the *Register* story that day, Dan Johnston told Judge Stephenson that the three students' right to freedom of expression under the First and Fourteenth Amendments had been denied by the Des Moines school district. To discipline students for wearing symbols of their concern about the war in Vietnam, as was done in this case, but not to take any disciplinary action against students appearing in class with political buttons or "Third Reich crosses" struck Johnston as hypocritical. The story also mentioned that Johnston had stressed that the armband demonstration had resulted in "no marches and no disturbances" by the three youths or anyone else.

For the defendants, Lovrien emphasized that school authorities must have the right to formulate reasonable rules and regulations. Prohibiting demonstrations, including the wearing of black armbands, in the classrooms and halls of the schools is a reasonable policy. Schools are for education, he submitted; other public places may be appropriate forums for protest demonstrations. Furthermore, Lovrien maintained, public-school students are a captive audience who should not be subjected continuously to the political opinions of a few armband-wearing students. Allan Herrick, who also participated in the closing, was quoted in the article as saying that the three students involved in this case were aware of the policy against armbands and that each was afforded more than one opportunity to remove his/her armband without penalty. Thus the students in question knowingly violated a reasonable rule for maintaining order in the schools; their rather mild punishment for their actions should be upheld and the ban on armbands should be continued.

With the completion of the final arguments Judge Stephenson "took the matter under advisement." That means that he retired to his chambers with the transcript of the trial, the exhibits submitted by the attorneys, and his own impressions of the witnesses and the lawyers. He gave no indication of when he would render his decision.

# CHAPTER 7

# Court Decisions in
# Des Moines and St. Louis

## The Judge's Ruling

The parties and the lawyers in *Tinker v. Des Moines Independent Community School District* had to wait five weeks after the close of the trial to learn of Judge Roy Stephenson's ruling. His "memorandum opinion," issued on Thursday, September 1, 1966, was only five and one-half typed, double-spaced pages. He found in favor of the defendants, denying the injunction and nominal damages sought by the Eckhardts and Tinkers and ruling that the original school district policy banning armbands was constitutionally justified. Although the judge's opinion accepted the basic legal position advanced by school district attorneys, some of his findings of fact and legal interpretations would prove useful to the plaintiffs on appeal.

After summarizing "the events giving rise to this controversy," Stephenson noted that he accepted as fact the plaintiffs' avowed dual purpose for wearing the armbands: to mourn the casualties in the Vietnam War and to urge an extension of the 1965 Christmas truce in the conflict. The motivation for the armband protest was not constitutionally important. But the fact that the trial judge recognized the humanitarian impulse behind the three students' symbolic expression (and did not place it in the same category with the more militant war protesters then making headlines in other parts of the country) was important to Christopher Eckhardt and the Tinkers.

Judge Stephenson reached the constitutional issue by the second page of the opinion. Here he noted that an individual's First Amendment freedom of expression is eligible for protection against legislation or actions of state government through the due process clause of the Fourteenth Amendment. This is the so-called "incorporation doctrine," to which Dan Johnston had referred in his trial brief. Judge Stephenson then accepted the plaintiffs' contention that the symbolic act of wearing an armband fell within the freedom of expression protected by the First Amendment. In support of this point he cited *Stromberg v. California* (1931) and *West Virginia State Board of Education v. Barnette* (1943)—two cases cited on this point by Johnston in his trial brief. However, to show that even federal jurists make mistakes, Judge Stephenson misspelled the name of the original plaintiff in the 1943 case as "Burnette."

After these concessions to the plaintiff students, Judge Stephenson's opinion began to tilt toward the school district. He noted that the protections of the free speech clause of the First Amendment are not absolute, accepting the "balancing position" that Allan Herrick had emphasized so heavily in the defendants' trial brief. The principal case that Judge Stephenson cited in support of the balancing position was *Dennis v. United States* (1951), a case *not* mentioned in either party's trial brief. The *Dennis* case confronted the question of whether the "Smith Act," an act of Congress passed in 1940 that made it illegal to belong to an organization advocating the overthrow of the government, infringed the rights of free expression of leading members of the American Communist Party. The federal district court, the court of appeals, and a majority of the U.S. Supreme Court all sided with the government position that the prosecutions under the Smith Act did not violate the First Amendment free speech clause. The passage from the *Dennis* case quoted by Judge Stephenson actually came from the opinion written at the appeals court level by Judge Learned Hand: "In each case [courts] must ask whether the gravity of the 'evil,' discounted by its improbability, justifies such invasion of free speech as is necessary to avoid the danger." Although the *Dennis* case has not been overruled by the U.S. Supreme Court, its sweep was substantially restricted by the Court in *Yates v. U.S.* (1957).

Judge Stephenson's opinion then applied his understanding of the law to the factual situation in the case. This section of his opinion essentially followed the trial brief of Allan Herrick and Philip Lovrien. He noted that the school officials have a responsibility to provide and maintain a "disciplined atmosphere" and that "they have an obligation to prevent anything which might be disruptive of such an atmosphere." He ruled that courts should move to set aside school policy only if the authorized officials act "unreasonably." At this point Stephenson took "judicial notice" (i.e., recognized the existence of certain facts, without the production of evidence, that have a bearing on the case) of the atmosphere of protest and controversy over the Vietnam War—nationally and in Iowa. He mentioned specifically the November 1965 March on Washington in which two of the plaintiffs had participated, the "wave of draft card burning incidents" that included two such cases pending in his court, and the two contentious school board meetings that had taken place in Des Moines after the armband incident.

Stephenson conceded that controversial subjects should not be excluded from the secondary-school classroom, but he agreed with the defendants that there need to be reasonable regulations. He maintained that, although the black armbands worn by a handful of Des Moines students in late 1965 may not in and of themselves have been disruptive, "the reactions and comments from other students as a result of the armbands would be likely to disturb the disciplined atmosphere required for any classroom." Given this situation, he concluded, the Des Moines school officials had a "reasonable basis" for adopting some form of regulation on the wearing of armbands. Even the banning of armbands from school, the judge stated, only infringed the plaintiffs' freedom of speech to a "limited extent." They could still wear the armbands outside of school, and they were free to participate in classroom discussions of the Vietnam War at appropriate times and in an orderly fashion. He concluded this point by declaring, "In this instance, however, it is the disciplined atmosphere of the classroom, not the plaintiffs' right to wear armbands on school premises, which is entitled to the protection of the law."

Since the trial briefs in *Tinker* had been prepared, two important cases from the Fifth Circuit Court of Appeals (the midlevel federal court whose jurisdiction encompasses the Deep South) had come to the attention of the attorneys and Judge Stephenson. In his closing argument at the trial, Johnston made reference to these cases, *Burnside v. Byars* (1966) and *Blackwell v. Issaquena County Board of Education* (1966). In the *Burnside* case, the circuit court held that a Mississippi school district's prohibition of the wearing of "freedom buttons" violated the students' freedom of expression; in *Blackwell* the same court reached the opposite conclusion. The buttons in question were inscribed with the acronym "SNCC" (Student Non-Violent Coordinating Committee). In *Burnside* there was a factual finding that the buttons had led to no disruption of discipline: thirty or forty students wearing the buttons aroused only a mild curiosity among other students. In the *Blackwell* case, however, the wearing of the SNCC-inscribed buttons led to disruptive conduct through the school, with some students attempting to pin buttons on students who did not want them and with many students throwing the buttons around their classrooms or out windows. The fifth circuit court held that a school district's prohibition of symbolic expression could be upheld only if there had been a factual finding that the disturbances that had taken place were "inexorably tied" to the symbolic expression. Stephenson referred briefly to both cases. He acknowledged that *Burnside* offered some support for the plaintiffs' contention that, absent proof of disruptions of the educational process, students' symbolic expression cannot be infringed. However, he emphasized that although *Burnside* was "entitled to respect and should not be brushed aside lightly," as the decision of another circuit it was not binding on the eighth circuit, of which the Southern District of Iowa is a part.

Judge Stephenson brought his opinion to a conclusion by submitting that an actual disturbance is not required to justify a cutting back on the freedom of expression. If "a disturbance in school discipline is reasonably to be anticipated," then "actions which are reasonably calculated to prevent such a disruption must be upheld by the Court." With that statement the judge denied the request for an injunction and nominal damages, assessed the court costs to the plaintiffs, and ordered that the judgment be entered.

## Reactions to the District Court Decision

Dan Johnston had thought from the beginning that it would be difficult to win his case at the district court level. He believed that Judge Stephenson's military background and conservative Republican political orientation would make it virtually impossible for him to vote in favor of war protesters of any ilk or to endorse the apparent affront to order and discipline presented by the Des Moines students' black armbands. But Johnston remembers being pleased at the time that he had been able to place into the record the fact that the school district punished his clients for wearing black armbands but failed to discipline students who wore religious medallions or political buttons. Although that point was not mentioned in the trial judge's decision, Johnston sensed that appellate judges at the circuit or Supreme Court levels might well find constitutional problems with the apparent double standard. Johnston was also pleased that the defendants' attorneys had not been able to introduce much testimony into the record of the case attesting to actual disruptions in the routine of the Des Moines schools stemming from the armband demonstration. Given the recent precedents offered by the fifth circuit court's decisions in *Burnside* and *Blackwell,* Johnston saw a good possibility of an appeals court noting the relatively mild student reactions to the armbands and seeing little justification for the school district's preemptive prohibitions. Finally, Johnston was surprised that Judge Stephenson would rely on *Dennis v. U.S.* as a leading authority for the proposition that freedom of expression is not an absolute value. Johnston called *Dennis* a case that "nobody followed anymore." In fact, the moment Johnston read that Stephenson cited *Dennis,* he thought "he just didn't get it." He suspected that, on appeal, either the circuit court or the U.S. Supreme Court would look askance at such a relic of the Cold War as *Dennis v. U.S.*

On the other hand, Edgar Bittle, the law clerk for the defendants' attorneys, was pleased both by the way the trial had unfolded and by how strong an opinion Judge Stephenson had written. He believed that Herrick and Lovrien had satisfactorily demonstrated that the armband protest had presented a serious threat to discipline in the Des Moines schools and that the legal precedents the defendants cited on the subject of school authority augured well for the school district's position. In addition, Bittle believed that Johnston's inexperience as a trial attorney had blunted his impact on the court. In preparing for the trial, Bittle recalls the defendants' attorneys regretting that they had not been able to persuade any Des Moines students to come forward to testify that threats had been made against those pupils wearing armbands. As a consequence, without corroborating testimony from students, the best Herrick and Lovrien could do to demonstrate that a "disruptive potential" existed was to allow administrators like Donald Blackman and E. Raymond Peterson to testify as to the threats. This was sufficient proof for Judge Stephenson at the district court level to rule that serious disturbances were possible in the wake of the armband affair. But would that suffice to carry this point on appeal?

The newspaper account in the *Des Moines Register* on September 2, 1966, was brief. In a one-column, non-bylined story on page 12, titled "Arm Band Case Appeal Urged," the *Register* reported that the ICLU was already calling for an appeal of Judge Stephenson's decision in the case. An unnamed representative on the ICLU's "legal committee" was quoted as saying that the organization "would continue to offer assistance if the two families decide to appeal." The ICLU representative also emphasized that Stephenson's decision conflicted with the recent fifth circuit decision on "freedom buttons." That same afternoon the *Des Moines Tribune* carried a long front-page story on Stephenson's decision. In contrast to the *Register*'s morning story, the *Tribune* elected to quote heavily from the judge's opinion and provided a brief synopsis of the case to that point. The only reaction to the district court decision noted in the article was a quotation from Johnston, emphasizing that the ICLU had offered to continue to pay some of the expenses should the Eckhardts and Tinkers choose to appeal the decision.

On Saturday morning, September 3, the *Register*'s lead editorial, "Schools and Free Speech," was on the black-armband case. The editorialist emphasized the contrasting analysis between Judge Stephenson's ruling in *Tinker v. Des Moines Independent Community School District* and the two "freedom button" cases from the fifth circuit court. After pointing out that the appeals court in the South drew a clear distinction between conduct that interferes with school activity and conduct that does not, the editorial pointed out that in *Tinker* Stephenson did not see the need to make such a distinction. As a result, the Iowa federal judge's analysis permitted a school district "to pre-judge an expression of political opinion." Then the editorial made an astute prediction: "If the Circuit Court of Appeals in this circuit upholds Judge Stephenson, the conflict with the Fifth Circuit probably will have to be resolved by the Supreme Court." The *Register* editorial concluded with middle-of-the-road sentiments similar to those that had characterized its editorials on the armband issue in December 1965 and January 1966: it agreed with Judge Stephenson that schools should have the discretion to formulate rules to promote and maintain discipline but concurred with the student plaintiffs that these schools should also be "hospitable to free expression and the exchange of ideas in and out of the classroom." The editorial also contained a classic example of journalistic hindsight that provided little comfort to Ora Niffenegger, E. Raymond Peterson, and other school officials: "We think the Des Moines school authorities would have been wiser if they had ignored the arm bands."

## Preparing for the Appeal

Should the plaintiffs in the black-armband case not be content to accept Judge Stephenson's decision, they could choose to appeal his decision to the U.S. Court of Appeals. Occupying the intermediate tier in the U.S. federal court system, the courts of appeals lie between the district court layer and the Supreme Court. Parties losing in the district court have an automatic right to appeal for another hearing in the appropriate appeals court. There are currently thirteen "circuits," divided on a geographic basis, making up the court of appeals. These circuits are staffed by judges who, like federal district judges and Supreme Court justices, are appointed by the President and "hold their offices during good behavior." Courts of appeals do not conduct trials of fact, but rather they hold hearings on legal points raised in the courts below. Appeals court hearings are based on the record of the proceedings in the district court, briefs of arguments prepared by the attorneys, and oral arguments offered by the attorneys before a panel of appeals court judges. The chief judge selects the judges—usually a panel of three—for each case docketed for appeal. For especially important cases, the court will sit en banc—meaning that all of the judges in the circuit will hear the case. The Southern District of Iowa is part of the U.S. Court of Appeals for the Eighth Circuit. The eighth circuit holds its hearings in St. Louis, Missouri.

As the Des Moines newspaper stories in early September 1966 made clear, the plaintiffs in the armband suit were ready to appeal the district court decision almost from the minute it was issued. Johnston knew that he had a good case to appeal and had no difficulty persuading the Eckhardts and Tinkers to allow him to take the necessary procedural steps to get the appeal moving. On Friday, September 16, the board of directors of the ICLU held its monthly meeting at Bishop's Downtown Buffet in Des Moines. The minutes of that meeting reveal that the

ICLU board heard a recommendation that the organization should continue to provide assistance to the parents and students in the black-armband case by helping to fund an appeal of Judge Stephenson's ruling. Subsequent ICLU statements indicate that the organization must have agreed to support the Eckhardt-Tinker appeal sometime in late September 1966. The minutes also show that Johnston, recently elected as a board member and vice chairman of the ICLU, continued to be privately retained by the complainants in the case.

On September 28, Johnston filed the necessary "Notice of Appeal" form with the office of the clerk of the U.S. District Court for the Southern District of Iowa to appeal Judge Stephenson's decision to the Eighth Circuit Court of Appeals in St. Louis, Missouri. The Eckhardts and Tinkers, as members of the losing party in the lower court, now on appeal became the "appellants." The Des Moines Independent Community School District and the approximately twenty named school district officials, as the winning party in court below, became the "appellees" in this action.

Over the next five weeks the copy machines in the Des Moines law offices of Jesse, Le Tourneau & Johnston (attorneys for the appellants) and Herrick, Langdon, Sandblom & Belin (attorneys for the appellees) were busy cranking out copies of the record in the district court case to be sent up to the court of appeals. Ultimately, the appellants (and also the appellees) would need to submit thirty copies of the record and twenty copies of their appellate briefs to the clerk of the circuit court, and another half dozen of each would be needed for their own use and, of course, for the attorneys for the other side.

While the appellants' attorney was busy putting together his paperwork for the appeal, the ICLU was undertaking an appeal for funds to support the clerical and copying expenses necessary for an appeal. On November 17, a letter, addressed to "Friends," went out from the ICLU over the signatures of the Eckhardt and Tinker families. In it the two families informed the recipients that they had decided to appeal Judge Stephenson's decision in the armband case to the Eighth Circuit Court of Appeals. The letter noted that the recent court of appeals "freedom buttons" decision from the South had bolstered the legal position of their children. The Eckhardt-Tinker letter also noted that the ICLU had assumed the costs of the case so far and was willing to continue its assistance in the future but that additional contributions to the ICLU, in the form of new memberships or money especially designated for the armband appeal, were needed. They requested money for the copying and filing expenses to the eighth circuit, estimated at about $500. The ICLU files do not contain information as to how much financial support was received as a result of this appeal.

## Whose Record?

On January 16, 1967, Robert C. Tucker, clerk of the Eighth Circuit Court of Appeals, received an official packet of legal materials concerning appeals court case number 18,642— *Tinker v. Des Moines Independent Community School District*—from the appellants' attorney, Dan Johnston. Among these materials were thirty copies of the record of the *Tinker* case at the district court level. (A court record is essentially the official documentary history of the case to that point.) Besides providing copies for the appeals court, Johnston simultaneously had copies sent to the attorneys for the appellees, the Des Moines school district. The copy of the record submitted by Johnston included copies of the following documents: the plaintiffs' original complaint in the armband lawsuit; the defendants' answer; the pretrial stipulations agreed to by both parties; edited summaries of the testimony of the witnesses at the district court trial on July 25, 1966; defendants' exhibit number 1; Judge Stephenson's "memorandum opinion"; and various procedural notifications. The document Johnston submitted was fifty typed pages in length.

The most interesting section of the record presented to the court by Johnston was the portion containing the edited summaries of the trial testimony; this amounted to about two-thirds of the document. In this section, what Johnston did—with the exception of one witness— was to edit out the attorneys' questions and present the witnesses' answers in narrative form. Overall, the narrative format allowed Johnston to condense the testimony substantially: whereas it had taken up more than 150 double-spaced pages in the official transcript of the district court trial, Johnston's narrative summary technique brought it down to about 30 single-spaced pages.

Had the attorneys for the appellees not objected, the version of the record presented by Johnston would have been the official documentary history of the case consulted by the appeals court. However, because the attorneys for the appellees did not believe the testimony summaries presented by the appellants were compete enough, they submitted on February 3, 1967, along with their appellate brief, thirty copies of a "Supplement to the Printed Record" for perusal by the appeals court. The school district attorneys justified the additional submission thus: "The defendants-appellees, deeming the printed record filed by plaintiff-appellants to be incomplete, hereby amend the same in the manner hereinafter particularly designated and pointed out." The additions presented by the appellees included the following items: narrative additions to the testimony of John Tinker, Donald Blackman, and Ora Niffenegger; several pages of verbatim testimony and attorneys' questions for Christopher Eckhardt; narrative summaries of the testimony of Leo Willadsen and Vera Tarmann; defendants' exhibits numbers 2 to 4; and a long portion of the defendants' deposition of Leonard Tinker.

All of the items in the appellants' statement of the record and the appellee's supplement to the printed record have been discussed previously, with one exception. That exception is the defendants' sworn and transcribed deposition of Leonard Tinker, placed in the record as defendants' exhibit number 8. The depositions of the three armband-wearing students—Christopher Eckhardt, John Tinker, and Mary Beth Tinker— were essentially tracked and restated in the testimony at the trial. But because neither side called Leonard Tinker to testify before Judge Stephenson, his deposition is an important and unique primary document in the case. The deposition of Leonard Tinker, summarized in the appellees' supplement to the printed record, is eleven pages in length, almost half the length of the entire supplement. Most of it is in narrative form, but a few sections are set out via the question and answer format taken verbatim from the transcript of the depostion.

Allan Herrick, who was administering the deposition, persisted in asking Leonard Tinker about any influence that SDS might have had on the armband protest. It became quickly clear to Dan Johnston, who represented Tinker at the deposition, that the school district attorney wanted to identify the black-armband demonstration with this radical student group. Tinker acceded that he was "familiar with it [SDS] generally." He also acknowledged there were college students who claimed to be SDS members at the meeting on December 11, 1965, in the Eckhardt home when the armband demonstration was being planned. But Tinker stated emphatically that "the people actually excluded from school were not members of the SDS. . . . [N]or were they directed by the SDS, nor were they organized by the SDS. They were not implementing the program of the SDS." He also explained that he had no knowledge of the reported picketing of the December 21, 1965, school board meeting by SDS members, which was later mentioned in the Des Moines papers. Herrick then asked him about a December 22 story in one of the Des Moines newspapers that reported that the Women's International League for Peace and Freedom, of which Margaret Eckhardt was then Des Moines chapter president, had joined with SDS in encouraging the wearing of black armbands in school. Tinker replied that he was familiar with the story but had no knowledge of the positions of the Women's International League for Peace and Freedom, just as he had no knowledge of SDS other than what he had already mentioned.

About the middle of the deposition Herrick asked Leonard Tinker about his children's decision to wear the black armbands. Tinker explained that he and his wife talked about the issue with their children that week but put no pressure on them to wear armbands. He said he even raised what he termed "a very serious objection" to their contemplated defiance of authority. But once it because clear that several of his children were going to wear armbands as a matter of conscience, he felt that he owed them his support. Herrick pressed him on the matter of defying authority. Tinker responded that he was mindful of the unpopular stand that his children were about to take in challenging school authority. He stated, "I believe in the exercise of authority. I believe authorities ought to be obeyed but not absolutely. There are times when they must also be questioned and it seemed to me this was one of these times." During the course of Tinker's explanation of his children's decision to wear armbands an amusing exchange took place. He was asked where his children obtained the black cloth for the armbands. He said that he supposed they found it around the house or that Lorena Tinker found it for them. Then in a comment that may or may not have been intended to be humorous, he said, "I wouldn't know whether there was that much black cloth in the house."

Leonard Tinker was asked about a meeting that he attended on December 19 at the Friends' House to plan strategy for the school board meeting two nights later. Herrick asked Tinker if there had been discussion at that meeting about physical attacks on armband-wearing students. Tinker responded indirectly by saying that "my youngsters were having a problem and some other youngsters were having a problem," but he also indicated that he did not recall any discussion that night about students being hit by other students over the armband issue. Finally, Herrick asked Tinker if he agreed with the statement that Craig Sawyer had reportedly made at the school board meeting on December 21 to the effect that the constitutional principle of free expression allowed him to support the right of a person to wear a black armband, a Nazi armband, or even an armband saying "down with the school board." Tinker said, "Oh, that's a long question, I'd rather not answer that." Herrick pressed Tinker on the matter, and Tinker still refused to answer. Then the record of the deposition states, "The question was not answered on the advice and instructions from counsel and similar questions were not answered for the same reason." It was at this point, as noted by Johnston years later, that he and Tinker had threatened to abort the deposition because they were so angry at Herrick. In any case, the Tinker deposition concluded shortly after this heated exchange.

## The Circuit Court Briefs

Besides the record of the proceedings in the district court, the attorney for the Eckhardts and the Tinkers as well as the attorneys for the Des Moines school district submitted appellate briefs to the eighth circuit. Twenty copies of Johnston's brief for the appellants and his version of the record were sent to the clerk of the circuit court in early January 1967. Copies of Johnston's brief were also sent to Herrick's law firm. Herrick sent copies of his brief to the circuit court and to Johnston in February 1967. Johnston elected to file a "Reply Brief" shortly after receiving the appellees' brief; the circuit court received it on February 23. The three briefs, the two from Johnston for the Eckhardt and Tinker families and the one from Herrick for the school district, would provide the principal analysis on which the circuit court judges would later base their decision. The general rule of appellate procedure in the United States is that appeals courts will not review matters of fact determined by a lower court unless clearly erroneous. Hence most appellate proceedings, this one included, revolve around legal issues that were in dispute at the trial or grow out of the lower court decision itself.

Johnston's appellants' brief began with a terse "statement of the case" in which he summarized the facts in the dispute. He emphasized that there was a minimum of disruption of regular routines on the days the armbands were worn. In addition he noted that while his clients had been disciplined for wearing black armbands, other students wearing religious symbols, political campaign buttons, and even Nazi insignia had not been disciplined. In fact, the policy of the school district to which his clients objected mentioned only armbands.

Johnston presented two main legal arguments in his brief. The first was that Judge Stephenson had erred in the constitutional standard that he had applied to review the symbolic speech of the three Des Moines students. Johnston maintained that the standard of *Dennis v. U.S.*, relied on by the district court, was inappropriate in this case. *Dennis* dealt with a prior legislative declaration (the "Smith Act") that deemed certain kinds of speech too dangerous or disruptive to be permitted (e.g., belonging to a group advocating violence). In the Iowa blackarmband case, however, there was no prior legislative determination of dangerous speech or conduct. In such a situation, Johnston argued, "the Court itself must determine whether the speech involves such likelihood of bringing about a substantive evil as to deprive the speaker of constitutional protection."

Instead of relying on the *Dennis* precedent, Johnston stated, the court should evaluate the conduct of his clients according to the standards of a different line of cases—those in which there had been no legislative finding of "clear and present danger" and in which intent to urge illegal conduct was not present. The fact situations of such cases involve matters such as the lease of public halls, the distribution of pamphlets, labor-management disputes, political speech making on a public sidewalk, a religious meeting on a public street or park, and refusal to salute a flag. The courts have viewed the governmental request to punish speech in such cases with much more skepticism than in a situation such as that presented by *Dennis*. The critical element that supported the punishment of such speech was the factual finding that the particular word or symbolism caused disorder or presented the clear possibility of disorder. Johnston emphasized that the factual record of the *Tinker* case provided "no evidence . . . that when Appellants were suspended there existed any threats of disorder, threats of violence, or riot, or that Appellants acted in a manner detrimental to peace and order." He granted that the school district feared the conduct of the armband-wearing students might be disruptive but pointed out that the record offered only "trivial" examples of disruption.

Then Johnston speculated as to "the true reason for the regulation against the arm bands." He argued that the testimony at the trial indicated that it was the "bias against . . . demonstration[s] thought to be out of the main-stream of popular contemporary political opinion." He cited statements of E. Raymond Peterson, the director of secondary education, and Ora Niffenegger, president of the school board, to support this contention. At this point he noted that the regulation at issue applied to only one form of symbolic expression—the wearing of black armbands. The district court record reveals that the displaying of religious medallions and political insignia was not prohibited or punished by the school district. Johnston stressed that freedom of expression is more important that decorum. He cited a passage from a 1949 U.S. Supreme Court decision, *Terminello v. City of Chicago:* "The vitality of civil and political institutions in our society depends on free discussion. . . . The right to speak freely and to promote diversity of ideas and programs is therefore one of the chief distinctions that sets us apart from totalitarian regimes."

Johnston's second argument was that the district court erred by not granting relief to his clients because there was no evidence showing that they had "materially interfered with the requirements of appropriate discipline in the operation of the schools." Judge Stephenson had ruled that although the armbands might not have been disruptive in and of themselves, they might have led to disruptive actions (or reactions) from other students. Johnston believed that this position should not pass constitutional muster. He observed that the assumption of the lower court appeared to be "that school officials have a rather absolute authority over the conduct of students which transcends even their most basic privileges as citizens." Finally Johnston referred to the fifth circuit case from Mississippi, *Burnside v. Byars* (1966), a case he said was "nearly identical" to *Tinker*. In the fifth circuit case, the factual record in the lower federal court revealed that students wearing "freedom buttons" were suspended not because they caused a disturbance but because they violated a rule. Since the fifth circuit struck down that Mississippi district court decision, he urged the eighth circuit to act similarly regarding the Iowa district court ruling. He, therefore, urged the court "to remand this cause to the District Court with instructions to grant the relief Appellants sought therein."

The appellees' brief on behalf of the Des Moines Independent Community School District and several named school officials was prepared by Allan Herrick, Philip Lovrien, and a third associate, Herschel G. Langdon. In its lengthy statement of the facts, it alleged that some of those attending the meeting on December 11, 1965, who planned the armband demonstration were college student members of SDS. The school district also went to great length to extract from the record all the references to nasty comments made to the students wearing armbands. The point, of course, was that the black armbands worn to Des Moines schools in mid-December did have an impact in terms of inciting "uncomplimentary remarks" and that it was the intention of the appellants, as John Tinker testified at the trial, "to influence public opinion about the matter of Viet Nam, to call attention to it." The school district's attorneys were trying to convince the circuit court that disruptions did take place in the normal order of educational activity during the time that the armbands were visible.

The school district's legal analysis had three parts. The first point, and by far the longest, was that Judge Stephenson's dismissal of the plaintiffs-appellants' claim was correct because the school district rule prohibiting black armbands was reasonable and within the discretionary powers of the school officials. A corollary of this position, of course, was that the armband-wearing students' First Amendment rights were not violated. The school district's attorneys pointed out that the law in Iowa and other states allows school authorities "to adopt reasonable rules and regulations governing the conduct of . . . pupils." The brief cited a number of state court decisions that, he maintained, supported the proposition that "it is not for the courts to consider whether the rule in retrospect was wise or expedient, so long as it was a reasonable exercise of the discretion vested in the school authorities." One of the cases cited was a very recent decision, *Independent School District of Waterloo v. Green* (1967), in which the Iowa Supreme Court upheld a school district rule that excluded married students from participating in extracurricular athletics. In its opinion, the Iowa court stated: "The duty of all courts, regardless of personal views or individual philosophies, is to uphold a school regulation unless it is clearly arbitrary and unreasonable. Any other approach would result in confusion detrimental to the management, progress and efficient operation of our public school system." On this point the school district brief also referred to *Burnside v. Byars* (1966), the fifth circuit decision that Johnston had cited with such enthusiasm. Even in that case, the school district maintained, the court of appeals recognized that "school officials have a wide latitude of discretion. . . . It is not for us to consider whether . . . rules are wise or expedient but merely whether they are a reasonable exercise of the power and discretion of the school authorities."

Then the school district returned to the balancing test of free expression that Herrick and Lovrien had emphasized in their trial brief. The brief argued that a majority of the Supreme Court had never held the First Amendment to offer absolute protection to speech. Perhaps the classic statement of the balancing test is found in *American Communications v. Douds* (1950), a case in which the Supreme Court upheld a provision of the National Labor Relations Act requiring that labor union officials attest that they are not members of the Communist Party. Language from the majority opinion in *Douds* was quoted with approval by the school district's attorneys: "When particular conduct is regulated in the interest of public order, and the regulation results in an indirect, conditional, particular abridgment of speech, the duty of the courts is to determine which of these two conflicting interests demands the greater protection under the particular circumstances presented."

At this point the brief turned to the two fifth circuit "freedom buttons" cases, one of which Dan Johnston had cited in his brief for the appellants. The school district attorneys observed that "the Fifth Circuit takes the position that school authorities may not prohibit a demonstration until it has progressed to such a point that school discipline has, in fact, been seriously affected. Defendants submit that this view is erroneous." Herrick and his associates then quoted with approval the trial court opinions in one of the freedom button cases: "[I]f

　　　　{ *The Struggle for Student Rights* }

... a disturbance in school discipline is reasonably to be anticipated, actions which are reasonably calculated to prevent such a disruption must be upheld by the Court." The school district attorneys felt that, given the controversy in the Des Moines schools over the war in Vietnam, there was reason to believe that an antiwar protest involving black armbands might reasonably trigger disturbances in the schools. The brief pointed to the following facts in evidence to suggest that the situation was volatile: the November 1965 Washington protest march in which at least two of the armband-wearing students had participated, the death in the Vietnam War of a former Des Moines high school student, and the testimony that a counterdemonstration was being planned should antiwar students wear black armbands to school in mid-December. They also alluded to the hostile remarks that John Tinker faced when he wore his armband as indicative of the tension in Iowa schools over the Vietnam War. With these matters in mind, the school district attorneys argued, it was reasonable for the principals and the director of secondary education to act as they did in banning armbands. To run a school district effectively requires discretionary authority, and the school district attorneys stressed that "school authorities are not obligated to wait until trouble occurs" before acting accordingly.

Then the attorneys for the school district attempted to point out the essential difference between the Des Moines armband case and the 1943 flag salute case cited so prominently by Dan Johnston. Lawyers and judges refer to this as "distinguishing" one case from another. According to the school district attorneys, the Jehovah's Witness students who petitioned not to be forced to salute the American flag during World War II were merely observing the tenets of their religious faith, whereas the armband wearers were demonstrating to advocate a point of view and to persuade others of the correctness of their point of view. Herrick and his associates admitted that Christopher Eckhardt and the Tinkers had the right to wear their armbands outside of school, but they asserted that in school the students' actions were subject to reasonable regulations necessary to maintain discipline.

The short second and third legal points raised by the school district attorneys in the last two pages of their brief were virtual reiterations of points two and three in the defendants' trial brief. The first of these two minor arguments was that individual defendants acting in good faith in the performance of official duties should not be liable for damages. In the second they claimed that the federal statute under which the case was being argued authorized a cause of action only against individuals, not against a school district. The appellees' attorneys argued that the court would not need to pass on either of these two minor points if it found in favor of the school district on the major First Amendment issue. The brief concluded by urging affirmation of the district court opinion of Judge Stephenson.

The appellants' reply brief was only a few pages long. Its major contention was that the balancing rule of free expression that enamored the school district attorneys should be applied by the court not instead of the so-called "clear and present danger" test, but in tandem with it. To understand this point requires some explanation. The clear-and-present-danger test of whether expression can be constitutionally regulated was formulated by the legendary Supreme Court justice Oliver Wendell Holmes, Jr., in *Schenck v. U.S.* (1919). In upholding the World War I Espionage Act that prohibited acts of disloyal speech, Holmes penned his much quoted and discussed words: "The question in every case is whether the words are used in such circumstances and are of such a nature as to create a clear and present danger that they will bring about the substantive evils the Congress has a right to prevent." Johnston argued that the balancing test should not be triggered until there is a finding that there is a clear and present danger that the exercise of free expression (in this case the wearing of black armbands) would result in the "substantive evil" (presumably a serious disruption of school discipline). According to Johnston, the school district attorneys had never demonstrated that there was a clear and present danger of significant disturbances stemming from a few students wearing black armbands. Johnston noted that a close reading of *American Communications Association v. Douds* (1950), the principal case from which the school district extracted the balancing test, supported his position. In *Douds,* the Supreme Court held that only after it was found that a clear and present danger existed was it necessary to determine whether the government interest was weighty enough to offset the danger to free speech. The few trivial examples of disturbance or threatened disturbance that the school district claimed stemmed from a few black armbands, Johnston declared, hardly constituted a clear and present danger.

## Oral Argument and Stalemate

After the submission of the briefs to the Eighth Circuit Court of Appeals, Case No. 18642—*Tinker, et al., Appellants v. Des Moines Independent Community School District, et al., Appellees*—was assigned to a panel of three judges. The hearing was set for April 1967. So at the appointed time, the attorneys—Johnston for the Eckhardts and the Tinkers, and Herrick and Lovrien for the school district—journeyed down to St. Louis and presented their case in oral argument before the appeals panel.

The oral argument of the *Tinker* case before the three-judge panel in St. Louis is impossible to reconstruct. There are no official transcripts of the arguments, newspaper coverage was virtually nonexistent, and lawyers' memories after almost thirty years yield little of substance. Johnston's one memory from the three-judge hearing is a humorous one. He recalls that he had placed a count for one dollar in nominal damages in the original complaint because he wanted to keep the issues in the case from being declared moot should the students graduate or no longer wish to wear armbands. He was asked, in good humor, by one of the appeals court judges if he was insisting on the dollar in nominal damages. Johnston recalls responding in kind: "No," he replied, "I didn't have the case on a contingent fee."

For whatever reason, the three-judge panel of the eighth circuit could not come to a decision in *Tinker*. So on April 26, 1967, the court ordered a reargument of the case before the judges of the eighth circuit en banc at its October 1967 session. The court noted that it was ordering the rare en banc hearing because of the importance of this case. So in mid-October 1967, the lawyers once again trooped back to St. Louis to present their arguments orally. Although there is, again, no official transcript of this hearing, a detailed article on the hearing appeared in the *Des Moines Register* a few days later.

The *Register* story began by citing a statement from Johnston's opening presentation that it was an unconstitutional "prior restraint" for school authorities "to come beforehand and make a regulation against students wearing arm bands, unless they knew if was going to be disruptive." Johnston then declared that the armbands caused little disruption in school routine in December 1965 but that the incident gave the Des Moines school authorities an excuse to suppress political demonstrations. On this point Johnston was challenged by Judge Donald P. Lay, who indicated that it seemed to him that school officials were willing to entertain "alternative points of view . . . expressed in class, whenever it's regulated." Johnston did not find such regulated expression adequate: "I submit this is not free speech at all. There is too much interference. What if President Johnson said you can argue against his policies only on Fridays?" Johnston emphasized that part of civic education is teaching students that it is sometimes necessary to challenge authority. And what better place is there to teach them this lesson than in the public schools?

Lovrien, who began the oral argument for the Des Moines Independent Community School District, maintained that it was the duty of school boards and other school authorities to "make reasonable rules and regulations." But sometimes, he stated, such rules limit conduct, including that of speech and expression. For example, he said, "no one disputes that officials shouldn't have the right to rule that talking in class, except when called on, is wrong." If a potentially disruptive situation presents itself, Lovrien declared, "it does not seem logical . . . to say a school must wait and see what happens, and then if something happens, pass a regulation."

Judge M. C. Matthes then asked Lovrien a question that addressed the "double standard" of symbolic expression that Johnston had raised on several previous occasions. The judge wanted to know why special measures had been taken to prohibit black armbands from the Des Moines schools when the wearing of other symbolic insignia, such as religious medallions or political campaign buttons, had never been challenged. Lovrien's response was that the wearing of such items was probably incidental and, besides, school officials may have thought that wearing a campaign button was part of the educational process. Another question to Lovrien came from Judge G.W. Heaney, who wanted to know why, instead of suspending students for wearing armbands, the school officials did not just hold assemblies explaining the rights of minorities and the right to protest under the U.S. Constitution. Lovrien's rejoinder was that to have done so would have taken valuable time from other subjects in the school curriculum. Lovrien then made a statement that the *Register* elected to highlight in bold-faced type: "If courts continue second-guessing [school] administrations and tell them what to do and not to do, I think we're in for a lot of administration by courts and not by the schools."

At this point Herrick took over the podium from his colleague. Johnston recalls that Herrick had a special way of relieving his associate in oral argument: "[D]own at the Court of Appeals, Lovrien started out making the argument. And then at some point, when Herrick had decided that Lovrien had said enough, Herrick would gather all of his papers up and start pounding them on end on the table, and that was the signal for Lovrien to sit down, [and] that Herrick was going to get up." Herrick, in his remarks, questioned whether the armbands worn by Christopher Eckhardt and John and Mary Beth Tinker represented their views or those of their parents. Johnston responded to this point by saying that, of course, these parents have had some influence in the formation of the views of their children but that these three youths expressed their own beliefs articulately and with great sincerity in their depositions and trial court testimony.

On the matter of which constitutional test should be applied to the wearing of armbands, Johnston submitted that "any disruption is trivial if there is no clear and present danger." Johnston was asked if he believed an individual should violate a law he believed to be unconstitutional. His response was that such an act would constitute civil disobedience and that, as such, the person committing the act should be prepared to accept the punishment. But, he added, "this does not necessarily show a disrespect for the law."

The attorneys and the parties did not have to wait long for the appeals court ruling—what there was of it. The decision came down on November 3, 1967, with the en banc court splitting 4–4. A decision by an equally divided court is regarded as an affirmation of the decision of the court below. Hence, Judge Roy Stephenson's decision—upholding the Des Moines school district's ban on black armbands—would stand, pending a reversal by the U.S. Supreme Court. The appeals court ruling was contained in a one-paragraph per curiam opinion. Latin for "by the court," *per curiam* is a phrase used to identify an opinion of a whole court as distinct from an opinion written by a single judge. A per curiam opinion is sometimes issued by a judicial body to mask the reasons for a disagreement on the court. The appeals court opinion in *Tinker* served just such a purpose. It contained no analysis whatsoever; it was essentially an order without justification. It read:

This is an appeal from a judgment entered September 1, 1966, by the United States District court for the Southern District of Iowa, Central Division, dismissing plaintiffs' complaint, based upon 42 U.S.C.A., Section 1983, seeking an injunction and nominal damages against defendants, the Des Moines Independent Community School District, the individual members of its Board of Directors, its superintendent and various principals and teachers thereof, for suspending plaintiffs from school for wearing armbands protesting the Viet Nam war, in violation of a school regulation promulgated by administrative officials of the School District proscribing the wearing of such armbands. . . . [citation deleted] Following argument before a regular panel of this court, the case was reargued and submitted to the court en banc. The judgment below is affirmed by an equally divided court.

In one sense, the terse court of appeals decision was a disappointment. After working hundreds of hours on their appellate briefs and oral arguments in the fourteen months since Judge Stephenson's district court decision, all the attorneys for both parties in the black-armband case had to show for their efforts was a 125–word paragraph. Still, there were grounds for optimism for both sets of litigants and their attorneys. For the Des Moines school district and its attorneys, the appeals court decision offered another vindication of the position that school officials must have the right to promulgate what, in their best judgment, are reasonable rules to handle potentially disruption situations. For Johnston and his clients, the ray of hope was less pronounced but still visible. Johnston remembered not being overly disappointed in November 1967 because he sensed then that the opaque 4–4 per curiam opinion of the Eighth Circuit Court of Appeals, which now was in conflict with the two fifth circuit "freedom buttons" rulings, called out for a definitive resolution by the United States Supreme Court. It is every young lawyer's dream to argue a case before the U.S. Supreme Court, and with the Iowa black-armband case, Johnston thought he might just get his chance.

# CHAPTER 8

# Attracting the High Court's Attention

## Certiorari

The brief opinion of the Eighth Circuit Court of Appeals in *Tinker v. Des Moines Independent Community School District* drew little attention from the Iowa media. Stories in the *Des Moines Register* and the *Des Moines Tribune* on the days immediately following the decision in St. Louis did little more than mention the issues, the litigants, and the appeals court's resolution of the case. The *Register* story indicated what was already a foregone conclusion—that the armband case would be appealed to the U.S. Supreme Court.

Dan Johnston felt so vehemently about the strength of his clients' case that he did not allow any dust to settle before putting in motion an appeal to the Court. On November 17, 1967, the Court of Appeals for the Eighth Circuit granted to Johnston, as attorney for the Eckhardts and the Tinkers, an "Order staying issuance of Mandate pending certiorari proceedings in Supreme Court, U.S." The eighth circuit order gave Johnston a thirty-day "stay" of their earlier decision in order to give him time to file a petition to the U.S. Supreme Court for a "writ of certiorari." If Johnston did file such a petition, the appeals court promised to extend the stay pending final disposition of the case by the Supreme Court.

The legal terminology here warrants explanation. A "stay" is a court order or decree that essentially freezes a legal proceedings or judgment. In this case, the stay meant that the decision of the appeals court—which affirmed Judge Stephenson's earlier dismissal of the complaint of the Eckhardts and the Tinkers and assessed court costs to them—would not be enforced until the U.S. Supreme made a ruling in the case. A "writ" is an order from a court directing the discharge of a specific act or authorizing that the act be done. "Certiorari" is a Latin word that means "to be informed of." The first writs of certiorari, which surfaced in English courts of law centuries ago, were orders by a superior court to an inferior court requiring the production of an authenticated, or "certified," record of a particular case tried by the lower court. The purpose of such an order is to enable the higher court to inspect the proceeding to determine if there were errors or irregularities that require correction. Granting a petition for a writ of certiorari has the consequence of ordering the lower court to send up the record of the case for review by the higher court. Dismissing a petition for certiorari means that the lower court's decision stands.

The path directed by a writ of certiorari is by far the most common route by which a lower court case reaches the U.S. Supreme Court. The writ of certiorari was established by a nineteenth-century congressional statute and, from time to time, has been modified by subsequent statutes. Perhaps the most important thing to keep in mind about the Court's jurisdiction under certiorari is that it is essentially discretionary jurisdiction. Rule 10 of the Rules of the Supreme Court of the United States ostensibly offers criteria for what makes a case "cert-worthy." It maintains that a "writ of certiorari is not a matter of right, but of judicial discretion, and will be granted only when there are special and important reasons therefor." Unfortunately for appellate attorneys, reasons listed for granting certiorari under rule 10 are essentially tautological, that is, a case is important enough to be heard through certiorari if the justices say it is important. Justice Frank Murphy, a liberal Supreme Court member in the 1940s, submitted that "writs of certiorari are matters of grace." The only substantive reason listed under rule 10 that tends to trigger the granting of certiorari more often than not is if there is a "circuit split," that is, if two or more of the courts of appeal have issued differing written opinions on a single legal point. Johnston, the attorney for the students, and Edgar Bittle, the law clerk who assisted Herrick in preparing the case for the Des Moines school district, both noted that the conflict between the eighth circuit opinion in *Tinker* and the fifth circuit opinion in *Burnside v. Byars* held promise that the Supreme Court would agree to hear the black-armband case.

At the time the petition for a writ of certiorari in the *Tinker* case was filed in 1967, about 90 percent of the Supreme Court's workload consisted of cases coming to the Court through certiorari. Today the figure is even higher because a 1988 statute eliminated most categories of mandatory appeal. Each year the Supreme Court meets to hear petitions and decide cases in an "October Term,"—a period of confidential discussions, opinion writing, and public sessions that begins in October and extends usually into June the following summer. During the 1967 October Term, 1532 petitions for certiorari were filed; only 156 were granted. Today the total figure of such requests exceeds 5000, and the total number of writs granted is even less than in the 1960s. To grant a writ of certiorari requires the vote of four of the nine justices. This "rule of four" is an informal custom that the Supreme Court developed as a procedural device in the 1890s to review certiorari petitions. It was first publicly acknowledged by the justices in 1924. Justices lean heavily on the advice of their law clerks in determining which petitions should be deemed certworthy. Hence, the task that Dan Johnston had before him was to draft a brief for a writ of certiorari that would catch the fancy of four justices (or their clerks).

---

## The Certiorari Briefs

In making their case to the U.S. Supreme Court for the granting of certiorari, the three students and their fathers as "next friends" were now designated as the "petitioners." The petitioners' certiorari brief was filed with the office of the clerk of the Supreme Court of the United States on January 17, 1968. To this point in the case, the Eckhardts and the Tinkers had been represented by Dan Johnston, who was serving as a volunteer attorney for the ICLU but paid with private funds raised by the litigants. That arrangement was about to be modified. The ICLU was (and still is) an affiliate of the national ACLU. The ACLU "Litigation Procedures and Practices" require state and local affiliates to consult with the national legal office in the preparation of cases bound for the U.S. Supreme Court. Such affiliates are also "strongly urged" to present drafts of Supreme Court briefs to the ACLU prior to final submission. Johnston dutifully consulted with the national body and proffered a draft of his certiorari brief to the ACLU for review. The final version of the petitioners' brief, although taking into account Johnston's suggestions, was substantially written by David Ellenhorn, a young ACLU attorney from New York. Ellenhorn and ACLU legal director Melvin L. Wulf also shared formal billing on the certiorari brief with Johnston. Johnston appreciated being relieved of much of the obligation to prepare the briefs in the *Tinker* case because he had just commenced a campaign for the Iowa Democratic Party's nomination for state attorney general. He had also just submitted his resignation as the ICLU's legal committee chairman. As Johnston later explained, at this point in the case "I kind of lost control" of the written portion of the argument.

The ACLU certiorari brief was indeed brief—only a total of seven pages (not including the attached lower court record and copies of the district and appeals court decisions). The statement of the facts in the case and summary of the decisions of the district and appeals courts took up just over a page. The brief emphasized that the pupils in question were active in Quaker and Unitarian religious organizations, perhaps to make it appear to the Court that their convictions had a theological basis and were not just the product of hasty antiwar passions. The statement of the case also emphasized that the petitioners "neither disrupted nor threatened to disrupt decorum or discipline within the schools"; this was a view that the school district would dispute in its own certiorari brief.

The brief's legal arguments tracked very closely those that Johnston had advanced before the court of appeals. It began by directing the justices' attention to the fifth circuit case of *Burnside v. Byars* and noted that the factual situations in the Mississippi case and the Iowa case were almost identical. In both cases the school administrators had prohibited modes of symbolic expression because they feared they would cause disruptions. In neither case was there a record of disruption. And in both *Burnside* and *Tinker*, the students were punished for breaking a rule, not for causing disruptions.

The courts below had seen the similarities in the facts in the Mississippi and Iowa cases, but the federal district court in Iowa and the court of appeals in St. Louis had ruled that the fifth circuit decisions were not binding on federal courts in the eighth circuit. So, for the ACLU attorneys, this petition presented the Supreme Court with a classic conflict-in-circuit-court issue. The fifth circuit held that there must be "material and substantial interference with … discipline in the operation of the schools." The eighth circuit, from which the petitioners were appealing, maintained that "the mere apprehension of 'reactions and comments . . . [which] would be likely to disturb the disciplined atmosphere . . . ' is sufficient to permit suppression of speech." The petitioners' brief asked the Supreme Court to resolve this difference by accepting the fifth circuit's position. The petitioners' brief characterized the fifth circuit position as reflecting the model of a school as a "democratic community," in which due process and freedom of expression are tolerated as in the larger adult society. By contrast, it referred to the eighth circuit position as set forth in *Tinker* as being "patterned after the parent-child relationship," in which children are deemed incapable of challenging authority. For the Eckhardts and the Tinkers, the proper "lesson" for the Court to teach in the Iowa black-armband case was that freedom of expression is "a lifeless right unless encouraged during school years."

The petitioners' brief concluded with a reference in a footnote to *Dennis v. U.S.,* the Cold War case relied on by the federal district judge in *Tinker* to support the proposition that the courts need not wait until trouble occurs to restrict free expression. The brief pointed out that the *Dennis* ruling was effectively repudiated by the 1957 case of *Yates v. U.S.* It was clear from the context that Ellenhorn wanted the Supreme Court to apply Justice Holmes's classic "clear and present danger" test to the black-armband fact situation, not the dubious "gravity of the 'evil,' discounted by its improbability" standard of the *Dennis* case.

In a U.S. Supreme Court case, parties contesting the petition for certiorari are known as "respondents." The respondents in this instance were the Des Moines school district as a corporate entity, various school district administrators, and the members of the school board. Once again they were represented by Allan Herrick, the long-time attorney for the school district, and various associates. Herrick himself and Philip Lovrien did most of the work on the Supreme Court briefs in the *Tinker* case.

The respondents' brief opposing the issuance of the writ of certiorari was about three times as long as the Ellenhorn/Johnston brief for the petitioners. For Herrick and his associates, the question was a simple one: should a school district be compelled to wait for a disturbance to take place, or should it be permitted to take necessary precautions? The armband-wearing students, the brief asserted, were seeking controversy: "[I]f their purposes . . . [had been] achieved they would have of necessity interfered with the management and operation of the schools." Had the ban on armbands not been instituted, the brief argued, there might have been many more students wearing armbands to school in late 1965 than the handful who actually did. And that would probably have led to more trouble.

In contrast to the one-page recitation of the facts in the ACLU brief, the respondents' brief devoted five pages to its statement of the case. It made a great deal of the national tension in late 1965 that provided a context for the Des Moines armband demonstration. It pointed out that several of those attending the December 11, 1965, planning meeting at the Eckhardt home were members of local college SDS chapters. It also noted that Christopher Eckhardt and his mother had attended the large anti–Vietnam War protest in Washington, D.C., just weeks before the armband demonstration in Des Moines. And it stressed that one of the antiwar tactics proposed by the Washington demonstrators was the wearing of armbands in support of an open-ended truce in the war. The brief also mentioned that the two public school board meetings on the armband issue were stormy affairs. Outside the hearing rooms were pickets and other demonstrators, many from outside the city. Maintaining order under such circumstances was "touch and go." From this casting of the facts, the respondents hoped to suggest that the armband protest was linked to divisive national issues that could become explosive, if not carefully monitored, in the Des Moines school system.

In a long section of the brief titled "Reasons for Not Granting the Writ," the respondents argued that the fifth circuit case of *Burnside v. Byars* presented a different issue than did *Tinker v. Des Moines* and thus that there was no conflict between the two circuit court opinions. Unlike the attorneys for the Eckhardts and the Tinkers, who had contended that these cases presented essentially the same issues, Herrick and his associates emphasized that the difference in the circuit court opinions was warranted due to the different factual contexts of the two cases. In their view, the record in the fifth circuit case from Mississippi did not reveal any actual disruption or likely probability of disruption of school activities by the wearing of the "freedom buttons." However, the brief insisted, the record in the Iowa federal district court contained evidence of tension in the local schools over the Vietnam War. The November 1965 protest march in Washington and a national wave of draft-card burnings had their Iowa analogues in local protests and pending Iowa draft cases. Moreover, the very fact that about two hundred vocal partisans had attended each of the two school board hearings on the Iowa armband issue demonstrated that national strain over the Vietnam War was strongly felt in Des Moines. This factual showing, the respondents' brief argued, provided a reasonable basis for a measure prohibiting a form of expression that might trigger actual disruptions in the Des Moines schools, namely the wearing of black armbands.

According to Herrick and his associates, Iowa state statutes and court decisions do not require that a school district wait until trouble breaks out before taking preemptive action. As to what measures might be appropriate, the respondents noted that the recent Iowa Supreme Court decision *Independent School District of Waterloo, Iowa v. Green* (1967) held that "the courts of this state are not concerned with the wisdom of discretionary acts on the part of school boards in adopting rules and regulations governing the operation, management and conduct of our schools." Courts, therefore, should not disturb a school regulation unless it is "clearly arbitrary and unreasonable." Several times in their certiorari brief, the respondents reiterated the importance of deferring to the judgment of school authorities.

The school district brief also reemphasized the balancing view of the First Amendment that its attorneys had stressed in their district and appeals court arguments. Freedom of expression, Herrick and his associates maintained, has never been found by the courts to be absolute: it must be weighed against other societal interests, including the need to maintain order and an established course of study in a state's public schools. To document the balancing view of the First Amendment, the respondents cited several Supreme Court decisions that had been mentioned in their district court and appeals court briefs, namely *Cox v. New Hampshire* (1941), *American Communications Association v. Douds* (1950), *Konigsberg v. State Bar of California* (1961), and *Adderley v. The State of Florida* (1966).

Near the end of the brief, the respondents advanced an argument in support of their view that the school district regulation banning armbands was a reasonable restriction on free expression. The relevant statement is this: "Surely the fact that out of 18,000 students . . . , it was only necessary to suspend five students for violating the rule . . . is a strong indication that most students viewed the rule as reasonable and proper." Earlier in the brief, the school district attorneys had strongly asserted that the climate of opinion in the Des Moines schools over the war in Vietnam was volatile and that disruptions of school routines were threatened. Yet now the respondents' attorneys were noting that only five out of eighteen thousand students in this tension-ridden situation caused enough trouble to be suspended.

The respondents' certiorari brief was received by the clerk of the Supreme Court on February 12, 1968. On March 4, the clerk of the Supreme Court issued an "order allowing certiorari" in the case of *Tinker v. Des Moines Independent Community School District*, No. 1034, October Term 1967. As is customary, the order did not mention when the oral argument in the case would take place.

Published orders of certiorari never indicate which justices vote for a petition. Occasionally one or two strong-minded justices will file a dissent to a granting of certiorari, thus revealing their own preferences. There were no written dissents to the granting of certiorari in *Tinker* case so, at the time, the votes on certiorari petition were not known. However, years after the fact, private papers of Supreme Court justices revealed the breakdown of certiorari vote in the *Tinker* case: five in favor (William Brennan, William O. Douglas, Thurgood Marshall, Potter Stewart, and Earl Warren) and four against (Hugo Black, Abe Fortas, John Marshall Harlan, and Byron White). Douglas, for instance, saw this as "a classic case of prior restraint." For Douglas, the reasonableness of the school district policy banning armbands could only have been demonstrated if the pieces of cloth had been worn and if some disruption had taken place. Hence, at the time of the granting of certiorari, Douglas was in favor of a summary reversal on the grounds of "prior restraint." As a later discussion in the conference of the justices would disclose, Douglas was willing to go farther than any of the other members of the *Tinker* majority in reversing the lower federal courts.

Another interesting wrinkle in *Tinker* is revealed in a February 19, 1968, memorandum addressed to Chief Justice Warren from one of his law clerks. It urged granting the certiorari petition in the armband case but recommended postponing the oral argument until after the announcement of a decision in a related case, *U.S. v. O'Brien*. The *O'Brien* case would test the constitutionality of a law making the burning of a draft card a federal crime. The memo read in part: "This case should be held for *O'Brien,* the draft-card burning case. . . . Pursuant to your directions, the opinion in *O'Brien* will hold that draft-card burning is not free speech. My aim is to reach that result on as narrow grounds as possible, so that the Court will still have the option in cases like this armband one to declare the First Amendment applicable. But this case is sufficiently similar to *O'Brien* to warrant holding it." Warren followed this advice. The decision in *O'Brien*—that the symbolic act of burning a draft card was not protected by the First Amendment—was announced on May 27, 1968. This was at the height of a massive student protest that had closed down Columbia University in New York City. The *Tinker* oral argument would not be held until the next term of the Court—in the fall of 1968.

Given their well-known positions on civil liberties issues, the certiorari alignment of the nine members of the Warren Court in *Tinker* was predictable with but two exceptions. As they had been consistent supporters of civil liberties in past constitutional decisions, Black's and Fortas's negative votes on certiorari are puzzling. Black would later dissent in the *Tinker* case, thus explaining in print why he was against the students' appeal from the start. But Fortas would end up writing the majority opinion *in favor of* Christopher Eckhardt and the Tinkers. How could Fortas vote against hearing the case, thus affirming the previous verdict for the school district, and then later write the landmark opinion to overturn the school district's position? According to Fortas's principal biographer, at the time of the vote on the certiorari petition Fortas was not convinced that the First Amendment entitled members of the judiciary to second-guess the discipline imposed by school administrators unless the record of a case shows abuse or discrimination. Nevertheless, Fortas wrote a note on the memorandum of one of his law clerks that "this is a tough case & [certiorari] probably will be granted." By the time of the Supreme Court's oral argument and the writing of his majority opinion in *Tinker,* Fortas was firmly back in the civil libertarian camp.

Another explanation for Fortas's shift from the certiorari vote to the vote on the merits of the case stems from the justice's friendship with President Lyndon Johnson and a simple matter of timing. When the certiorari vote was taken in March 1968, Fortas's friend and patron was in the White House and under siege by antiwar protesters. However, when the case was ready for decision in February 1969, Johnson

was no longer president. So Fortas's vote defending the rights of protesters was not politically embarrassing to the president.

A few days after the Supreme Court grant of certiorari in the *Tinker*
case, the *Des Moines Register* editorialized: "The Supreme Court de-
serves credit for willingly tackling the tough questions posed by the
Iowa case. School administrators increasingly confronted by politically
active and militant student bodies will be grateful for any guidance
the Supreme Court can give." Later in March, the *Roundup,* the student newspaper of Roosevelt High School, published an article on the
Supreme Court's granting of full review of the black-armband case,
which featured some quotations from Christopher Eckhardt, now a
senior at Roosevelt. Eckhardt expressed optimism about the Supreme
Court review of the case: "Things seem to be getting better and better. The first case [district court] we lost. In the second, no decision
could be reached [three-judge appeals court], and in the third, we got
a tied vote [en banc appeals court]. Each ruling gets progressively
better." Eckhardt also stated in the article that he had no idea he would
be involved in such an important case when he had first worn his
armband to school over two years earlier. He added that he did not
regret his action and that he was still as committed as ever to the application of the First Amendment to the public schools: "As long as you
are not hurting yourself or others, as long as you are not infringing on
the rights of others, and as long as it is done peacefully, I see no reason
for denying free student expression in the schools."

## A Friend of the Court?

Although there were only two official parties to the legal action in
*Tinker v. Des Moines,* three full-dress briefs were submitted to the
Supreme Court. The brief for the Eckhardts and the Tinkers as petitioners was filed with the clerk of the Supreme Court on June 1, 1968.
The brief from the respondents for the school district was received by
the clerk on June 24, 1968. A third brief, completed in early May 1968,
was received by the Supreme Court well before the briefs from the
petitioners and respondents.

This was an amicus curiae brief. The term translates literally as
"friend of the court." An amicus brief is usually submitted by a profes-

sional group, organization, or institution of government not involved in a case as an actual party to the litigation but still interested in the outcome of the case. On rare occasions an individual may submit an amicus brief. The privilege of filing amicus briefs at the U.S. Supreme Court level is governed by the Rules of the United States Supreme Court. Rule 42, for example, permits interested organizations or persons to file as amici if they have consent of all parties to the action. If one of the official parties refuses to honor a request from a potential amicus, the party can appeal directly to the Court itself. Amici, in seeking permission to file, usually allege that they possess information that may be useful to the Court in deciding the case. In reality, most amici wish to be heard because they support the position of one of the parties to the dispute; thus they are more often friends of one of the parties than friends of the court. Amici generally wish to mount an argument consistent with their own organizational policy views. Although amicus briefs are especially common in cases involving civil liberties, judicial scholars disagree about how much attention the justices actually pay to amici.

The amicus brief submitted in the *Tinker* case was proffered by the United States NSA. The NSA was (and is) a confederation of college and university student governments. In the late 1960s it represented student governments at more than three hundred institutions. Dan Johnston had been a national officer of NSA before he commenced his legal education at Drake University. NSA had an interest in the Des Moines armband case because it saw any limitation on the rights of secondary-school students as having potential consequences for college-level students. A decision in favor of the Des Moines school district, NSA argued, would give support to those college authorities who believed that freedom of expression on college campuses should be subordinate to institutional rules and regulations. At the very time that NSA was preparing its brief, a wave of student protests on college campuses, highlighted by a clash at Columbia University in New York City, was sweeping the country. A decision against Christopher Eckhardt and the Tinkers would send a message that the courts were more willing to support the dictates of university administrations than the individual rights of college students. The NSA had another interest in the *Tinker* case. Many of the high-school students who might benefit from an endorsement of the right to peaceable symbolic expression would later attend American colleges. Being able to exercise free speech at the high-school level would enhance independent thinking and help equip students for the contentious discourse on college campuses. Furthermore, anything that nurtured freedom of expression among students, NSA maintained, would benefit the nation as a whole by preparing citizens for informed and open debate in an increasingly complex political environment.

Following the usual summary of the facts in the case, the NSA brief, prepared by Roy Lucas of the University of Alabama School of Law and Charles Morgan Jr. of Atlanta, presented several arguments in favor of the Eckhardt/Tinker position. First, it maintained that public-school administrators cannot constitutionally suppress the symbolic expression of students unless it "imminently threatens orderly operation of the classroom or other school facility." The leading case cited by NSA in support of this position was *West Virginia Board of Education v. Barnette* (1943). The brief contended: "[T]he interest in preventing speculative disturbances caused by students whose friend had been killed in Vietnam is . . . [no] different from requiring students to salute the American flag in order to please friends whose fathers or relatives might have been risking their lives in World War II." The *Barnette* decision, the NSA brief declared, had been consistently cited with approval by the Supreme Court in cases dealing with order in the public schools.

The standard for determining whether expression could be prohibited or punished in the schools, the NSA brief declared, must be the traditional "clear and present danger" test first articulated by Justice Holmes in 1919. Quoting with approval a 1962 case from Georgia, the NSA noted that, under the clear-and-present-danger standard, "the substantive evil must be extremely serious and the degree of imminence extremely high before utterance can be punished." The record in the *Tinker* case, according to NSA, revealed "the transparency of any argument that orderly operation of the school was endangered by the wearing of armbands." Regarding the likelihood of future disorder as a justification for banning the armbands, the NSA brief submitted that such a speculative cast "would leave the First Amendment rights of these students to the whims of the least secure of their mentors."

Another argument stressed by NSA was that the school administrators' proscription of black armbands was issued in anticipation of a possible demonstration. Hence it was a "prior restraint." The NSA reminded the justices that throughout American constitutional history courts had been loath to sanction prior restraints. On those rare occasions that U.S. courts have upheld prior restraints, the cause has been a weighty one such as national security. In addition, prior restraints that have passed constitutional muster have generally been narrowly drawn. In this case, the danger that might have arisen from the threatened expression was not established in the court record, and the prohibition laid down by school authorities was, in the words of NSA, "patently overbroad." The amicus brief also submitted: "Arm bands hardly differ from normal attire such as boy scout uniforms, scarves, school sweatshirts, or yo-yo sweaters." One of the arguments of the school district in the lower federal courts had been that the wearing of armbands threatened school order because the armband wearers themselves would be targets for anger or violence. But the NSA reminded the justices that American courts have consistently held that a person's First Amendment rights cannot be constrained because of the "possibility of adverse reaction by others" to the form of expression chosen. In other words, the Court should not allow the difficulties that might confront someone because of speaking his or her mind—the so-called "thug's veto"—to serve as a justification for denying that individual the right of free expression.

The amicus brief then moved into the realm of psychology. It presented an argument that denying free expression to the Des Moines students would "defeat and chill [these] young people in what may well be their initial efforts at independent evaluation of political questions." If secondary-school students are to be allowed to mature intellectually, they must be allowed to use ideas "associated not only with mathematics and chemistry, but also with the Bill of Rights." To support this point, the NSA brief alluded to a varied literature on the benefits of permitting free thought and expression for adolescents. The brief also cited the findings of psychologists that "indicate that a maximum of free student expression would encourage the development of creative students, and would deter, to a degree, the stifling effects of group conformity."

The NSA brief concluded with an analysis of how various federal district and appeals courts have treated the matter of student expression of ideas. Here the brief confronted the fact that most circuits have not been tolerant of student free expression when alleged by authorities to threaten order in the schools. Essentially the NSA encouraged the Court to strike off in a different direction and use the *Tinker* case as a springboard to write a new chapter in the history of student rights.

———

## The Eckhardt/Tinker Brief

By the summer of 1968 the *Tinker* case had been argued before a federal district judge, a three-judge appeals court, and an eight-judge en banc appeals panel. Written documents previously submitted in the case included the original complaint and answer, the trial briefs for Judge Stephenson's original hearing, two sets of appeals court briefs, the certiorari briefs to the Supreme Court, and various versions of the lower court record. It is not surprising, therefore, that the Supreme Court briefs for the petitioner students and respondent school district had a deja vu quality about them. There was really very little new to say.

The main argument presented by the Eckhardt/Tinker brief was, of course, that the three students had been denied their constitutional right to freedom of expression by the school district order prohibiting them from wearing black armbands and then suspending them for violating this order. In support of this contention, the brief first directed the Court's attention to a line of cases establishing the proposition that state governments and school district administrators as state employees "may not interfere with the individual rights of students in the guise of providing an education for them." The leading case cited was the now familiar 1943 flag-salute case, *West Virginia Board of Education v. Barnette*. One passage from Justice Robert Jackson's majority opinion in *Barnette* seemed especially appropriate to the students' attorneys:

> The Fourteenth Amendment, as now applied to the States, protects the citizen against the State itself and all of its creatures—Boards of Education not excepted. These have, of course, important, delicate, and highly discretionary functions, but none that they may not perform within the limits of the Bill of Rights. That they are educating the young for citizenship is reason for scrupulous protection of Constitutional freedoms of the individual, if we are not to strangle the free mind at its source and teach youth to discount important principles of our government as mere platitudes.

In this connection, the brief also quoted the famous language from *In Re Gault* (1967) that the "Bill of Rights is not for adults alone." The students' brief then reiterated a point that had been advanced in their certiorari brief, namely that schools should be treated as "models of our democratic society," not operated in loco parentis.

Perhaps the most crucial section of the brief addressed the issue of prior restraint and the school administrators' alleged fear of disorder. The brief maintained that "the form of expression chosen by petitioners was dignified, orderly, and peaceful." The wearing of armbands did not interfere with the rights of others. The record, at least as Ellenhorn and Johnston read it, revealed that "no disorder had taken place, and there was no threat of disorder." The leading case cited to bolster Johnston's "no prior restraint" contention was *Near v. Minnesota* (1931). The students' brief acknowledged that John Tinker had been the recipient of a few adverse comments for displaying his armband but pointed out that "such banter typically and routinely occurs in classrooms and halls without disrupting school." After the ban on armbands had been instituted, and after several students had been suspended, the school administration, according to the Ellenhorn brief, offered several after-the-fact rationales for the suspensions. These included the concern that students disagreeing with those wearing black armbands would don different-colored armbands; fears that friends of a former Des Moines student who had died in Vietnam would be hurt or angry; and worries that those wearing the original black armbands would be subjected to harassment and even violence. The brief for the students labeled such reasoning as "too remote and conjectural to override the guarantee of the First Amendment."

The brief commended District Judge Stephenson for recognizing that the wearing of black armbands was a symbolic act eligible for the protect of the First Amendment's free expression clause, but it strongly disagreed with his application of the standard selected for determining whether the First Amendment's protections should have been activated. Stephenson had determined that it was "'reasonable' for the school officials to anticipate that the wearing of armbands would create some type of classroom disturbance and, thus, that the prohibition of the armbands was a 'reasonable means of preventing such a disturbance.'" Because Stephenson accepted the school district argument that it was reasonable to assume that disruptions might take place if armbands were permitted at school, he upheld the school district's banning of this form of symbolic protest. However, the students' brief contended that Stephenson had applied the wrong First Amendment standard. It noted that the Supreme Court has ruled that expression should not be proscribed "on the basis of . . . notions of mere reasonableness." The quoted statement was doubly telling because it was drawn from *Dennis v. U.S.*, the 1951 decision upholding Smith Act, hardly a friendly decision for the petitioners. To apply a reasonableness standard as Stephenson did would open First Amendment jurisprudence to ad hoc resolutions of individual cases, not to adjudication based on principles. The correct standard, the one urged on the Supreme Court by the students' brief, was the traditional "clear and present danger" test. This was the standard accepted by the fifth circuit in the "freedom button" cases. The much discussed "conflict in the circuits" could be resolved by reversing Judge Stephenson.

The petitioners' brief criticized Stephenson for going outside the official record in the case to find "facts" suggesting the possibility of disruptions if armbands were worn to Des Moines schools. Stephenson had asserted that the debate over the Vietnam War in Des Moines had intensified recently due to draft-card burnings and other demonstrations, making the schools ripe for disruptions. The petitioners' brief emphasized that the actual record of the case demonstrated that the reactions to the black armbands on December 16 and 17, 1965, had been more quizzical than hostile. If the school authorities really believed that there was a serious threat to the armband-wearing students, the petitioners' brief maintained, those officials should have appropriately disciplined the offending students rather than suspending Christopher Eckhardt and the Tinkers for merely trying to express themselves in a dignified, nonviolent fashion.

The final argument advanced by the Eckhardt/Tinker brief was that the three students had been suspended not for disruptive conduct, but for violating the armband prohibition. This was not an "incidental" encroachment on their free expression. The ban on armbands was fully intended to suppress a particular type of symbolic expression on a single subject. The proscription against armbands was, according to the Ellenhorn brief, "a prohibition addressed directly to a particular controversial statement of political opinion, not an even-handed regulation designed to control a valid state interest." It was at this point that the brief directed the justices' attention to the double standard in the toleration of symbolic expression in the Des Moines public schools. It pointed out that the record showed that other forms of symbolic expression—Nazi crosses, religious medallions, political buttons, and displays of school spirit—had been permitted for years in the city's schools without leading to any disruption of the normal curriculum. Thus, the students' attorneys submitted that the singling out of black armbands for prohibition was "stimulated by hostility on the part of the school authorities towards the particular views or because of their controversial nature."

The petitioners' brief concluded by asking the U.S. Supreme Court to reverse the judgment of Judge Stephenson, as affirmed by the court of appeals, and to issue instructions to grant the relief that had been requested by the Eckhardts and the Tinkers more than two years earlier. The Court and the students' attorneys only had to wait three weeks for the rejoining brief from the school district.

## The School District Brief

The Supreme Court brief for the respondents, the Des Moines Independent Community School District, presented a summary of the facts in the dispute that was about twice as long as the corresponding factual section in the Supreme Court brief for the student petitioners. Perhaps the reason for its heavy reliance on the facts was that the respondents wished to stress the disruptive (or potentially disruptive) context in which the armbands appeared. As such, this factual presentation flowed into a doctrinal point that the school district felt needed to be made forcefully and with repetition: that the "rights" of students to express themselves symbolically needed to be balanced against something more important, namely student learning in a peaceful setting.

More than in any of the previous legal documents submitted on the case, the school district's Supreme Court brief stressed the alleged role of SDS in the armband dispute. SDS had become progressively more strident in its rhetoric and more violent in the years that the armband case was working its way through the courts. In the fifteen-page section on the facts, SDS activity was explicitly referred to five times: SDS was mentioned as participating in the November 1965 antiwar protest in Washington, D.C., that sparked the Eckhardts and the Tinkers to action; SDS was cited as having a presence at meetings in Des Moines both before and after the armband protest; and SDS's alleged participation in the picketing outside the school board meetings in the winter of 1965–66 was also noted. In the later "Argument" section of the brief, SDS was mentioned an additional six times. The seed that the brief apparently wished to plant in the justices' minds was that outside agitators—particularly the unpopular SDS—had a major role in the armband case.

Allan Herrick, who had taken the leading role in assembling the school district brief, was no friend of SDS. According to Edgar Bittle, Herrick was "personally offended" by positions and activities of SDS and other antiwar groups. As a World War I veteran and a staunch conservative, Herrick had no sympathy for anyone who criticized the American government. Furthermore, Herrick did not believe that Christopher Eckhardt and the Tinker children had made their own decisions to wear armbands in December 1965. Herrick believed that besides stemming from SDS or some other radical group's agenda, the armband demonstration had been instigated by the students' activist parents. Herrick's brief for the school district made much of the fact that it was the adult Eckhardts and Tinkers and not the three students who had attended the planning meeting on December 11, 1965. The fact that many of the winter 1965–66 meetings held to plan the armband protest and respond to the school district's prohibition order had been held in the Eckhardt home was mentioned several times in Herrick's factual summary. The brief also noted that, while Christopher Eckhardt and the Tinker children participated in a number of demonstrations prior to December 1965, they were almost always accompanied in these ventures by their parents. According to Bittle, "Herrick felt that children should do what their parents told them to do, and what parents should tell their children to do is to obey the rules and not rock the boat in school."

The respondents advanced three major contentions in the "Argument" section of their brief. The first was that the school district "did not deprive petitioners of their constitutional right of freedom of speech under the United States Constitution." The leading case cited in support of this contention was *Blackwell v. Issaquena County Board of Education* (1966), the fifth circuit companion case to *Burnside v. Byars*. In

*Blackwell* the appeals court upheld the school regulation prohibiting the wearing of "freedom buttons" as "a reasonable rule necessary for the maintenance of school discipline." At this point there was no mention of the *Burnside* case, in which the appeals court had struck down the banning of freedom buttons in another school district. The difference in the two Mississippi cases was that in *Blackwell* the buttons had sparked substantial controversy, including violence, while in *Burnside* the buttons had caused minimal trouble. It is not surprising that the attorneys for the Des Moines Independent Community School District gave more weight to *Blackwell* than *Burnside*. The brief quoted with strong approval the fifth circuit's statement that decisions in such cases involving school district prohibitions "must be made on a case by case basis."

To carry the argument that the school district ban on armbands had a reasonable foundation, Herrick and his associates had to persuade the Court that the wearing of armbands had substantially disrupted school business as usual or that the threat of punishment for wearing armbands had scared off large-scale demonstrations and preserved the peace. The school district attorneys tried to have it both ways. Their brief noted that "there were accounts of physical violence over wearing arm bands. Either Bruce Clark or Ross [Peterson] said somebody had struck him." In the alternative, if the Court did not see the violence as substantial, the brief went on to point out that "except for the prompt action by the school administration, the problem might well have developed into the type of demonstration that has been witnessed throughout the country in the past two or three years." Because only five of eighteen thousand Des Moines public-school students had to be disciplined for violating the order prohibiting armbands, Herrick and his associates maintained that the administrative order itself had likely preempted trouble.

The school district attorneys concluded this first section of their "Argument" with a reference to the 1966 U.S. Supreme Court case of *Adderley v. State of Florida.* Here, speaking through Justice Hugo Black, the Court had upheld a state university's right to prohibit the occupation of campus buildings by students protesting racial segregation. The decision rejected the right of "people who want to propagandize protests or views . . . whenever and however and wherever they please." The brief also cited with favor Justice Black's admonition that the

"Constitution does not forbid a State to control the use of its own property for its own lawful and nondiscriminatory purpose."

The second major argument presented by the respondents was that "disturbances in schools are not properly measured by identical standards used to measure disturbances on the streets, in eating houses or bus depots." Here the brief relied heavily on a dissent by Justice Black in *Brown v. Louisiana* (1966). In this case the Court majority upheld the right of "adult Negroes" to remain in a public library for a short time to protest the policy of segregation. Justice Black, while strongly disapproving of segregation, still emphasized that a public building was not a proper place for a demonstration. He stated: "In the public building, unlike the street, peace and quiet is a fast and necessary rule, and as a result there is much less room for peace officers to abuse their authority in enforcing the public building part of the statute." Using this language as a foundation, the Des Moines school district attorneys took the opportunity once again to mention the alleged SDS connection: "[W]hatever rights the Students for [a] Democratic Society . . . has . . . to demonstrate their views, they should not be permitted to infiltrate the schools with such demonstrations and disrupt the scholarly discipline that is necessary to a school room."

The third and final point in the respondents' argument was that the rule prohibiting the wearing of armbands in the Des Moines schools should be upheld because it was "reasonably calculated to promote discipline in the schools." Here the brief finally dealt with the fifth circuit case of *Burnside v. Byars.* In that case the appeals court had granted an injunction lifting the ban in one school district on the wearing of the SNCC-inspired symbols of protest. The attorneys for the students had stressed that this was a strong precedent for the exercise of symbolic expression. However, Herrick and his associates maintained in their brief that in *Burnside* the appeals court granted only a *temporary* injunction. They concluded that this was not as weighty a precedent as the petitioners would have the Court believe. Furthermore, the school district attorneys used the differences in the facts in the *Blackwell* and *Burnside* cases to make a point crucial to their case, namely that appeals courts should decide each such case on its own facts, recognizing that the First Amendment must balance the right to free expression with the maintenance of public order. If a restrictive order is reasonably calculated to deal with an imminent threat, then it should be judged to be constitutional. This was the argument that the respondents had successfully advanced at every previous stage in the black-armband proceedings. To support this point before the Supreme Court, the respondents' brief discussed several state and federal decisions that had applied the balancing test. From one of the U.S. Supreme Court cases, *Konigsberg v. State Bar of California* (1961), the school district attorneys extracted the following language:

> Throughout its history this Court has consistently recognized . . . [that] freedom of speech is narrower than an unlimited license to talk. . . . [R]egulatory statutes, not intended to control the content of speech, but incidentally limiting its unfettered exercise, have not been regarded as the type of law the First or Fourteenth Amendment forbade Congress or the States to pass, when they have been found justified by subordinating valid governmental interests a prerequisite to constitutionality which has necessarily involved a weighing of the governmental interest involved.

The school district attorneys then turned to the relevant state and federal cases on the discretion of public school authorities to enact and implement regulations. Their reading of the case law was that courts, including the U.S. Supreme Court, had upheld school district regulations governing the conduct of pupils unless the regulations had been deemed "unreasonable." The leading Iowa decision cited by Herrick and his associates, as was the case in the courts below, was *Independent School District of Waterloo v. Green* (1967), in which the Supreme Court of Iowa upheld a school district order barring married students from participating in extracurricular activities. The respondents' brief quoted with approval the following statement from *Green:* "The duty of all courts, regardless of personal views or individual philosophies, is to uphold a school regulation unless it is clearly arbitrary and unreasonable."

Applying this standard to the facts in the Iowa armband dispute, the school district attorneys once again returned to their assertion that the protesting students were spurred on by outside agitators and activist parents. The petitioners' brief referred to the senior Eckhardts and Tinkers as "professional protesters and demonstrators" and once again reminded the Court of the specter of SDS, which, they maintained, "saw an opportunity to infiltrate the Des Moines schools with their propaganda." Fortunately, the brief declared, the school district "nipped this plan of infiltration in the bud." If the school administration had not acted promptly, major disruptions in the city schools might well have occurred. Herrick urged the Court to take "judicial notice" (that is, recognize the existence and truth of certain facts without presentation into evidence) of the spate of student protests in the late 1960s. The school district attorneys believed that the Des Moines schools had been spared large-scale disruption because of the ban on armbands. Nevertheless, they pointed out that there had been some disruptions on the two days in December 1965 that armbands had been worn: the punching of one or two students and threats to John Tinker and Mary Beth Tinker. The respondents wished the Court to conclude that sufficient trouble over the armband issue had taken place in Des Moines in the winter of 1965–66 to warrant their prohibition, and that the school district's prohibition order had preserved the community from a future wave of protests and disruptions.

Before concluding their brief and requesting affirmation of the decisions of the courts below, the respondents confronted the case heavily relied on by the petitioners, *West Virginia v. Barnette* (1943). Johnston had employed this decision to brace his contention that the First Amendment protects the freedom of speech in the public-school classroom. For the respondents, *Barnette* had no application to the armband situation because the wearing of black armbands was a political act without the religious element of *Barnette.*

Whether the school district's position would prevail on this and other legal points would not be known until the following year. Before the Supreme Court would rule on the armband dispute, however, Allan Herrick and Dan Johnston would have the opportunity to make their case in person to the nine justices.

# CHAPTER 9

# Oral Argument in Washington

During the week that *Tinker v. Des Moines Independent Community School District* was argued before the Supreme Court of the Unites States, the war in Vietnam was the dominant news story in America. Over half a million U.S. soldiers were then stationed in Southeast Asia. The American death toll in the war had reached almost thirty thousand; the estimated North Vietnamese body count was over four hundred thousand. By the late fall of 1968, the conduct of the war in Vietnam had become the leading focus of student protest, eclipsing even civil rights. On October 31 President Johnson had ordered a halt to the bombing of North Vietnam in order to stimulate peace talks with the North Vietnamese. The talks had stalled, however, because of the South Vietnamese government's refusal to negotiate with the communist National Liberation Front. On the very day that the *Tinker* case was argued before the Supreme Court, the headlines in major American papers proclaimed that President-elect Nixon endorsed President Lyndon Johnson's efforts to continue the war in Vietnam while, at the same time, trying to bring all parties to the peace table. The headline in the *Des Moines Register* on November 12 put it simply: "Nixon: Johnson Speaks for Me."

## High Court Protocol

Tuesday, November 12, 1968, was not a pleasant day in the nation's capital. The temperature was in the middle thirties, with a mixture of rain and snow. During the morning the nine justices of the United States Supreme Court handed down a decision overturning a state antievolution law that had been challenged by a young Arkansas biology teacher named Susan Epperson. This was a victory for civil liberties in a case reminiscent of the 1925 Scopes "monkey trial" in Dayton, Tennessee.

The heart of the day was reserved for the oral argument in case number 21 of the 1968 October Term, *Tinker v. Des Moines Independent Community School District.* Christopher Eckhardt and his parents were in attendance in the elegant courtroom in the Supreme Court Building on First Street Northeast and Maryland Avenue, as were many members of the Tinker family. John Tinker, however, had had difficulty making air connections due to an early-season snowstorm in the Midwest and did not make it to Washington in time to witness the oral argument.

The Eckhardts and the Tinkers were represented before the Court by Dan Johnston. The Des Moines Independent Community School District's side of the case was presented by Allan Herrick. The selection of Herrick to present the case for the respondents was a given. Herrick had been the school district's principal attorney for years. He was an experienced appellate advocate who had advised the school district throughout the case and had had a major role in all the written submissions. The choice of Johnston to argue the Supreme Court appeal for the Eckhardts and the Tinkers as petitioners was less clear-cut. The ACLU had experienced advocates available who would have loved to have taken over the oral argument in this bellwether civil liberties case. The ACLU's David Ellenhorn had taken the lead role in writing the Supreme Court brief in *Tinker,* and Melvin Wulf, a veteran advocate, was also waiting in the wings. However, Johnston wanted to make the argument himself. He had lived with the black-armband case for almost three years and did not want to hand it over to an ACLU "hired gun" for the final act. In addition, the Eckhardt and Tinker families felt that Johnston had earned his moment of glory. So it was Johnston who began the argument for the petitioners with the traditional salutation, "May it please the Court."

The oral argument is an obligatory and dramatic stage in a major Supreme Court case. The Court conducts oral arguments in only one hundred to two hundred cases a year. Most oral arguments, as was the case in *Tinker,* are an hour in length—thirty minutes for each side. The "Notice to Counsel" sent to the attorneys advises them to pay strict heed to the time limits. When a lawyer has five minutes left in allotted time, a white light flashes on the podium. When the time expires, he or she is confronted by a red light. Attorneys are admonished to conclude their arguments immediately when the red light appears unless they are responding to a question put by a justice. Legend has it that Chief Justice Charles Evans Hughes, a commanding presence on the Court in the 1930s, halted a flustered lawyer in the middle of the word "if."

Lawyers, of course, prepare exhaustively for oral argument before the Supreme Court. As the scheduled date for the oral argument approached, the attorneys for both sides in the *Tinker* case subjected their presentations to the criticisms of fellow attorneys. Johnston recalls that the ACLU arranged for several former Supreme Court law clerks to grill him in a "moot court" setting. Similarly, Edgar Bittle, working with the school district attorneys, remembers Herrick practicing his presentation in front of several of his colleagues.

Because the justices can hurl questions at the attorneys at any time during their presentations, even the best planned argument can be side-tracked or cut short by a query from the bench. A justice's questions may suggest interest or support for an advocate's position, or they can appear contrary or even malicious. Counsel appearing before the Supreme Court are advised by experienced appellate advocates to respond to justices' questions simply and directly. Since the justices expect attorneys to be able to depart from their prepared remarks when challenged, advocates able to speak extemporaneously under pressure have a decided advantage over lawyers who prefer set presentations. The justices are also accustomed to respect and deference. Therefore, attorneys before the Supreme Court are cautioned never to exhibit arrogance or impatience.

Some of the tension of a presentation before the Supreme Court is mitigated by informal features of the setting. The tables of attorneys are positioned so close to the Court's bench that counsel can occasionally overhear whispered comments from the justices. A few justices have been known to maintain running colloquies throughout an oral argument that have nothing to do with the case at bar. In addition, from the bench during oral argument some justices summon clerks or aides to run errands. William O. Douglas was notorious during oral argument for sending out for books and other research materials to allow him to write his tracts on conservation and travel. And a few justices

take it upon themselves to reassure nervous advocates. Johnston remembers thinking, "If anything really went bad, [Chief Justice] Earl
Warren would come down off the bench and put his arm around [me]."

## The Justices

The other major players at this crucial juncture in the *Tinker* case were,
of course, the nine robed justices of the nation's highest court. The men
who sat in final judgment of the weighty constitutional issues in the
Iowa black-armband case were a distinguished and varied group of
jurists.

The "center seat" on the Supreme Court bench is occupied by the
chief justice. In November 1968 that position was held by Earl Warren, one of the most heralded and beloved justices in American history. Warren was a big man with an impressive head of white hair. He
was nominated as chief justice by President Dwight Eisenhower in 1953.
Just a few months after taking his seat, Warren wrote the unanimous
decision in *Brown v. Board of Education* (1954), striking down school segregation and initiating a legal onslaught against racial discrimination.
Warren was a Californian who had been a three-term governor and
former state attorney general. But while on the Court he became both
leader and symbol of a liberal constitutional revolution that could not
have been predicted given his partisan Republican background. The
famous decisions of the "Warren Court" included not only civil rights,
but also judicially mandated legislative reapportionment, defense of
individuals accused of crimes, and support for the civil liberties of
people having the temerity to criticize their government. Warren's
leadership of the Court from 1953 to 1969 allowed him to write or bro-
ker majority decisions on most of the great issues coming before the
American judiciary in the 1950s and 1960s. His leadership skills as well
as his legal acumen enabled him to hold together a brilliant but contentious group of associate justices. At the time of the oral argument
in *Tinker* Warren was seventy-seven. He had recently announced his
intention to resign at the end of the term (summer 1969) and allow the
new president, Richard Nixon, to name his successor. Given his judicial voting record in civil liberties cases, Warren was very likely to

side with Christopher Eckhardt and the Tinkers, upholding their right to symbolic expression.

The senior associate justice was Hugo Black, appointed to the Court in 1937 by President Franklin Roosevelt. Black would serve on the Court until a few days before his death in 1971, thus making him one of the longest-serving justices in the country's history. Appointed because he was a strong advocate of FDR's New Deal, Black made himself into one of the Court's greatest legal scholars. He sought to read the U.S. Constitution literally and, whenever possible, to seek out the views of the framers of the core document or its amendments. Belying his youthful membership in the Ku Klux Klan and his opinion supporting the internment of Japanese-Americans in *Korematsu v. U.S.* (1944), Black had been a judicial supporter of racial justice and individual liberties for most of his more than three decades on the Court. He had generally sided with the chief justice on the great decisions of the Warren Court. However, his recent opinion in *Adderley v. Florida* (1966), affirming the convictions of black students who had conducted a sit-in protest against segregation at a Southern jail, made his vote in the *Tinker* case uncertain. Would he read the First Amendment broadly and uphold the right of students to wear armbands to school, or would he vote to deny this form of symbolic expression because it went beyond what he conceived of as the literal meaning of the First Amendment?

The other Roosevelt appointee on the Court was a westerner and self-made man, William O. Douglas. Douglas took his seat on the Court in 1939 and did not retire until 1975. His thirty-six-year tenure is a Supreme Court record for longevity. Douglas was a vigorous outdoorsman, conservationist, and world traveler. As an exponent of the "work hard, play hard" philosophy of life, Douglas would regularly rush from a session on the Court to a fishing expedition or an international vacation. Even more than Black and Warren, Douglas was a champion of the underdog. His judicial record defending civil liberties was perhaps unsurpassed on the Supreme Court. Douglas was less concerned with adhering to precedent than with doing what he felt to be the right thing. His majority opinion in *Griswold v. Connecticut* (1965), striking down a state anticontraception law, offers a good example of Douglas's result-oriented jurisprudence. Although the U.S. Constitution no where mentions the word "privacy," Douglas felt that a married couple's decision to use birth control was theirs alone. He thus posited that the "penumbra" of several protections of the Bill of Rights could, if linked together, compose a right to privacy that would ascend to constitutional status. Douglas and Black had written concurring opinions in *West Virginia v. Barnette* (1943), a key precedent cited by Dan Johnston in all of his legal arguments in the *Tinker* case. If there was a sure vote for the Iowa students' right to wear black armbands, it was Douglas's.

The next most senior associate justice on the Court in 1968 was John Marshall Harlan II. The grandson of a previous justice—the first John Marshall Harlan—this 1955 Eisenhower appointee had been a Rhodes Scholar, a brilliant lawyer for a prestigious Wall Street firm, and, for a short time, a U.S. court of appeals judge. Harlan was a principled conservative, a defender of stare decisis (adherence to precedent), and a skilled legal craftsman. He generally found himself at odds with the liberal, activist jurisprudence of the Warren Court. For instance, he expressed strong dissents in the Court's several legislative reapportionment decisions. Harlan did, on occasion, support the rights of freedom of expression and freedom of religion, but he most often found himself supporting the instrumentalities of government in First Amendment cases. He was thus a likely vote in favor of the Des Moines school system in the *Tinker* case.

The third Eisenhower appointee on the Court was William Brennan, previously a New Jersey Supreme Court judge. Brennan was appointed in 1956 and would serve until 1990. Because Brennan, like Warren, was decidedly more liberal once on the Supreme Court than in his previous public life, Eisenhower regarded his appointment as a "mistake." Although Brennan had a hand in many of the great decisions of the Warren era, recognition of his critical role in constitutional law would not emerge until after Warren and most of the other liberal justices of the 1960s had died or retired. Overshadowed by the more strident Black and Douglas, Brennan was a safe vote in defense of the freedom of expression, the protection the rights of the accused, and civil rights. Brennan wrote the majority opinion in *Baker v. Carr* (1962), one of the leading legislative reapportionment decisions. In his final decade on the Court, 1980 to 1990, Brennan became an articulate voice in opposition to the Republican-appointed justices of the 1970s and 1980s. He believed that the Constitution should be interpreted broadly and that the intention of the framers of the document, if such intention could ever be deciphered, should not bind courts of a later century. In a case like *Tinker*, Brennan was a certain vote in favor of the protesting students.

The fourth and final Eisenhower appointee still serving on the Court in the 1968 October Term was Potter Stewart. He was confirmed in 1959 and would serve on the Court until 1981. Stewart was the author of the famous line about obscenity, "I know it when I see it." Stewart, like many members of the Warren Court, hailed from a family of judges. He was active in the moderate wing of the Cincinnati Republican Party in the 1940s and 1950s before his appointment to the U.S. court of appeals. Stewart boasted that he adhered to no overriding legal philosophy, that he simply decided the cases before him as he thought best. Scholars who have studied Stewart's decisions agree that he was a truly "nondoctrinal" jurist. If there was any key to his constitutional leanings, it was Stewart's apparent support for the autonomy of state governments. He was a defender of states' rights without falling prey to racism. He dissented in the leading rights-of-the-accused case, *Miranda v. Arizona* (1966), and the landmark children's-rights case, *In Re Gault* (1967). Thus, judging from his prior record on the Supreme Court, Stewart would likely support the school district in *Tinker*.

Byron R. White was the lone appointee of President John Kennedy on the Supreme Court during the 1968 October Term. In college White had been a fine student and a star athlete; he followed his baccalaureate degree with a Rhodes Scholarship. Immediately prior to his Supreme Court appointment White had served the Kennedy administration as a deputy attorney general. In this capacity he took a leading role in civil rights enforcement in the South. He was initially perceived as a Kennedy liberal, but legal scholars disagree as to whether White remained true to his liberal pedigree during his three decades on the Court. A former law clerk maintains that White did not base his Supreme Court decisions on abstract principles or technical doctrine but on "a pragmatic estimate as to how effective his choice would be." For example, White voted with the majority in the legislative reapportionment cases of *Wesberry v. Sanders* (1964) and *Reynolds v. Sims* (1964), dissented in the landmark criminal justice case of *Miranda v. Arizona* (1966), remained on the side of school integration in *Swann v. Charlotte-Mecklenburg Board of Education* (1971), but disagreed strongly with the majority in the 1973 case of *Roe v. Wade*, which limited state power to regulate abortions. Just as White had once gloried in competition on the gridiron, he threw himself into pickup basketball games with his much younger law clerks and took pleasure in the give and take of oral argument. How White would view the Iowa armband case was hard to predict.

The final two members of the 1968–69 Supreme Court were appointed by President Lyndon Johnson. Thurgood Marshall, appointed to the Court in 1967, had been the U.S. solicitor general under Johnson prior to his service on the Court. From the 1940s to the early 1960s, Marshall had been the country's most distinguished civil rights lawyer. As chief counsel for the National Association for the Advancement of Colored People (NAACP), Marshall's greatest recognition occurred in connection with his successful representation of African-American plaintiffs in the leading school desegregation case, *Brown v. Board of Education* (1954). The first African-American appointed to the Court, Marshall was a vigorous, friendly man. His jurisprudence was more pragmatic than theoretical. A former clerk commented that "Marshall's career as a practicing lawyer and as a justice . . . exemplif[ies] how far good judgment can take a person." Known for his strong endorsement of Johnson's "Great Society" and his unflagging support for individual rights, Marshall is also remembered for his string of dissents in capital punishment cases and his authorship of powerful opinions in race-relations and equal-protection cases. Marshall was another sure vote for the students in the *Tinker* case.

The final member of the Supreme Court in 1968–69 was Abe Fortas, the justice who would ultimately be selected to write the opinion in *Tinker*. Fortas had been an outstanding law student at Yale University in the early 1930s; there he came under the crusading influence of law professor and later Supreme Court colleague William O. Douglas. In the 1930s Fortas served in two of Franklin Roosevelt's New Deal agencies. From 1940 until his 1965 appointment to the Supreme Court, Fortas operated as a high-powered Washington lawyer. In 1948, Fortas's legal brilliance and political savvy helped Lyndon Johnson prevail in a disputed election to the U.S. Senate. Thereafter Johnson regarded Fortas as a close friend and adviser. Fortas was a strong supporter of individual rights: as a lawyer he successfully defended a small-time crook in the leading right-to-counsel case, *Gideon v. Wainwright* (1963); on the Supreme Court, Fortas's best-known decision was probably *In re Gault* (1967), the case that established that juveniles have rights in courts of law.

Given his judicial liberalism and his strong opinion in *In re Gault*, Fortas appeared to Court-watchers in the fall of 1968 to be a likely vote for Christopher Eckhardt and the Tinkers. It would not be known until years later that Fortas had voted against certiorari in *Tinker* in March 1968 because he had not been persuaded at that time that courts should intervene in school disciplinary matters "except where discrimination or clear abuse is involved." His vote against certiorari might also have stemmed from an unwillingness to embarrass his friend, President Lyndon Johnson. For whatever reason, Fortas would later change his mind and characterize the student protest as "akin to pure speech" and thus deserving of constitutional protection. But had Fortas's position on certiorari prevailed in March 1968, the Supreme Court would have refused to hear the *Tinker* appeal, Fortas would not have written his majority opinion in the case, and the lower federal court rulings against the student litigants would have persisted.

While the *Tinker* case was under review, the man who would ultimately write the majority opinion was undergoing a very difficult time. Abe Fortas had been nominated by Lyndon Johnson in June 1968 to replace the retiring Earl Warren as chief justice. It turned out to be an ill-starred nomination. As a lame-duck president, Johnson did not possess the political clout to get his old friend's appointment through the Senate confirmation hearings. The hearings became a battleground for Republican criticisms of the Great Society. In addition, Fortas's financial relationship with a wealthy businessman, Louis Wolfson, brought his ethics as a justice into question, thus further undermining his prospects for confirmation as chief justice. A month before the *Tinker* appeal was argued, intense political pressure forced LBJ to withdraw Fortas's nomination for the chief justiceship. Attacks on Fortas's ethics would continue during the time the Tinker case was under review. Just over two months after the announcement of the *Tinker* opinion, the unrelenting criticism would force Fortas to resign from the Court, thus cutting short a promising judicial career.

# May It Please the Court

Dan Johnston began his oral presentation to the U.S. Supreme Court on November 12, 1968 with a reference to the evolution law case, *Epperson v. Arkansas,* decided earlier that day. He noted that the case he was arguing and *Epperson* both dealt with the rights of individuals in the nation's public schools. The difference was that *Epperson* concerned academic freedom for public school faculty while the *Tinker* case dealt with the rights of students to express their political concerns symbolically. Justice Abe Fortas interrupted to make sure that Johnston was not saying that *Tinker* was a First Amendment establishment clause case. Johnston quickly acquiesced to this clarification, indicating that *Tinker* was a First Amendment case "in the sense of expression of view," not a dispute involving religious worship. Johnston later recalled that, given Fortas's quibble, he sensed he "was in trouble right away, right out of the box." He suspected that Fortas, the author of the majority opinion in *Epperson,* may have secured the support of several other justices on that case by promising that their votes on *Epperson* would not dictate their votes on *Tinker.* According to Johnston's surmise, several justices had not yet decided how they would vote on the armband case and, therefore, Fortas was quick to emphasize that *Epperson* and *Tinker* were different kinds of cases—the former involving freedom of religion and the later being a free-speech case.

Confessing to have been a bit rattled, Johnston moved on quickly. As he put it, "your adrenaline is really up." He summarized the facts that gave rise to the case, reviewed the procedural passage of the case in the lower federal courts, emphasized the reasons that his student clients had worn armbands to school, and stressed the fact that the Des Moines secondary-school officials had decided to ban black armbands in advance of any incidents. In his accounts of the events of mid-December 1965, Johnston underscored that no disturbances had been spawned by the armbands or the suspensions that followed.

Approximately five minutes into his presentation Johnston was interrupted by Justice Byron White, who asked him if his defense of the right to wear armbands would be different if students wearing the armbands had taken it upon themselves to stand up in class to explain the purpose of the pieces of cloth. Johnston responded that if such a set of facts had prevailed, "we would not be here." White then launched into a series of short, quickly posed questions concerning whether Johnston's student clients wanted to convey a message through the display of their armbands. Johnston attempted to tread a fine line in his responses to White: he said that the student petitioners had wished to get a point across with their armbands but that the pieces of cloth did not cause the other students to take their minds off academic subjects for very long.

Johnston later characterized White's line of questioning as a "cross-examination." He felt that White was firing his questions so fast that he did not have a chance to answer. In fact, the transcription of the oral argument reveals that White asked nineteen separate questions in this period of about three minutes. On several occasions the justice interrupted Johnston in midword with another question. Johnston recalls being irritated that White was interfering with the flow of his presentation and using up his limited time for oral argument. Despite his frustration, Johnston responded respectfully to White, referring to him as "your honor" or "sir," eschewing the more traditional manner of address, "Mr. Justice." Finally Johnston found a way to blunt White's concern about disruptions. He acknowledged that the armbands "might have distracted some students, just as many other things do in the classroom." White queried, "But which the school has forbidden?" Johnston rejoined, "But which the school also allows to continue." Johnston then reminded Justice White and the entire the Court that, while the Des Moines schools prohibited black armbands, the school administration had not banned political campaign buttons or religious symbols from school property.

At this point Chief Justice Earl Warren and Justice Thurgood Marshall entered the discussion about the symbols permitted in the Des Moines schools. Both seemed intrigued when they learned that the students claimed the right to wear the armbands anywhere on school property but that the hastily contrived school district policy had banned black armbands from the cafeteria and the halls as well as classrooms. In acknowledging that this was in fact the result of the administrative prohibition, Johnston asserted that the policy was too broad, did not directly target potential disruptions or distractions in the classroom and, therefore, "will not stand the test of freedom of speech under the First Amendment." Here Johnston was referring to the "overbreadth" doctrine in constitutional law, which demands that statutes regulating speech must be tailored to specific evils within an allowable area of government control or be ruled unconstitutional for overbreadth. Johnston pointed out that the record contains no indication that teachers or administrators had any reason to believe that armbands would be disruptive. Moreover, when the petitioners and a handful of other students wore armbands on December 16 and 17, 1965, no disruptions ensued. In response to a seemingly friendly question from Chief Justice Warren, Johnston acknowledged that a narrower regulation banning armbands from school classrooms might be "sustainable" under the First Amendment. White again joined the fray, asking why this made a difference. Johnston replied that there was no evidence that Christopher Eckhardt and the Tinkers were suspended just for wearing armbands to class but that they were suspended for violating the broad policy against wearing armbands on school property. In fact, he noted that Christopher Eckhardt never wore his armband in class because he had turned himself in to his high-school office at the beginning of the day in question.

Because several justices were posing various hypothetical questions, Johnston found that he had to slip his substantive comments into his answers to the justices' queries rather than attempting to return to his planned presentation. For example, when Chief Justice Warren asked if the armbands could have constitutionally been prohibited if they had sparked fistfights, Johnston agreed. He noted that such a record of violence or threatened violence might have justified a ban on disruptive symbols—as was the situation in the fifth circuit "freedom buttons" case cited in his brief. More appropriately, Johnston maintained, under the precedent of *Terminello v. Chicago* (1949), the state should take action by disciplining individuals physically engaging in disruptive actions rather than by compromising the freedom of expression of those merely voicing their opinions. But, he hastened to emphasize once again, there was no evidence of violence or serious threats of violence in the lower court record of the *Tinker* case. The students in the Iowa case had not been suspended for causing a disruption; they had been suspended for violating a school district policy. Johnston perhaps had in mind the "prior restraint" argument from his Supreme Court brief, although he did not take the opportunity at this juncture to raise the point explicitly or mention the leading prior-restraint decision, *Near v. Minnesota* (1931).

In the face of continued prodding from several justices, Johnston was willing to admit that the armband worn by John Tinker on December 17 had provoked discussion about the Vietnam War in a classroom setting as well as in the halls and in the cafeteria. But he emphasized that the armband did not "significantly or substantially or materially" interfere with the normal classroom activities. Furthermore, he insisted that a student who physically or verbally disrupted a class because he objected to John Tinker's armband should be punished but that John Tinker should not. He also said that he wished to distinguish between the simple symbolic act of wearing an armband and the act of making a speech in class or conducting a protest march in the hallway while wearing an armband. According to Johnston, the pure symbolic speech should be constitutionally protected; the other acts—"speech plus"— if done in a school setting should not.

At this point a justice queried as to whether the case was "moot" (whether the issues originally raised had ceased to exist). Because the armband-wearing students had been allowed back into school without penalty or punishment after the 1965–66 Christmas vacation could a good argument be advanced that the petitioners had not suffered any negative consequences from the armband episode in December 1965? Johnston pointed out that each of the students had testified before the district court judge that, as long as the Vietnam War continued, they might again consider wearing black armbands to school as a form of symbolic protest. Thus the school district policy against wearing black armbands presented a continuing restriction on their chosen form of symbolic expression. Johnston also reminded the justices that his clients had sued for nominal damages of one dollar to compensate them for the handful of days of school that they were under suspension. Even if the Vietnam War should end before the Court decided the *Tinker* case, the damages—albeit slight—had been sustained. Thus, in Johnston's clients' minds, this was more than an academic controversy.

Once again Johnston attempted to wend his way back to a matter that he had planned to address: what is the proper balance between the right of a school to maintain discipline and the right of students to express their opinions? Before he could state his position he was challenged by Justice Harlan, who accused the students' attorney of wanting to descend "pretty deep in the trenches of ordinary day to day discipline." Johnston's response was that the Court must occasionally draw such a line between school discipline and freedom of expression, just as it did in the World War II flag-salute case, *West Virginia Board of Education v. Barnette* (1943), and the evolution case just decided, *Epperson v. Arkansas* (1968). This immediately got a rise out of Justice Fortas, who once again admonished Johnston for confusing the freedom of expression and establishment clauses of the First Amendment. Fortas then launched into a short series of hypothetical questions about whether Johnston believed that student appearance—such as long hair or outlandish clothing—should be a protected form of constitutional expression. Johnston first attempted to avoid answering the questions. But, when pressed, he ventured the opinion that matters of appearance do "not present per se First Amendment problems such as we have here." At this point, seeing that his time was rapidly dwindling, Johnston concluded that there should not be a special rule for schools under the First Amendment. He submitted that "we would like to have the same principles applied in the school or perhaps especially in the school that are applied elsewhere." With this provocative statement, Johnston requested that the few minutes of his time remaining be reserved for rebutting points raised by the respondents. He had hoped to save five minutes, but the heavy barrage of questioning, especially from Justice White, had left him only about three minutes.

Allan Herrick, in presenting the arguments of the respondent Des Moines Independent Community School District, asserted that the *Tinker* case essentially presented three constitutional issues. The first was whether school officials have to wait until disruptions take place in order to act or whether they can exercise their best judgment to head off potential trouble before it starts. The second, according to Herrick, was how far the judiciary should go in reviewing the discretionary decisions of school district officials. The third issue was whether disturbances (or potential disturbances) in schools should be measured by identical standards as disturbances "on the streets."

In addressing the first issue, Herrick noted that American courts have consistently held that the freedom of expression is not absolute and that it must be balanced against the need to maintain order. As he alluded to the 1966 decision of *Adderley v. Florida*—where the Supreme

Court had denied a group of students the right to stage civil rights protests on the grounds of a jailhouse—he was interrupted by Justice Marshall. This fast-paced, revealing exchange ensued:

Q. [Marshall] How many students were involved in the *Adderley* case? Several hundred, weren't there?

A. [Herrick] It was quite a large number.

Q. How many were involved in this one [the *Tinker* case]?

A. Well, it is a question of what do you mean by "involved."

Q. How many were wearing arm bands?

A. There were five suspended for wearing arm bands.

Q. Any wearing arm bands that were not suspended?

A. Yes, sir, I think there were two.

Q. That makes seven. . . . Seven out of 18,000? And the School Board was advised that seven students wearing arm bands were disrupting 18,000? Am I correct?

A. I think, if the Court please, that doesn't give us the entire background that builds up to what was existing in the Des Moines Schools at the time the arm bands were worn.

In listening to this exchange, Christopher Eckhardt was struck by how adroitly Marshall had placed Herrick on the defensive. He remembers that, immediately after Herrick admitted that only seven students had been involved in the armband demonstration, Marshall "just kind of [sat] back in his chair and . . . [shook] his head a little bit" as if to indicate that the school district's argument on this point was not very effective. Herrick labored on, attempting to convince the Court that the armbands had caused or at least threatened disruptions and, therefore, that the school system had acted in good faith in banning the armbands. At several places in the course of his presentation Herrick argued that a public secondary-school classroom was not the place for a political demonstration. The students in a class, he submitted, were a captive audience, and the appearance of black armbands in their midst might provoke strong responses. At the very least, symbols of the anti-war movement could distract attention from the subjects being taught; in the extreme the wearing of such armbands might lead to violence.

Given the questions from the bench that Herrick's statements sparked, it appeared that Marshall and several other justices remained unpersuaded. For example, when Herrick asserted that the school system and the community were "aroused" by the possibility of black armbands appearing, he was challenged to identify such evidence in the district court record. This launched Herrick into a recitation of his version of the genesis of the armbands in Des Moines, emphasizing the ties of the Eckhardts and the Tinkers to the November 1965 anti–Vietnam War march on Washington and the alleged role played by SDS and the Women's International League for Peace and Freedom in this march and in a few students' decision to wear black armbands to school in December 1965. As in his Supreme Court brief, Herrick attempted to link SDS, which had disrupted the Democratic National Convention just a few months earlier, with the armband affair.

Herrick also noted that John Tinker had been verbally harassed at school on December 17, 1965, for wearing his armband and that he had stated in his deposition that another student—either Bruce Clark or Ross Peterson—had been struck. But John Tinker had not stated whether the alleged attack had taken place on school property. That led to the following exchange:

> Q. [Unnamed Justice, probably Marshall] Would I be correct in assuming that if violence had occurred at any of the three schools, the Des Moines school officials would have known about it?
>
> A. [Herrick] I wouldn't want to say that this is true because I wouldn't know.
>
> Q. Would it be normal? And my second question would be if the School Board knew about it, wouldn't they put in evidence about it? What evidence did the School Board . . . [cite] . . . when they adopted this resolution? Is it on paper any place?
>
> A. No. I think, your Honor—"

Eventually Herrick was forced to acknowledge that the "matter of disruption . . . [had been] very brief."

Not being able to demonstrate actual disruptions from the official record, Herrick fell back on the contention that the very *threat* of disruptions was sufficiently great so as to warrant the banning of the armbands as a prudent course of action. He put it in a cliche: "Sometimes an ounce of prevention is a lot better than a pound of cure." Again and again throughout his presentation, Herrick referred to what he characterized as an "explosive situation" in Des Moines in the mid-1960s. He cited the more than two hundred individuals—"many of them outsiders"—who had attended each of the two school board meetings on the armbands. He noted that the school officials had been worried about demonstrations, counterdemonstrations, and even violence if armbands were worn. Just as he mentioned the alleged SDS connection to the armband protest several times in his Supreme Court brief, Herrick made additional allusions to SDS in his oral argument. He also maintained that the recent death in the Vietnam War of a former Des Moines student had inflamed community passions to such a degree that violence could erupt if black armbands appeared. A justice then asked Herrick, in part rhetorically, "Do we have a city in this country that hasn't had someone killed in Vietnam?" Herrick reluctantly conceded, "No, I think not."

The school district attorney then mentioned an Arkansas case, *Pugley v. Sellmeyer,* that had been cited in his brief. In that case the Arkansas Supreme Court had upheld the right of a school system to forbid the wearing of face paint and cosmetics. In its opinion, the state supreme court had ruled that it would sustain duly instituted school policies unless there was a clear "abuse of discretion" or that the policy was not "reasonably calculated to effect the purpose intended of promoting discipline." For Herrick, if a school district's administration acted in a reasonable way to address a potentially disruptive situation, courts should bow to the school district's assessment of what needed to be done. But a justice interjected that, in contrast to *Tinker,* the Arkansas case did not involve a First Amendment claim. Herrick conceded that a First Amendment issue was raised by the Eckhardt-Tinker symbolic speech, but he submitted that that concern should be balanced against the need to maintain an atmosphere conducive to teaching and learning in the classroom. He stated, "I believe the schools are there to give these children an education, and I think Des Moines is one of the great spots in the nation where they have done it. And I feel that anything that threatens that type of scholarly atmosphere in the classroom ought to be prohibited."

This led one member of the Court back to a query about how much disruption the armbands actually caused to instruction in the Des Moines schools on December 16 and 17, 1965. This justice noted that the record showed that one mathematics class had been given over to a discussion of the armband protest. Neither the justice alluding to this incident nor Herrick mentioned that the class in question was conducted the day before the armbands were worn and that the discussion was initiated by Mary Beth Tinker's math teacher, not by Mary Beth or any of the other students. This same justice raised the matter of what other symbolic tokens had been permitted in the Des Moines schools. Herrick replied that he was aware that Iron Crosses and political buttons were occasionally displayed by students, without sanction, and that this practice had been noted in the record of the case. The issue of the double standard posed by tolerating religious and some political paraphernalia but not black armbands was not pursued by the Court or by Herrick.

Finally Herrick was asked about the application of the holdings of several other cases to the fact situation in *Tinker*. Herrick chose to respond to this question by saying that "every case must be reviewed on its own facts, and I think that is the difficulty in the Court getting into the situation." One of the cases mentioned by the Court at this late juncture in the oral argument was *Meyer v. Nebraska*, a 1923 Supreme Court decision that had struck down a state law banning the teaching of German in that state's public and private schools. *Meyer* was an unusual case to mention in this context. It had more to do with the Fourteenth Amendment's due process clause than the First Amendment's freedom of expression clause, and it was not cited in any of the parties' Supreme Court briefs. Before the tenuous link to *Meyer* could be established, however, Herrick's time expired.

Johnston, who had reserved a few minutes for rebuttal, began by highlighting the school district's willingness to permit religious symbols and mainstream political buttons in the classroom while at the same time banning armbands intended to convey feelings about the Vietnam War. Johnston pointed out that the only school district policy treating symbolic expression by students involved armbands. In contrast to the argument made by Allan Herrick that "an explosive situation . . . made this a special circumstance," Johnston argued that the record of the district court trial in *Tinker* did not reveal that any great tension prevailed in December 1965 in the Des Moines schools. Whereas the school district attorney had maintained that the test for determining the constitutionality of the ban on armbands should be one of "reasonableness," Johnston vehemently disagreed. He argued that, under the doctrine of *West Virginia Board of Education v. Barnette* (1943), the mere reasonableness of a school policy was not sufficient to uphold that policy if it offended privileges protected by the First Amendment. For the students' attorney, the reasons behind the school district's proscription of armbands "do not provide sufficient grounds for subornation of freedom of speech."

Throughout the oral argument Johnston was frustrated that Justice Black—long one of his judicial heroes—did not appear willing to extend to school children the protections of the First Amendment. By the rebuttal Johnston recalls that his feelings toward Black had gone beyond frustration and were verging on anger. It was one thing for Black to appear to disagree with Johnston's position, but Johnston felt that Black was trying to steal his time by asking "silly questions." One such question came right at the end of the rebuttal: "Which do you think has the most control in the school, the pupil policy of teaching the pupils, or the authorities that are running the schools?" In other words: "Who's in charge?" As his time ran out, Johnston recovered as best he could: "The authorities . . . are running the school under the authority given to them by the Constitution of the United States and within the provisions of that constitution, and the whole nub of our case is that they have exceeded their powers." With that statement Johnston thanked the Court, and oral argument ended.

Although Johnston had been nervous before the oral argument in *Tinker,* he knew he had a strong case. Years later he would remark that a bad presentation can "probably blow a marginal case, but this was not a marginal case." Even the pointed exchanges he had had with Justices Black, White, and Fortas did not detract from his general satisfaction with his performance and the likelihood that his clients would prevail.

Among those in attendance at the oral argument was Lorena Tinker. She remembers that most of the justices seemed by their questions to be sympathetic to Johnston and hostile to the school district attorney. She felt that Herrick had hurt his case by expressing anger that any students would "dare to defy the authority of the schools." For Lorena Tinker, just as for Christopher Eckhardt, the best moment in the oral argument was when Justice Thurgood Marshall successfully undercut the school district position by getting Herrick to acknowledge that only a handful of the eighteen thousand Des Moines students wore armbands in December 1965. She also remembers Marshall nearly falling asleep at other times during the lawyers' presentations.

On November 13, 1968, the *Tinker* oral argument and the *Epperson* decision shared equal billing in the nation's press. For example, in an article titled "High Court Studies Classroom Protests," the Washington *Evening Star* emphasized that the issue in the background of the *Tinker* case was the "legality of increasing protest movements on college campuses, as well as in high schools." The *Star* article also mentioned that, despite a few cutting questions from Hugo Black and Byron White, the justices "seemed outwardly sympathetic to the students' legal case." The November 13 *Des Moines Register* carried a front-page story on the arm-band case, titled "D.M. Appeal on Arm Bands to High Court." Although providing a summary of the armband case to date, it contained little information on the oral argument. Next to the *Register*'s page-six continuation of this story was a sobering article, titled "Two More Iowans Die in Vietnam." Neither young man was from Des Moines, but they were both about the same age as Christopher Eckhardt and John Tinker.

# CHAPTER 10

# The Supreme Court Rules

## The Conference

As strange as it may seem, a Supreme Court decision often appears anticlimactic to those most intimately involved in the long litigation leading up to the Court's review. All the heavy lifting is completed well before the day on which a decision is announced. Lawyers for the parties pour great effort into their briefs and oral arguments. Individuals and groups with vested interests in the issues presented by a Supreme Court case often attend the oral argument. At the conclusion of the oral argument the case is submitted to the Court. The parties, their attorneys, the legal community, and the general public learn nothing more about a case until the decision is read in a public Supreme Court session sometime later in the term. All they can do is wait and worry.

A few days after an oral argument is completed, the nine justices gather in their private conference room within the Supreme Court Building to discuss cases that they have recently heard. The conference room is beautifully paneled, with a fireplace, a chandelier, and a complete set of *U.S. Reports* (the volumes containing the Court's decisions) in one of the walled bookcases. Generally twice a week during a term the Court conducts a conference to screen certiorari petitions, discuss cases on the current docket, and transact other business. When it is time for a conference to commence, a buzzer summons the justices from their offices elsewhere in the building. As the justices file into the conference room, they shake hands with each other. Although there are strong intellectual and occasionally personal disagreements among the justices, the ritual of handshaking before conferences (as well as before oral arguments) is maintained in an attempt to preserve harmony on the Court. Under a painting of Chief Justice John Marshall and around a handsome table, the justices seat themselves in high-backed leather chairs. The chief justice is ensconced at one end of the table; the senior associate justice occupies the other end; the remaining justices sit in assigned places on the long sides of the table. No clerks, secretaries, aides, or visitors ever attend conferences of the Supreme Court. The most junior associate justice guards the door, dispatching and receiving any messages.

Supreme Court tradition holds that conference discussion on a case begins with the chief justice and then proceeds in descending order from the most senior associate justice down through the Court's most recent appointee. This procedure allows for the senior justices to make their views felt first. Then the tentative votes are cast in reverse order so that junior justices will not be swayed by the votes of their senior colleagues or the chief justice. Chief Justice Warren's rein on the Court was loose enough to permit frequent unstructured give-and-take discussion. After the votes have been cast, if the chief justice is in the majority, he assigns the writing of the opinion to one of the majority voting justices (himself included). If the chief is not in the majority, the senior associate justice makes the assignment from the justices voting with him. Justices in the majority are free to write "concurring opinions"—opinions agreeing with the decision of the majority for different reasons than those specified by the "opinion of the Court." Justices not in the majority may, if they choose, write separate dissenting opinions.

After the assignment of the opinion, the real work of the justices begins. The justice assigned to write the opinion prepares a draft, frequently benefiting from the advice, research, and writing skill of one of his/her law clerks (usually recent law school graduates with outstanding academic records). When the draft is completed, it is circulated to other members of the Court, including those not in the tentative majority, to see how many of them will "join" the opinion. At the same time, any justices who elect to produce concurring or dissenting opinions will similarly distribute drafts of their opinions and solicit the votes of colleagues. Justices may change their votes on a case until the decision is announced in open court. The confidentiality of the conference and the opinion writing is virtually absolute. On only a handful of occasions in the Court's history has word of a pending decision been leaked in advance of its announcement. However, years after the fact, scholars are sometimes permitted to probe the private papers of the justices for notes, memoranda, or draft opinions on crucial cases. Through this review, details about the Court's decision making on a particular case, unknown to the public and the media at the time of the decision, can be disclosed.

## Behind the Scenes

The Supreme Court discussed the *Tinker* case at its conference on Friday, November 15, 1968, three days after the oral argument. Tally sheets kept by the justices disclose that there had been five votes in March 1968 in favor of granting certiorari in the appeal (William Brennan, William Douglas, Thurgood Marshall, Potter Stewart, and Earl Warren) and four votes against hearing the case (Hugo Black, Abe Fortas, John Marshall Harlan, and Byron White). The tally sheets also note that, on the merits of the case, seven justices at the conference expressed votes in favor of reversing the lower federal courts and thus supporting the students' right to wear armbands. Only two of the justices (Black and Harlan) voted to affirm the lower courts' endorsement of the school district position.

Conference notes kept by the justices—often only marginally legible—allow glimpses into the thinking of the members of the Court on the black-armband case. Chief Justice Earl Warren spoke first. His conference notes and those of some of his brethren indicate that he favored deciding the case on the ground of "equal protection." In his view, Christopher Eckhardt and the Tinkers were denied equal protection of the laws under the Fourteenth Amendment because of the Des Moines school district's double standard: it acquiesced in allowing students to wear Iron Crosses and other symbols, but it singled out a form of conduct of which it disapproved—wearing black armbands to protest the Vietnam War—and proscribed it.

One of Earl Warren's law clerks in the 1968 term of the Court prepared a nineteen-page "bench memo" on the *Tinker* case. It was dated November 8, 1968—just four days before the oral argument in the case. The memo advances the following value judgment: "Resps' [Respondents'—the school district] brief is very disappointing." The memo goes on to note that the school district brief concedes that the wearing of black armbands is speech but that such speech can be regulated or prohibited only if it poses a "clear and present danger" to the school's educational activities. However, the memo points out that the lower court record mentions only a single incident of violence at school stemming from the armbands, that other armband-sparked disturbances occurred outside the classroom, and that disturbances at the January 1966 school board meeting resulted from the administrative regulation itself and not from the conduct of the students. The memo concludes that "the resps clearly failed to meet this test" and that "where such conduct is obviously intended and understood as a manifestation of political or social protest, it is protected by the 1st amendment." The position that Warren would take on the *Tinker* case in the conference was consonant with the points raised in his clerk's memo. In addition, because Supreme Court clerks frequently circulate memos among themselves, it is possible that the November 8 clerk's memo to the chief justice may have had influence throughout the Court.

As the senior associate justice, Hugo Black spoke next. Notes of his judicial colleagues indicate that the Court's longest-serving member favored affirming the lower court decisions on the broadest possible grounds. Justice Thurgood Marshall's notes capture the essence of Black's hostility to the student position in a phrase: "children being allowed to run riot." William O. Douglas's cryptic notes also reveal the tenor of Black's concerns: "—schools are in great trouble . . . children need discipline . . . the country is going to ruin . . . this is no 1st Amendment problem . . . question is whether the rule is reasonable." It was clear from these colleagues' notes that Black would be filing a dissent, no doubt a blistering one.

Douglas, the next longest serving member of the Court in 1969, took exactly the opposite position from Black, his traditional ally on constitutional issues. Conference notes indicate that Douglas supported the broadest possible reversal of the lower court decisions in *Tinker*, thus upholding the right of symbolic expression of the three student petitioners. A bench memo to Douglas from one of his clerks, dated February 16, 1968, urged him to vote to grant certiorari because this was "a classic case of prior restraint." But at the conference on November 15, 1968, Douglas indicated that he could agree with an opinion of the Court that found a narrower ground for the decision.

John Marshall Harlan indicated (without much elaboration, judging from the conference notes) that he would affirm the court of appeals decision. William Brennan, also without much elaboration, said that he supported the chief justice's position and favored reversal. Potter Stewart stated that he agreed with Chief Justice Warren on the equal protection issue, but that he could not support an opinion of the Court that denied school authorities the right to discipline students.

Byron White had plenty to say about the *Tinker* case in the conference. He was willing to vote for reversal of the lower court decisions, but he did not favor Warren's equal protection argument or Douglas's broader prior restraint position. White wanted to make sure that school authorities retained the power to discipline students causing disruptions. He did not like the idea of armbands—or any symbols—getting in the way of the lessons taught by teachers. What persuaded him to side with the emerging Court majority—although he would eventually write his own short concurring opinion—was a belief that the facts of the case did not reveal any serious disruptions of school routine. A phrase in Marshall's notes summarized White's position: "they [the school district] have not done a good job [of demonstrating that the armbands were disruptive] and therefore [should] loose [lose?]." White was also troubled that the Des Moines school district's prohibition order, by banning armbands from entire school campuses and not just classrooms, was too broad.

The most junior appointees on the Court, Abe Fortas and Thurgood Marshall, both indicated in the conference that they "could go with Byron"—that is, favor reversal on the narrow ground suggested by White. Marshall, after mentioning his inclination, said little. Fortas was more voluble: he stated that school authorities must control their schools, but they must also have a compelling justification for restricting the free expression of students in terms of school functions. For Fortas, the record showed no justification for the restrictions instituted by the school district.

The dominant impression that emerges from a careful reading of the several justices' notes of the conference on the *Tinker* case is that Douglas's broad prior restraint reasoning was discarded early as a rationale for seven justices who favored reversal. The chief justice's equal protection argument was attractive for a time. But once White had a chance to outline his more temperate view, the plurality of the Court came over to his position. Then why didn't White write the opinion? Given the absence of clear evidence in the papers of the justices, and given the fact that Chief Justice Warren (the assigner of the opinion) never commented on this issue, no definite answer can be advanced. However, some speculation is in order. In the assignment of opinions, one consideration of the assigning justice is to distribute as evenly as possible the writing of the Court's majority opinions. As the Court's second most junior justice, Fortas was due a few more opinions in the 1968–69 term. In addition, the chief justice may have felt that Fortas, an able negotiator, could do a better job of holding together the majority than the more strong-willed White. In addition, Fortas's liberalism was more consonant with the dominant pro-civil-liberties tenor of the Warren Court than was White's judicial philosophy. Finally, it is possible that Warren selected Fortas for this opinion because he had already established himself as the Court's "expert" on children's rights with his recent opinion in *In re Gault* (1967).

Once it was established who would write the Court's opinion, the justices went to work. Court records indicate that Fortas began circulating his first draft of an opinion to other members of the Court in early December 1968. Warren, as chief justice, kept a tally sheet on the status of support or dissent from the Fortas opinion. It noted that Brennan and Marshall signed the Fortas opinion in December, and Warren "joined" in early January 1969. The tally sheet does not indicate when Douglas joined. White produced a draft of a brief concurring opinion on January 9. Two days prior to that, Stewart wrote a brief memo to Fortas: "I am in general agreement with your opinion for the Court. . . . However, at the risk of appearing eccentric, I shall not join any opinion that speaks of what is going on in Vietnam as a 'war.' If you prefer not to go to the trouble of making the necessary verbal changes to meet this objection . . . , I shall simply write a brief concurrence." Fortas would later make this change, but Stewart would find another point in Fortas's eventual opinion about which to quibble. He would express it in a concurring opinion submitted on January 24, 1969.

The dissents posed their own special concerns. John Marshall Harlan submitted his draft dissent to the Court on January 7, 1969. Two days later Hugo Black wrote Fortas, apologizing that it was taking him such a long time to produce his own dissent. He blamed the mail service and the fact that he felt he could not rest his dissent on the views Harlan expressed. In truth, because Black liked to fiddle with his prose through several drafts, his opinion writing was often slower than that of his colleagues. Not surprisingly, his judicial papers contain many hand-written and typed drafts of his dissent in *Tinker.* Another factor slow-ing down the production of the dissenting opinions in *Tinker* was that Black and Harlan had each made less than flattering references to the other's constitutional views in early drafts of their dissents. Black had referred to Harlan as being the only remaining exponent on the Supreme Court of the "old" (early-twentieth-century) doctrine of "reasonableness" under the Fourteenth Amendment. In turn, Harlan had stated in a footnote to his draft that Fortas's majority opinion "arouse[ed] in me a collateral satisfaction" because it sparked a "dis-senting essay" from "my Brother Black" which "reveals . . . his extraor-dinary capacities for . . . colorful self-mesmerizing characterization of the constitutional views of others." For these two longtime legal ad-versaries to agree to delete the verbal jabs at each other required some negotiations and a little bit of time. Constitutional law can make strange—and not very comfortable—bedfellows.

The Supreme Court never announces on which day it will decide a case heard previously in the term. So lawyers and interested parties are seldom in attendance to hear directly the disposition of the dis-pute that concerns them. Reporters and Court-watchers can occasion-ally get a hint that an important decision will be issued on a particular day if they happened to notice the spouses of some of the justices in the Supreme Court Building. Otherwise a decision is issued without any preparation or warning—as was the situation with *Tinker v. Des Moines,* announced in open court on February 24, 1969.

## The "Opinion of the Court"

During the week that the Supreme Court decision was announced in the black-armband case, riots took place on the campus of the Uni-versity of California, Berkeley over minority-student demands for a separate college of ethnic studies. Among the many other campuses experiencing rioting in this period were Duke University, the City College of New York, and the University of Wisconsin. President

Nixon said that he supported the "get tough" policy with student demonstrators advocated by Notre Dame President Father Theodore Hesburgh. The campaign pledge of the new president to end the Vietnam War had not been fulfilled during his first month in office. Most expert commentators doubted that much could be done quickly to extricate the United States from the Southeast Asia "quagmire." In late February the U.S. troop commitment to Vietnam was close to its historic high—539,000. Foreign correspondents reported that heavy North Vietnamese rocket and mortar rounds were being fired into Saigon and other South Vietnamese cities; they were comparing this attack to the Tet Offensive of the previous year. The Pentagon set the draft call for April 1969 at 33,000—one of the highest levels since the onset of the Vietnam War. The Iowa Selective Service planned to call up 473 young men in April.

On February 24, 1969, a mild winter day in the nation's capital, the U.S. Supreme Court held a public session to transact a variety of business. It announced the denial of certiorari in over a hundred lower court cases, granted certiorari in five cases, noted jurisdiction in ten cases, issued orders in seven pending cases, and read opinions in about twenty cases. The myriad rulings and decisions concerned such varied subjects as the constitutionality of a federal labor law requiring union officials to swear they were not communists; the legality of the five-month prison sentence against comedian Dick Gregory for resisting arrest during a demonstration in Chicago; a state's legal ability to bar a "jailhouse lawyer" from helping a fellow inmate prepare legal documents; the legality of a proposed railroad merger; and the constitutionality of a state practice of sterilizing "mentally deficient" persons as a condition of releasing them from institutions. The decision, though, that would receive top billing by the press in a summary of the Court's action for that day was the Iowa black-armband case, *Tinker v. Des Moines.*

Justice Fortas's opinion of the Court ran to just over eleven pages in the official volume of Supreme Court opinions, the *U.S. Reports.* In the post–World War II era, this is a relatively short opinion for a constitutional case. Fortas began with an introduction of the three student petitioners and a terse recitation of the events of mid-December 1965 that led to the controversy. To mollify Justice Stewart's concerns about nomenclature, Fortas referred to Iowa students as calling for a truce in the "hostilities" in Vietnam rather than using the term "war." Elsewhere in the opinion Fortas employed such euphemisms as "conflict" and "involvement" to describe the military situation in Southeast Asia. Fortas's account of the facts and procedural history of the case occupied only about a page and a half. To the likely consternation of school district attorney Allan Herrick, Fortas did not mention SDS's putative connection to the armbands anywhere in his opinion.

Fortas noted that the district court was correct in classifying the wearing of black armbands as a "type of symbolic act that is within the Free Speech Clause of the First Amendment." The first clear hint that the Court was going to find in favor of the student petitioners came on the third page of the opinion, when Fortas announced that "the wearing of arm bands in the circumstances of this case was entirely divorced from actually or potentially disruptive conduct by those participating in it. It was closely akin to 'pure speech' which, we have repeatedly held, is entitled to comprehensive protection under the First Amendment." Later in the opinion Fortas would distinguish "pure speech" from matters of appearance or conduct that might disturb school administrators, for example, questionable clothing, jewelry, or hair styles. Then Fortas concluded that symbolic acts of pure speech should not be denied to teachers and students in the public schools. In a much-cited statement, he maintained that "[i]t can hardly be argued that ... students or teachers shed their constitutional rights to freedom of speech or expression at the schoolhouse gate." In support of this proposition, he cited Supreme Court cases going back almost fifty years, principally *Meyer v. Nebraska* (1923), in which the Court upheld the "property right" of an instructor to teach a foreign language.

Fortas emphasized that statutes interfering with the liberty of teachers, students, or parents had been consistently ruled unconstitutional by the Court. Among the cases cited to substantiate this proposition was the Court's decision concerning the liberties of Jehovah's Witness children and parents, *West Virginia Board of Education v. Barnette* (1943), which struck down a state's compulsory flag-salute statute. This was a case that Dan Johnston had cited favorably in every one of his legal briefs and in his oral argument to the Court a few months earlier. It appeared that the Supreme Court was reading the *Barnette* case as just the kind of friendly legal precedent that Johnston argued it to be. Fortas also cited the Arkansas evolution decision, *Epperson v. Arkansas* (1968)—

the case decided the same day that *Tinker* was argued, in which Fortas himself had written the majority opinion—as supporting the right of free expression in the schools. Apparently Fortas was no longer troubled by the possible confusion between *Epperson* and *Tinker* that he had brought to Johnston's attention in oral argument.

Having established that armbands are symbolic speech and that students and teachers do not give up constitutional rights while on school property, Fortas moved to the issue of balancing the right to practice this form of expression with its degree of interference with public order. Essentially Fortas accepted the reading of the lower court record provided by Johnston. He found the wearing of armbands to be "silent, passive . . . unaccompanied by any disorder or disturbance on the part of petitioners." Furthermore, he stated that "there is here no evidence whatever of petitioners' interference . . . with the school's work or of collision with the rights of other students to be secure and to be let alone." Outside of class, he stated that the few hostile remarks against armband wearers did not constitute sufficient disruption to justify a limitation on students' free expression. If any violence resulting from the armbands did take place, Fortas noted, it did not occur on school property.

Relying on the district court's finding that no appreciable disturbances took place because of the armbands, Fortas proceeded to address the issue of whether the Des Moines school authorities had good reason to proscribe armbands, given their apprehension of possible disruptions. Fortas noted that any departures from consensus may be unsettling: comments in class or, for that matter, anywhere else on campus may spark an argument. The American historical experience, in Fortas's words, bespeaks a "sort of hazardous freedom . . . that is the basis of our national strength." A "mere desire to avoid . . . discomfort and unpleasantness" is not enough to sanction a ban on certain types of conduct.

For Fortas, the constitutional standard gleaned from *Burnside v. Byars* (1966)—that the proscribed right must "materially and substantially interfere with the requirements of appropriate discipline in the operation of the school"—was not met by the Des Moines school district in *Tinker*. Fortas noted that, while the school district's after-the-fact "official memorandum," mentioned several reasons for the armband prohibition, the articulated reasons did not include "anticipation of . . . disruption." Rather, Fortas believed, the actions of the school administrators in banning the armbands were based on a desire to avoid any controversy that might derive from the armbands themselves.

Finally Fortas reached the double-standard issue. Because the record showed that some students wore religious and political symbols without sanction but that other students were suspended for wearing black armbands to express concerns about the war in Vietnam, there appeared to Fortas and the Court majority to be a constitutional inconsistency. School officials must grant students a fair and equal treatment under the law. "State-operated schools," Fortas maintained, "may not be enclaves of totalitarianism." In this context, Fortas came back to a view expressed earlier in the opinion, namely that schools should be tolerant of differences and diversity. Education works best—here Fortas paraphrased Justice Brennan's words from a 1967 opinion—if it is practiced with "a robust exchange of ideas which discovers truth out of a multitude of tongues, [rather] than through any kind of authoritative selection.'"

Because Fortas believed that the school environment extended beyond the classroom, he argued that students should be free to express themselves symbolically on controversial subjects on the playground, in the cafeteria, and in the halls between classes. Moreover, as he noted in a footnote, a school campus is a public place that should be open to the expression of diverse opinions; it is unlike the jail enclosure that was the subject of *Adderley v. Florida* (1966), where the Supreme Court found less of a basis for the free run of ideas. Fortas stated that the Court was willing to tolerate the "reasonable regulation of speech-connected ideas," but that it was not willing to confine such activities to a telephone booth, a printed pamphlet, or a school classroom.

Justice Fortas concluded his opinion for the seven-justice majority by reiterating that the lower court record did not reveal that any disturbances occurred on school premises as a result of the armbands. Nor, he reemphasized, did the record present any facts that might reasonably have convinced school officials that small black strips of cloth on the sleeves of a handful of students in a large urban school district threatened disorder. With these statements, Fortas ordered the reversal of the decisions of the Eighth Circuit Court of Appeals and the

Federal District Court of the Southern District of Iowa, and he remanded *Tinker v. Des Moines* to the lower courts for relief in line with the views expressed in his opinion.

Fortas's majority opinion in *Tinker* did not refer to *U.S. v. O'Brien* (1968), the draft-card-burning case of the previous term. In that decision, the Court had held that setting fire to a draft card at an antiwar rally, in violation of a 1965 amendment to the selective service law prohibiting the destruction of draft registration certificates, was not protected speech. Fortas had considered filing a separate concurrence in *O'Brien* because he felt that Chief Justice Warren's first draft of an opinion of the Court in that case did not go far enough in recognizing the constitutional legitimacy of symbolic speech. But when the Chief Justice softened his opinion to leave the door open for symbolic speech that would pass muster under the First Amendment, Fortas joined in the Court's opinion. According to a Fortas biographer, what differentiated *O'Brien* from *Tinker* in Fortas's constitutional philosophy was that five students quietly wearing armbands in a large school system were much less disruptive than draft cards being ignited at a public rally. This seems to be a fair interpretation, because Fortas's opinion of the Court in *Tinker* continually stressed the limited, non-threatening behavior of the armband-wearing Iowa students.

---

## Three Short Opinions

After Justice Fortas read the Opinion of the Court in *Tinker v. Des Moines,* two of his brethren presented concurring opinions and two delivered dissents. The concurring opinions and one of the dissents were less than a page each in the *U.S. Reports* and can be discussed quickly. The dissent delivered by Justice Hugo Black demands greater attention.

Justice Potter Stewart's concurrence, dated January 24, 1969, on Chief Justice Warren's tally sheet, was the last opinion completed in the *Tinker* case. In his earlier memo, Stewart had objected to Fortas's use of the term "war" to describe the hostilities in Southeast Asia. Although Fortas had duly removed the offending three-letter word from his opinion, Stewart found something else to bother him, and thus he produced a concurrence rather than joining the opinion. Stewart wrote that he did not accept "the Court's uncritical assumption that, school discipline aside, the First Amendment rights of children are co-extensive with those of adults." He quoted from one of his previous opinions: "[A] child—like someone in a captive audience—is not possessed of that full capacity for individual choice which is the presupposition of First Amendment guarantees."

Justice White was even briefer in his concurrence than Stewart. Although he was willing to side with the majority in reversing the lower courts, he registered two points on which he disagreed with Fortas's reasoning. The first is hard to grasp because it is expressed so cryptically. White wrote: "[T]he Court continues to recognize a distinction between communicating by words and communicating by acts or conduct which sufficiently impinge on some valid state interest." The second is understandable but undeveloped. White pronounced: "I do not subscribe to everything . . . said about free speech . . . in *Burnside v. Byars* (1966) . . . , a case relied upon by the Court." Given White's obvious interest in the black-armband case, as demonstrated by his enthusiastic participation in the oral argument, and given the fact that the Court accorded his comments great weight in its conference on the case conducted three days after the oral argument, the brief and undeveloped concurring opinion he ultimately produced in *Tinker* is disappointing.

The dissent delivered by John Marshall Harlan was not surprising, given his traditional reluctance to overturn decisions made by governmental agencies. Harlan argued that school authorities should be given the benefit of the doubt in actions taken to maintain discipline and order. The rule that he proposed for a situation such as this was that a school policy should be upheld unless it could be demonstrated from the factual record that the policy "was motivated by other than legitimate school concerns—for example, a desire to prohibit the expression of an unpopular point of view, while permitting expression of the dominant opinion." Because Harlan found nothing in the record to call into question the good faith of the Des Moines school administration, he voted to affirm the lower court rulings. As Harlan had promised Hugo Black, the unflattering characterization of his senior colleague's jurisprudence that he had included in an earlier draft of his dissent was removed from the version that Harlan submitted for the *U.S. Reports*.

# An Angry Dissent

Hugo Black, although one of the mainstays of liberalism on the Warren Supreme Court, dissented eighteen times during the 1968–69 term of the Court. This was the highest number of dissents of any member of the Court that term, higher even than the contentious William Douglas or the conservative conscience of the Court, John Marshall Harlan. No Black dissent that term, however, was as stinging as his paean to the proper deportment of children in *Tinker v. Des Moines.* It began as a crude set of handwritten notes; it graduated to a draft written completely in Black's virtually indecipherable hand; then it was typed; then it was edited and retyped several times before delivery in Court. Even as he was preparing to deliver his dissent, Black made several last-minute changes in the wording in his reading copy.

When decisions are announced in open court, some justices prefer to read from their opinions verbatim; others elect to excerpt and quote from critical sections of their opinion; and sometimes a justice chooses to speak extemporaneously. On this occasion, Justice Black spoke for about twenty minutes, off-the-cuff and from the heart. The first sentence of the opinion left no doubt as to his view of the black-armband case: "The Court's holding in this case ushers in what I deem to be an entirely new era in which the power to control pupils... [in the public schools] is... transferred to the Supreme Court." Near the beginning of the public delivery of his opinion, Black emphatically stated, "I want it thoroughly known that I disclaim any sentence, any word, any part of what the Court does today."

For purposes of argument Black was willing to accept the majority view that wearing black armbands to convey political ideas is protected by the free speech clause of the First Amendment. However, Black did object strongly to "students and teachers... [using] the schools at their whim as a platform for the exercise of free speech—'symbolic' or 'pure.'" Black emphasized that he had long believed that units of American government under the U.S. Constitution do not have the right to censor speech, but he qualified this by quickly adding: "I have never believed that any person has a right to give speeches or engage in demonstrations where he pleases and when he pleases." Later in the opinion Black made the point this way: "It is a myth to say that any person has a

{ *The Struggle for Student Rights* }

constitutional right to say what he pleases, where he pleases, and when he pleases." To support his point Black made reference to the majority opinion in *Cox v. Louisiana* (1964), which held that the rights of speech and assembly under the First Amendment "do not mean that anyone with opinions or beliefs to express may address a group at any public place and at any time." Black neglected to say that the majority in *Cox*, over his dissent, upheld the right of students to picket a Baton Rouge courthouse.

Black then went on to offer his particular reading of the lower court record in *Tinker*. In contrast to the majority justices, Black maintained that the record showed several instances in which the wearing of the black armbands disrupted the Des Moines schools in December 1965: students made comments, poked fun, and issued warnings; John Tinker felt "self-conscious"; and Mary Beth Tinker's mathematics teacher had one period's lesson "wrecked" by discussion regarding the wearing of the armbands. For Black, the record showed that the armbands distracted students from their classwork and "diverted them to thoughts about the highly emotional subject of the Vietnam war." By contrast Fortas, for the majority, had found "no evidence whatever of petitioners' interference, actual or nascent, with the school's work or of collision with the rights of other students to be secure and to be let alone." It is certainly legitimate to wonder if Fortas and Black were reading the same lower court record. Black concluded this section of his dissent with a lament: "[I]f the time has come when pupils of state-supported schools ... can defy and flaunt orders of school officials to keep their minds on their own school work, it is the beginning of a new revolutionary era of permissiveness in this country fostered by the judiciary."

Next Black accused the Court majority of returning to an outdated judicial doctrine that permitted courts to impose their own views of "reasonableness" on state agencies. In the late nineteenth and early twentieth centuries, conservative justices on the U.S. Supreme Court had occasionally controlled enough votes to succeed in striking down state reform laws—concerning such subjects as maximum hours, child labor, and unsafe working conditions—because they were deemed "unreasonable" by the justices. In essence, the Court imposed its own vague understandings of what was reasonable upon the law, in contrast to the views of the people as expressed through their legislatures. This judicial doctrine was usually termed "substantive due process" because it involved the Court imposing on the substantive law its own view of what was "reasonable" pursuant to the due process clause of the Fourteenth Amendment. The clash over this constitutional test of legislation, as Black correctly noted, was settled in the mid-1930s when the Court's majority, under pressure from President Roosevelt, discarded the old "reasonableness" test. Black accused the majority of the *Tinker* Court of "resurrecting that old reasonableness due process test" in this free speech case. In the final version of his dissent, however, Black struck out the unflattering reference to Justice Harlan's view of reasonableness that had appeared in an earlier draft.

The difference between the line of old cases alluded to by Justice Black under the reasonableness test and the Iowa black-armband case is that the early-twentieth-century court clashes involved economic regulation, while the state policy struck down by Fortas's majority opinion in *Tinker* had no economic dimension. The black-armband case simply posed the question of whether a state agency's regulation of freedom of expression was justified in order to maintain the peace. Black conveniently did not acknowledge this distinction. In fact, Black went so far as to cite *West Virginia Board of Education v. Barnette* (1943) as one example of a case rejecting the reasonableness test, even though the Court in that instance struck down a state's compulsory-flag-salute policy in the schools. In short, Black offered a truncated reading of the cases in order to support his view of the First Amendment.

It is correct that Fortas's majority opinion found the regulation in *Tinker* to be "unreasonable." But Fortas's analysis was based on the standards of the First Amendment in which the right to free expression is balanced against the possible threat to public order from such expression, not on the repudiated view of property under the Fourteenth Amendment that Black attempted to throw in the face of the *Tinker* majority. On his personal copy of Black's dissent, Fortas scribbled next to the discussion of standards for First Amendment review: "We're relying on *Black* not *McReynolds*" (Fortas's emphasis). The allusion here was to James McReynolds, a conservative member of the Court from 1914 to 1941, who was a strong proponent of economic substantive due process. In several places on his copy of Black's dissent, Fortas placed exclamation marks next to comments that he apparently found incredible or distressing. For example, Fortas could not believe that Justice Black, the Court's great civil libertarian, wrote the words "uncontrolled liberty is an enemy to domestic peace." In the margin, a surprised Fortas wrote, "Hugo Black!!"

In the final four pages of his dissent, Black cited only one court decision. But these pages resound with Black's simple but powerful rhetoric about the need to maintain discipline in the schools and in society in general. A few passages from Black's opinion will help to provide the flavor of his prose. For example, in emphasizing that youths in school need to behave in order to learn, Black declared:

> The original idea of schools, which I do not believe is yet abandoned as worthless or out of date, was that children had not yet reached the point of experience and wisdom which enabled them to teach all of their elders. It may be that the Nation has outworn the old-fashioned slogan that 'children are to be seen not heard," but one may, I hope, be permitted to harbor the thought that taxpayers send children to school on the premise that at their age they need to learn, not teach.

Black insisted that the social problems America was witnessing in the late 1960s were exacerbated by a lack of discipline in the schools. "School discipline," Black submitted, "like parental discipline, is an integral and important part of training our children to be good citizens." Because Black believed that the *Tinker* decision would further erode discipline in the schools, he feared dire consequences for society as a whole:

> One does not need to be a prophet or the son of a prophet to know that after the Court's holding today that some students in Iowa schools and indeed in all schools will be ready, able, and willing to defy their teachers on practically all orders. This is the more unfortunate for the schools since groups of students all over the land are already running loose, conducting break-ins, sit-ins, lie-ins, and smash-ins. Many of these student groups, . . . have already engaged in rioting, property seizures and destruction.

Although Black did not say so, perhaps he had in mind SDS, mentioned prominently by Allan Herrick in oral argument. Black acknowledged that the students in the *Tinker* case were practicing a very mild form of protest. But, in his view, a case like this could open the floodgates:

It is no answer to say that the particular students here have not yet reached such high points in their demands to attend classes in order to exercise their political pressures. Turned loose with law suits, damages and injunctions against their teachers . . . , young, immature students will not soon believe it is their right to control the schools rather than the right of the States that collect the taxes to hire the teachers for the benefit of the pupils. This case, therefore . . . subjects all the public schools in the country to the whims and caprices of their loudest-mouthed, but maybe not their brightest, students.

Further, with a sarcastic jab at the majority opinion, Black proclaimed: "I, for one, am not fully persuaded that school pupils are wise enough even with this Court's expert help from Washington, to run the 23,390 public schools systems in our 50 States." Black concluded his blistering opinion thusly: "I wish, therefore, wholly to disclaim . . . that the Federal Constitution compels the teachers, parents, and elected school officials to surrender control of the American public school system to public school students. I dissent."

The Court's senior member had spoken, but it was unclear as that February day ended as to which side would really have the last word in the armband case. Regardless of the reaction, Justice Black was clearly proud of his essay. On the day after he read his decision into the record, he sent a copy of the opinion to his son with a note saying, "Sterling, You will be interested." It was signed "Daddy."

Justice Black's opinion notwithstanding, the lower federal courts acted quickly to execute the ruling mandated by the Court's majority. An order filed with the Eighth Circuit Court of Appeals on March 2, 1969, directed that the petitioners in *Tinker* should recover $326.65—$150 for "clerk's costs" and $176.65 for "printing the record"—from the Des Moines Independent Community School District. That order ended the formal legal activity in *Tinker v. Des Moines*. But the meaning and impact of the decision did not reach closure quite so easily.

CHAPTER II

# Armbands Yes, Miniskirts No

## The Media Reaction

On February 25, 1969, a story on the Supreme Court's action in *Tinker v. Des Moines* appeared on the front page of the *New York Times*. The *Times*'s account emphasized that the Court's decision in *Tinker* only dealt with symbolic speech and did not set down specific guidelines for other forms of student expression. Nevertheless, the article predicted that the decision in the armband case might have the consequence of limiting the administrative review of student newspapers and restricting the purge of school libraries and curricula of "objectionable" materials. The following day the *Des Moines Register* and a number of other American papers carried a story on the armband case bearing the byline of a *Los Angeles Times* reporter. Titled "Campus Rioters Warned by Court in D.M. Ruling," the thrust of the story was that the *Tinker* decision had determined that the unobtrusive wearing of armbands by students in midwestern secondary schools was constitutionally acceptable, but that protests causing "substantial disorder or injuring the rights of others" would not be sanctioned. The article noted, "Four times in the opinion by Justice Abe Fortas, the Court went out of its way to point out, in effect, that a school in Des Moines was no Berkeley, no Columbia, no San Francisco State College." The article claimed that even the liberal majority of the Court was sending a clear message that it would not overturn the actions of university administrators who had suspended or expelled campus protesters.

The news accounts of the *Tinker* decision in the press were followed quickly by editorials. The *New York Times* weighed in with its comments on the armband decision on February 26 in a piece titled "Armbands Yes, Miniskirts No." After noting that the *Tinker* majority properly upheld nondisruptive symbolic expression of political ideas without tampering with school dress codes, the *Times* editorial declared, "The majority of the justices felt—we think, rightly—that a line could and should be drawn between free expression and disorderly excess. A close reading of the facts and decision shows that there is no license given here to riot, to interfere with classroom work or to substitute the Court for the thousands of school boards." In an editorial simply titled "The Armband Case" that appeared on February 27, the *Des Moines Register* insisted that the Supreme Court's *Tinker* decision properly upheld the right of nondisruptive political speech. In contrast to the fears expressed by Justice Black, the *Register* editorial emphasized that the Court's majority opinion did nothing to undercut the authority of school officials to deal with disciplinary problems. Then the editorialist made a point that the Des Moines newspaper had been making for the last three years, namely that this acrimonious dispute would never have arisen if school officials had not "panicked and overreacted to plans by a handful of youngsters to show up in school with some black cloth on their arms." The editorial also stated, "The Supreme Court ruling is an admonition to school officials that panic is no substitute for calm judgment and common sense when free speech is at stake."

A contrary view of the *Tinker* decision was expressed a few days later by a *Register* Washington correspondent and syndicated columnist, Richard Wilson. Agreeing with Justice Black's doomsaying, he wrote: "The high court has sent tremors running through the educational system by its dictum that symbolic free speech may emerge from the mouths of babes at school . . ." Writing that the Supreme Court had placed the "Good Schoolkeeping stamp of approval" on the expression of Christopher Eckhardt and the Tinkers, Wilson referred to the armband demonstration as a "children's crusade." According to Wilson, the *Tinker* decision had "seriously deranged" higher education. The Court did not yet realize the "density of the thicket into which . . . [it] has advanced." Wilson's opinion piece also referred to a recent episode at Iowa's Grinnell College when a handful of students, objecting to the appearance on campus of a male representative of *Playboy* magazine, proceeded to disrobe during his speech. Wilson pondered: Does the *Tinker* decision protect a "nude-in" as symbolic speech?

# Litigants and Lawyers

Christopher Eckhardt was advised of the Supreme Court decision when a reporter from a Minneapolis newspaper called him in Mankato, Minnesota, and extended his congratulations. Eckhardt, who was then attending Mankato State University, did not immediately comprehend what the reporter was talking about until he announced: "You won your Supreme Court case. And how do you feel?" Eckhardt, caught off guard, could only think to respond that he was "overjoyed." The reporter then wanted him to comment on the more radical turn that student protests had taken since the mid-1960s. Eckhardt replied that he did not support violence, saying, "That wasn't our case." That night Eckhardt and several of his friends from Des Moines who were attending Mankato State "celebrated hearty." A few months after the decision, Christopher's father published an article on the case for the *Journal of Human Relations*. Near the end of the article, William Eckhardt quoted a passage from Justice Black's dissent in which the Court's most senior member termed the majority's decision in *Tinker v. Des Moines* "the beginning of a new revolutionary era of permissiveness in this country." William Eckhardt's rejoinder to Justice Black—the final statement in his fifteen-page article—was "Let's hope so! Without permissiveness, democracy is a word without meaning."

John Tinker was a freshman at the University of Iowa in Iowa City in 1969. He was an art major, but he admits now that he was really "majoring in protests." Like Christopher Eckhardt, John found out about the Supreme Court decision in a call from a reporter. As John remembers it, the call came "totally out of the blue," and virtually all he said to the reporter was that he was "glad" and "excited." Later that day John called his parents and they talked about the case. When John was able to get together with his family several weeks later they had "a little celebration," toasting their success with ginger ale and ice cream. Two months after the Supreme Court decision John had time to put his thoughts in better order regarding the case that bears his name. He made the following strident statement about the significance of the armband case in the context of the educational process:

> This decision has come at a time when many Americans are afraid of students. . . . It is ironic . . . that they should think that by claim-

ing certain rights we were in some way destructive of the educational system.... If school systems cannot... provide students with the rights to which they are entitled, then they will be changed, and should be.... The Armband Case should provide a... springboard for further students rights. I believe that this is in the best interest of our country and of the democratic system as a whole.

Leonard Tinker and Lorena Jeanne Tinker had relocated to St. Louis, Missouri, by the time the decision in *Tinker v. Des Moines* was announced. Lorena Tinker remembers feeling at the time that the decision itself was "sort of an anticlimax" because she and her family had already expended so much energy on the case. Two weeks after the Supreme Court decision, the *St. Louis Post Dispatch* ran a profile article on the Tinker family. In the story Lorena Tinker related a touching story about her youngest daughter, Hope. In the aftermath of the December 1965 black-armband demonstration and the various threats against the Tinker family, Hope—who was ten years old that winter—was quite depressed, and she began to paint pictures of peace signs against large backgrounds of black. As the months and years wore on and the courts found against her siblings, the black swallowed up more and more of her pictures, and the peace signs grew proportionately smaller. However, when Hope learned of the family victory at the Supreme Court level, her artistic work changed. She created a bright yellow image of a peace dove and a glowing candle. There was no black anywhere in this painting.

Mary Beth Tinker was a high school student in St. Louis, living with her parents, when the Supreme Court decision was announced. As she remembers February 1969: "It hit the media in a real big way, and I was just really unprepared for all that." As a student trying to make her way in a new high school, she found her celebrity status embarrassing. Two months after the Supreme Court decision, Mary Beth Tinker published an eight-page article on the armband case in *Youth,* a magazine intended for high-school-aged students, published by the United Church of Christ and the Episcopal Church. Some of her statements in the article indicate that she had become, by 1969, more radical in her personal beliefs about the Vietnam War than had been the case three and a half years earlier. She stated:

[T]he "movement" in this country has progressed beyond black armbands. People are thinking that the Vietnam war is just one bad product of a basically corrupt society. People are not content to mourn silently for Vietnam's dead. They want to act in a way that will get to the basis of a government that would carry on such a war, a government that drafts boys to fight and die unwillingly in it, and that starves its poor to pay for it.

In her article, Mary Beth also criticized the very judicial system that had just found in her favor: "In these days when . . . 'the times are a-changing' almost from day to day, it still takes our court system three years to reach a decision on only one small part of the total question of academic freedom. I seriously wonder if this will be fast enough to keep up with the people and their needs."

Dan Johnston was working in his Des Moines office in late February 1969 when he received a call from a reporter for the *Des Moines Register*, asking for a comment on the Supreme Court opinion. Johnston responded that he was not surprised by his clients' victory. He had assumed that they had an excellent chance to win the armband case from the very beginning, but admitted that he had not done much head counting since he had walked away from the Court back in November 1968. He was, of course, disappointed that he had received such a chilly response in the oral argument from Justice Black. He suspected that he was not going to win Black's vote unless the justice was swayed by the fact that the Des Moines school district permitted other forms of political symbolism in the classroom. He hoped that Black would see the inconsistency of the school district's position, but the oral argument convinced him that he was not reaching Justice Black and would "probably" not receive the vote of Justice White. He also said that he had had no sense as to how Justice Harlan might vote because "he was [so] quiet" in the oral argument. Otherwise, Johnston felt that the remaining justices were going to side with his clients. He turned out to be amazingly prescient, guessing wrong only on White.

Johnston's adversary in the armband case, Allan Herrick, was, of course, disappointed to lose the case before the Court. What particularly upset the school district's chief counsel, however, was Fortas's statement for the Court that the record of the lower federal court proceedings contained no finding of disturbances stemming from the wearing of the black armbands. Herrick felt that there were references to disturbances in the district court record but that Fortas had ignored or overlooked them. Edgar Bittle recalls that Herrick may have known Abe Fortas through American Bar Association activities and that he "didn't have a lot of time for Fortas anyway." After Fortas resigned from the Court under a cloud of scandal about two months after the *Tinker* decision, Bittle recalls a conversation with Herrick in which the armband case was mentioned. The senior attorney's response was: "Well, that opinion was written by Fortas and we know what happened to him."

Bittle, by 1969 a regular member of Herrick's Des Moines law firm, believed that Judge Roy Stephenson had written a "pretty good decision" at the district court level. But he acknowledged years later that Justice Marshall's pressing of Herrick on the disturbances/lack of disturbances issue during oral argument may have undermined the school district's position before the Supreme Court. Bittle stated that if he had been in charge of the appeal, he would have "softened" the unflattering description of Leonard Tinker and downplayed the alleged role of SDS in the case. According to Bittle, Herrick believed that ministers, such as Leonard Tinker, should devote more time to soliciting money for their churches instead of just "raising hell." In the larger sense, however, Bittle maintained that the *Tinker* decision served to prod the Des Moines school district to move in the "right direction" by encouraging it to craft realistic disciplinary policies.

---

## The Legal Community

Law professors and law students pay close attention to leading decisions of the nation's highest court. Their reactions to these decisions are, of course, discussed in law school lecture halls and seminar rooms. But they also regularly find their way into legal periodicals, generally called "law reviews" or "law journals." Virtually every American law school publishes a law review; some law schools issue several. Law review articles thus provide a good insight into the way the legal community responds to decisions of the Supreme Court. Law professors vie competitively to write heavily footnoted essays for law reviews, and law students feel privileged to be selected by their law review staff to prepare case notes or comments.

In the year following the announcement of the Supreme Court decision in *Tinker v. Des Moines,* law school periodicals published about fifteen student-authored notes or comments and five major articles on the black-armband case. This body of the legal community's analyses of the Supreme Court's leading freedom of expression decision of the 1968–69 term defies an easy recounting. But a summary of the most important arguments can be provided in a few paragraphs. Of those essayists expressing an opinion on the resolution of the case, about half felt that the Court's opinion was warranted, with the other half finding common ground with one or the other of the dissents.

Most of the law review articles discussed the conflict between the Fifth and Eighth Circuit Courts of Appeal that led to the Supreme Court accepting review of the *Tinker* case. The Fifth Circuit Court of Appeals had held in 1966 in *Burnside v. Byars* that a regulation banning symbolic expression (in this case civil-rights buttons) was "without force" because the conduct proscribed did not "materially and substantially interfere with the requirements of appropriate discipline in the operation of the school." The Eighth Circuit Court of Appeals, in ruling on the appeal in *Tinker,* had explicitly rejected the standard to test school regulations promulgated in *Burnside.* Several of the law review essayists recognized that the fact situations in *Tinker* and *Burnside* were virtually identical; hence resolving the conflicts in these circuits made sense. Moreover, as an essayist in *Harvard Civil Rights and Civil Liberties Law Review* emphasized, the majority in *Tinker* placed the burden of justifying any interference with students' freedom of expression on the school authorities themselves. This marked a departure from past legal standards for determining the First Amendment rights of students.

Several of the essays noted that the holding in *Tinker* might have resolved this case but that it left much uncertainty for courts in the future confronting different modes of student expression. Justice Fortas had specifically said in his majority opinion that the decision did not apply to hair length, dress, or deportment. But many of the cases coming to appellate courts in the late 1960s—during a time of cultural rebellion for high-school and college students—concerned appearance and general conduct. Were these legitimate First Amendment concerns or not? The *Tinker* majority did not help school administrators on the front lines of the cultural battles of the Vietnam War years. In fact, as an essayist in the *Georgetown Law Journal* pointed out, within a year after the *Tinker* case the Supreme Court had already refused to hear many cases involving student appearance and conduct. In his mind, the precedent was limited to student political speech, not free expression in the schools generally. Even in the sphere of political speech, however, the *Tinker* holding was still too vague for the taste of some scholars writing in late 1960s law reviews. One essayist noted that the black-armband case said nothing about the more common form of student protest in the 1960s, the publication of underground student newspapers.

About a third of the law reviews publishing articles or notes on the *Tinker* case in the year after the decision was issued expressed the view that the Supreme Court had not paid sufficient respect to the strains on secondary-school administrations in the 1960s. Given the penchant of some high-school students to engage in conduct that distracts fellow students and teachers from the academic lessons at hand, did not school administrators have the right to institute policies designed to minimize behavior that would tend to divert attention, such as the wearing of emblems of protest? For many essayists in the legal community, the *Tinker* decision unjustly elevated the right of a small number of students to protest over the right of all students to an education.

For those writers taking the position that the school district's interest in order was undercut by the holding in the black-armband case, the dissenting opinion of Justice Black was their touchstone. For example, the writer of a case note in the *Loyola Law Review* echoed Black's view that the classroom is for learning, not political demonstrations: "School is not the place to wear a badge or emblem that would spark controversy. . . . A series of arguments about a highly inflammatory subject such as Viet Nam can very easily disrupt the operation of any class." A case note on *Tinker* in the *Wake Forest Law Review* maintained that "a court without professional training should hesitate to reverse an administrator's recommended method of operating his school. . . . There is no reason for thinking the average judge inherently has the qualifications to take charge of the disciplinary problems of the schools."

Justice Black's dissenting opinion drew criticism as well as praise from the legal community. For example, an essayist in the *Suffolk Law*

*Review* found Black's "children are to be seen not heard" philosophy to have "the practical effect . . . [of depriving] the student of his constitutional rights merely because he enters the door of the schoolhouse." A view frequently expressed in legal periodicals was that Black's dissent was indicative of his increasingly hostile attitude toward student protests as the Vietnam War and the civil rights movement became progressively more divisive in the late 1960s. Some writers characterized the Black dissent as a testy complaint of an aging court liberal, retreating from freedom of expression positions that he had championed earlier in his career.

For those in the legal community expressing support for the Supreme Court's decision in *Tinker v. Des Moines,* a characteristic view was one expressed in the *Harvard Law Review's* annual recapitulation of the 1968–69 term of the Court. The anonymous writer of the law review's section on freedom of expression praised the Court for extending real—albeit limited—freedom to express political ideas in school. The writer recounted that the Court in *Tinker* had held that the First Amendment "protects a learning process in state schools which is open, vigorous, disputatious, disturbing—a robust dialectic in which error is combatted with reason, not fiat." Finally, in his conclusion of the section on the black-armband case, the *Harvard Law Review* essayist submitted simply: "the Court adopted the view that the process of education in a democracy must be democratic."

Published in the immediate wake of the February 1969 decision, the most strident defense of the Supreme Court holding in *Tinker v. Des Moines* was "Mary Beth Tinker Takes the Constitution to School." It appeared in a 1969 issue of the *Fordham Law Review* and was written by Theodore Denno, a professor of political science. Denno's article was a flowery apologia for the freedom of expression and a virtual celebration of Fortas's majority opinion. Near the beginning of the essay, Denno stated, "*Tinker* is a pathfinder in that children themselves, claiming the common rights of citizenship . . . , have been recognized by our supreme constitutional tribunal as proper subjects of those rights." The article is replete with the rhetoric of the late 1960s, including frequent references to the "generation gap." The essay also attacked the traditional view of childhood voiced in Black's dissent and questioned "whether Justice Black . . . personally remember[s] a happy and carefree childhood." In challenging the "regimentation and busy work atmosphere of the public schools," Denno argued that the black-armband-wearing Des Moines students had performed an important public service. Denno concluded his unconventional law review article with a statement that might have caused even the most ardent supporters of the armband demonstration to wince:

> A society which is too proud to listen to its children, too afraid that they may "disturb" it, is probably a society too afraid to look itself in the eye. During the course of history there was probably precious little difference between Mary Beth Tinker's message of the black armband and the twelve year old boy who spoke to the elders in the temple. This time the men in the black robes got wise. How will it be with the rest of us?

---

## Dear Mr. Justice

The legal papers of Supreme Court justices contain some fascinating examples of the public's reactions to major decisions. Justice Abe Fortas, for instance, received a number of letters in the wake of *Tinker v. Des Moines*. Fortas's correspondents—most of whom were critical of his position—wrote not so much to object to the right of students to wear black armbands as to express their worries regarding where this decision might lead. For example, a school principal from Portland, Oregon, wrote to inquire, in light of the armband decision, "whether the schools are now . . . to be used as propaganda organs for any and all organizations . . . who [wish to] . . . distribute their sometimes corrosive literature." He attached to his letter a copy of a neo-Nazi leaflet that had been confiscated in his school after it had been distributed without authorization. The Portland principal declared that if his school's right to ban the distribution of such literature must now be tested in light of the *Tinker* decision, "the purpose for which the schools have been established will indeed be subverted." In a similar vein, a U.S. Navy captain wrote to Fortas, "[Y]ou and those justices who joined themselves with you in the majority opinion are wrong. So wrong. Wrong philosophically, humanly, morally and realistically."

A few letters mentioning *Tinker v. Des Moines* were directed to the Supreme Court as a whole. One example was a letter from a woman from Shawnee Mission, Kansas, who described herself as "a liberal who went too far." She wrote, "I agree, dissent should be permitted, with reason. But at the child's level?" Another such document was "an open letter to our erstwhile friends in the Supreme Court," written by a Kansas City minister. The clergyman personalized his letter, indicating how he had treated his own sons when they requested that family decisions be reached by majority vote. The Reverend reported, "I immediately served notice upon them that they were not living in a democracy under my roof but that it was most certainly a dictatorship and that I was the dictator." Using his experience as a model, he instructed the Court that its recent decisions on children's rights, *Tinker* paramount among them, "will serve to create a turmoil in future relationships between authority and those under it [that] you'll not (probably) live to contend with; but we and others after us may well be saddled with the struggle to undo your folly." In the final sentence of his letter, the clergyman reaffirmed his message to the Court in the form of a personal admonition to his children: "If my kids ever try to take advantage of your recent decisions in high school or college they'll find out just who the real supreme court is."

By far the greatest number of letters addressed to the Supreme Court in the aftermath of *Tinker v. Des Moines* were written to Justice Hugo Black. The legal papers of Justice Black include 260 letters related to *Tinker,* all but eight expressing agreement with his views. A fair assumption is that Black's impassioned defense of order and traditional values struck a sympathetic chord with many Americans troubled by what they perceived as the turmoil in the nation's schools in the late 1960s. Black penned handwritten notes on many of the favorable letters, indicating that a form letter be dispatched in response.

Among those praising the Court's oldest member for his dissent in *Tinker* was this note from a California lawyer: "Your dissent . . . in the Des Moines, Iowa, High School case was one bright ray of sunshine that brought hope and encouragement to the hearts of millions of Americans. I salute you and encourage you to continue your battle for righteousness and sanity." A woman from a small town in Kentucky conveyed similar sentiments: "Thank you and let me again say you are a man among men and a true and loyal American. Oh! Lord, how I wish there were more like you, we would have a much better world to live in."

A number of letters to Justice Black came from appreciative secondary-school personnel. For example, a school counselor from Augusta, Georgia wrote, "As a counselor in a junior high school, I appreciate and admire your stand angrily dissenting in the Iowa Students' case." She later stated that more discipline was necessary in the schools, not less. Then she continued, "Maybe if your fellow Justices could sit where I sit for one day, a reversal of the present decision would be made." In a similar vein, a superintendent from Glasgow, Missouri, wrote, "We wish to applaud you on your recent dissent.... Every day we witness this very obvious lack of respect for authority exercised by the young people we come in contact with in our school system.... Again we thank you for taking a stand and want you to know there are other people who agree with you and support you." The superintendent's letter was signed by twenty-two members of his school system, including principals, teachers, counselors, secretaries, and even the "cafeteria manager."

Justice Black's dissent had suggested that many of the problems in American schools—at both the secondary and college levels—stemmed from weaknesses in the American family and in society in general. Most of those writing him favorable letters shared this conviction. Like Black, they blamed an all-too-pervasive "permissiveness." A man from Catonsville, Maryland, wrote, "Permissiveness seems to be the name of the game.... One hears quite a bit about lack of communication between parent and child. I say Hogwash! When I was a youngster, my mother had a very good means of communication. It was called 'Hairbrush.' And I seldom failed to get the message." A Springfield, Illinois, physician also commended Black for his battle against permissiveness: "[Y]ou speak eloquently my feelings and those of so many of my countrymen whose responsibility it is to keep our cities, counties, and states strong and effective against this new sweeping plague of Permissiveness over the entire United States." He continued, "I'm sick and intolerant of permissive parents, permissive teachers, permissive law enforcement agencies, permissive legislators, and permissive courts. And I am particularly disappointed and ashamed of the many permissive Supreme Court decisions which have been coming down in recent years." In all, the Illinois doctor used "permissive" or "permissiveness" eight times in his two-page letter.

All of the justices receive unsigned letters from time to time. Most of these are probably from harmless cranks, but some threaten injury or are otherwise disturbing. Justice Black received a handful of anonymous letters shortly after the *Tinker* decision was announced. One read, "You don't have to worry about the laws breaking down. We are organizing a secret club to bring criminals to justise [sic]. We won't dress any different but will FIX all trouble makers in our school. Everyone says we are helpless but we know different." The postscript read, "There are 8 of us."

As the senior member of the Supreme Court in 1969, Black saw his amazingly robust health commented on by a good percentage of those writing to him about the *Tinker* decision. A West Coast attorney, for instance, wrote that he hoped that Black would "continue in good health and feel up to staying on the Court for a long time." An Alabama attorney writing to Justice Black on March 5, 1969, congratulated him on reaching his eighty-third birthday. And an Illinois physician invoked the memory of a recently departed relative in praising Black's opinion. He wrote, "My father would have been about your age, Justice Black were he alive today. I believe he would have stood with me and cheered your 'wrathful outburst.'" On the other hand, Black's age was singled out for concern by some of those voicing criticisms of his dissent in the black-armband case. For example, one man wrote the Supreme Court a postcard a few days after the armband decision, saying, "As a former admirer of Justice Black, I would like to suggest that he has reached the age where he should graciously retire the judicial robe, even at the risk of a Nixon appointment." A less sympathetic postcard writer addressed this comment to Justice Black: "Your [sic] 80 and losing your faculties yet you determine people's future."

Besides the concern about Black's age and health, expressed in the small number of critical letters addressed to him, there was a characteristic theme: that Hugo Black of the 1969 *Tinker* decision was not the liberal Hugo Black that he had been for most of his Supreme Court tenure. A Union College undergraduate, for example, wrote:

With your dissenting opinion in this case you are, curiously, opining counter to your own previous record as a civil libertarian. . . .

Sadly for the cause of individual liberties which you yourself once championed, you have placed the rights of the society above the rights of the man in a case involving no visible personal or property damage.

A couple of the individuals writing Justice Black were blunt to the point of crudity. In a letter addressed to "Honorable Black," one writer stated, "You kind sir would put a straight jacket on America and send it back to the stone age. We are civilized people and not barbarians." A college student in New York also expressed his feelings inelegantly: "I had always assumed that a man of your background and reputation of insight and erudition would not be prone to such neanderthal political, social and educational opinions."

Finally, a handful of individuals writing to Justice Black posed rhetorical questions to challenge the dissenting justice's perspectives on student behavior. For example, a man from California wrote to ask, "How are we to prepare our young people to become full and responsible citizens if they are not allowed to experience the opportunity to exercise, peacefully, the rights of citizenship?" Another correspondent, writing on American Federation of Teachers stationery and identifying himself as a high-school teacher with a special interest in constitutional law, submitted similar queries:

> How are we to expect our young to assume responsibility and participate in our society constructively and meaningfully if we condemn and restrict them by standards we do not condone for ourselves? If they are to be prohibited from expressing their concerns within the institutions in which they spend a great portion of their productive hours, institutions which purport to prepare them to think and to function effectively in the rest of society, where and when then are they to learn responsibility and constructive effectiveness?

# CHAPTER 12

# From Black Armbands to Risque T-Shirts

It has been almost thirty years since the U.S. Supreme Court decision in *Tinker v. Des Moines Independent Community School District* afforded a victory for freedom of expression for American students. The war in Vietnam and the polarized culture of the country in the 1960s that gave rise to the Des Moines black-armband demonstration and the ensuing events detailed in this book have faded from the scene. Some of the individuals who were part of the controversy in the *Tinker* case have died, but many major and minor figures in the dispute are very much alive. In addition, the core judicial precedent in *Tinker v. Des Moines* persists, although it has been undercut by events of the last quarter century and the decisions of a new, more conservative Supreme Court.

## Supporting Cast and Setting

Ora Niffenegger, the President of the Des Moines School Board at the time of the armband demonstration in the mid-1960s, remained on the board until losing a close election in 1976. Some attributed Niffenegger's defeat to his age—seventy in 1976. Ever one for the clever quip, Niffenegger agreed that age was a factor in his defeat: "I have one foot in the grave and the other on a banana peel." While being interviewed in the mid-1980s, Niffenegger showed a *Des Moines Register* reporter his file of yellowed clippings on the armband dispute. He conceded then that the administrative decree prohibiting armbands may have been a mistake; but in his mind, the issue in the case was whether the school administration had the authority to impose the ban. He believed then that it did and had not changed that opinion in twenty years.

Arthur Davis, one of the two members of the Des Moines school board who disagreed with Niffenegger and supported the students' right to wear armbands in school, has stayed active in central Iowa public life since the 1960s. Generally perceived as moderate in his political orientation, Davis was elected mayor of Des Moines in 1995. He served in this capacity until deteriorating health forced his sudden resignation on March 31, 1997.

Since the late 1960s, large segments of Des Moines's middle class have moved to the suburbs. As central Des Moines has lost population, new suburban communities—particularly to the west of the city—have boomed. As a result, the capital city's tax base has declined and the physical condition of the public schools has deteriorated markedly. Des Moines's Theodore Roosevelt High School, where Christopher Eckhardt attended school in the 1960s, opened its doors in 1923. Today it still has an elegant facade and handsomely landscaped grounds, but the roof leaks, the heating/ventilation system is sorely in need of replacement, and many of the administrative offices are cramped. The very title of a March 17, 1995, editorial in the *Des Moines Register*—"Roosevelt's Fading Grandeur"—makes the point. A study conducted in the early 1990s, known as "Vision 2005," proposed changes in Des Moines's public education, including a massive physical overhaul of the city's schools. The price tag for Vision 2005 has been projected at over $300 million. Bearing such a high cost will require creative financing. One such financial option was to increase the sales tax in the city and apply a portion of the revenue generated to school construction and maintenance. With the defeat of a sales tax referendum in December 1996, however, the prospects for meeting the challenge of Vision 2005 do not appear encouraging.

Another Des Moines institution essential to an account of the black-armband dispute is the *Des Moines Register*. As the leading paper of Iowa—its motto for years has been "The Newspaper that Iowa Depends Upon"—the *Register* figured heavily in this story: the announcement of the ban on black armbands first appeared in the *Register;* the students' flouting of the decree was described by the paper in detail; the controversy involving the school board meetings was front-page news for several weeks; the various court decisions were thoroughly reported; and the anniversaries of the *Tinker* case were marked with additional stories. Although the format and the type fonts are different, some of today's *Register* would be familiar to individuals who have not taken the time to examine the Iowa newspaper since the 1960s. James

Flansburg, the reporter who broke the story of the January 1966 "secret" school board meeting, remained on the *Register*'s staff until his retirement in January 1997. Although his column, titled "The Old Reporter," has vanished from the op-ed page, the *Register* has promised to continue to publish occasional pieces by Flansburg. Donald Kaul, the paper's controversial political and social commentator who wrote several columns on the armband dispute thirty years ago, was dropped from the *Register* in the eighties. However, much to the dismay of Iowa's conservatives, the paper's management brought Kaul's satirical "Over the Coffee" column back to the op-ed page of the paper a few years ago. The *Register* continues its leading role in the coverage of Des Moines events, especially since the closure of its evening *Tribune* in 1982. If anything, the *Register* does a better job of probing capital-city activities in the 1990s than it did in the previous decades because its management has made a conscious decision to concentrate the paper's focus on central Iowa. Nevertheless, the closing of news bureaus outside of the Des Moines area, the termination of same-day delivery in the western part of the state, and the diminishing coverage of international news has made the 1990s *Register* a weaker newspaper in the eyes of its critics than the *Register* of the 1960s.

Louise Noun, the president of the ICLU when the armband case took place, currently lives in an elegant high-rise apartment building overlooking the golf course at Des Moines's exclusive Wakonda Club. She continued as a volunteer leader of the ICLU well into the 1970s and has been active in a number of other human rights and civic causes for half a century. Noun's collection of works by female artists is of museum quality. The sale in 1992 of one of her most valuable pieces—a Frida Kahlo painting—provided sufficient capital to create an endowment for an Iowa Women's Archives, a collection that now bears her name. Her extensive civic activities have led to her receipt of numerous awards, including two honorary college degrees and induction into the Iowa Women's Hall of Fame. Noun's autobiography, *Journey to Autonomy: A Memoir*, was recently issued in a second edition.

The ICLU continues to defend the rights of Iowans thirty years after the black-armband affair. In spite of Justice Fortas's injunction that the *Tinker* ruling should not be extended to cover "length of skirts . . . type of clothing . . . hair style or deportment," many of the 1970s cases that the ICLU involved itself in concerned these very issues. Other issues occupying the ICLU since the *Tinker* decision are typical of many other state chapters of the ACLU: conscientious objection, creationism in the schools, commencement prayers, student newspapers, the rights of welfare recipients, child custody, women's rights, police practices, and censorship in public libraries. In 1995 the ICLU took a leading role in defeating a capital-punishment bill in the Iowa legislature. It is still fair to say, however, that *Tinker v. Des Moines* was the ICLU's greatest hour. The organization continues to feature the Iowa black-armband case in its promotional literature and in its in-house historical accounts.

Allan Herrick, the principal attorney for the Des Moines Independent Community School District, practiced law in central Iowa until his death at the age of ninety-three. His assistant in the *Tinker* case, Edgar Bittle, took a job with Herrick's firm after his graduation from law school and continued to practice law with Herrick for a number of years until the firm divided. Today he counts school law as one of his specialties. In 1994 Bittle wrote a retrospective, first-person account of the Iowa black-armband case, titled "The *Tinker* Case: Reflections 25 Years Later."

Herrick's adversary in the armband case, Dan Johnston, has led a varied public life in Iowa and elsewhere. While he was assembling appellate briefs on *Tinker v. Des Moines,* Johnston was the legal director for the ICLU and served a term in the Iowa legislature. In 1968 he ran an unsuccessful campaign for the position of Iowa attorney general, losing that election in the same month that he argued the black-armband appeal before the Supreme Court. He was in private practice in Des Moines until 1972. To show how quickly times changed: Johnston was asked in 1971 to deliver the annual commencement address at Roosevelt High School—part of the city school system that he had taken to court just a few years earlier. After five years of legal work in Washington, D.C., and New York, Johnston returned to Iowa in 1977 to accept an interim appointment as Polk County prosecutor. Johnston won several elections to continue as the chief prosecutor for Iowa's most populous county, serving until 1985. His tenure was distinguished by improved organization in the county prosecutor's office, but it was marred by a contentious investigation into a case involving a missing Des Moines paperboy.

In 1984 Johnston came under fire from political opponents for maintaining a consulting relationship with a New York foundation—requiring frequent travel to that state—while drawing his salary as county prosecutor. On three separate occasions the *Register* editorialized against Johnston's attempt to hold down the full-time position as a county prosecutor while shuttling back and forth to New York. In December 1984 Johnston announced his intention to resign as country prosecutor, indicating that he had decided to move to New York. About a month after the announcement of his resignation from the county prosecutor's position, Johnston was the principal speaker at his own going-away party. In an emotional talk, Johnston surprised many of those in attendance by saying that he was a homosexual and had decided "to stand up . . . and be counted in the cause of my gay . . . brothers and sisters." During the last ten years Johnston has worked in New York at the Vera Institute, an organization studying the judicial disposition of criminal cases. He also has acted as a trustee for five real estate investment trusts. In 1987 New York Mayor Edward Koch chose him to serve as one of the civilian members on the city's police review panel.

Johnston claims never to tire of being referred to as "the kids' attorney in the *Tinker* case." When asked how he would rank, in the context of his professional life, his representation of the Eckhardts and the Tinkers before the Supreme Court, Johnston says without hesitation that it has been the high point of his legal career. Then he half-jokingly adds, "It's all been downhill from there." In a speech in 1992 he passed along similar sentiments: "Don't get a case like this, with clients like this, when you're 30 years old. The rest of life is dull." When asked to reflect on the significance of the *Tinker* case, Johnston maintains that "it opened the public schools and the colleges to antiwar organizing . . . and was a major factor in bringing the Vietnam War to an end."

---

## The Central Characters

Members of two families who brought the legal action in the black-armband dispute have also led interesting lives in the quarter century since the armbands were worn to school. William Eckhardt and Margaret Eckhardt were in Oakville, Ontario, when their son's case was decided by the U.S. Supreme Court. There William Eckhardt held a position as a research psychologist at the Canadian Peace Research Institute. In the fall of 1969 the interdisciplinary *Journal of Human Relations* published William Eckhardt's fifteen-page article "The Black Arm Band Story: A Community Case Study of Conflicting Ideologies and Values." The Eckhardts stayed in Canada for more than a decade and then moved to St. Louis. William Eckhardt died in 1992. Margaret Eckhardt now lives in Florida with her son Christopher.

Leonard Tinker and Lorena Jeanne Tinker were residing in St. Louis at the time of the announcement of the Supreme Court decision that bore their family name. Leonard Tinker was still on leave from the Methodist Church, serving as a representative of the AFSC. Lorena Tinker was in the final stages of writing a Ph.D. dissertation in psychology at Iowa State University. In 1972, when Leonard Tinker became the regional head of the AFSC in the Ohio Valley, the family moved to Dayton, Ohio. After Leonard Tinker died in 1978, Lorena Tinker relocated to St. Louis and later to Corpus Christi, Texas. She moved to her current home in a picturesque rural Missouri location in 1990. Her youngest daughter, Hope, is a physician and resides in a nearby town.

Lorena Tinker's wood-heated Missouri home is jammed with files, newspaper clippings, and pictures of her children and grandchildren. She believes that her notoriety in the armband dispute and her reputation as an antiwar activist were "liabilities" in her graduate study and in subsequent college teaching positions. From conversation and observation it is clear that Lorena Tinker maintains an almost 1960s-like passion for social justice. She has combined this passion with her scholarly interests in educational psychology, as evidenced by a seventy-three page bibliographical essay on "Attitude Formation and Attitude Change" that she published in 1991 for a journal called *Peace Research Reviews*. In addition, she has not ceased her active commitment to peace. She proudly reveals that she was jailed for a night during the Persian Gulf War because she refused to leave a military recruiting office. In her seventies, Lorena Tinker still has a sparkle in her gray eyes and a solid grasp of recent events.

Since 1969 John and Mary Beth Tinker have endured countless interviews and have been asked to take part in many discussions of the issues raised in *Tinker v. Des Moines*. Neither has sought out attention for participation in a famous Supreme Court case. But attention has followed them nonetheless. On most occasions John and Mary Beth have willingly responded to journalists and scholars seeking insights on their case, but at times over the last quarter century each has sought to create distance between themselves and those who seek to understand the 1960s through contact with the "Tinker children."

John Tinker attended the University of Iowa for a year and a half. After leaving college, he obtained conscientious-objector draft status. Beginning in college and continuing to the present, John has immersed himself in social action: first the antiwar movement, then the anti–nuclear power movement, and more recently environmental issues and human rights in Latin America. Since the Supreme Court case John has held numerous odd jobs: he has driven a laundry truck, worked at a radio station, and operated a store called "Inventor's Supply." Most recently he has been involved in computer consulting and in the operation of a large used electrical equipment warehouse. In the warehouse he maintains an enterprise he calls "Peace Parts," which involves collecting the discarded but still useable technology of industrial society— such as old computers, typewriters, and telephones—and bringing or sending them to Latin American countries. For most of the last twenty-five years John has resided in small towns in Iowa. Today John is slender, slow talking, and reflective. A beard that was in evidence in 1994, he says, "comes and goes."

Over the years, especially at the anniversaries of the *Tinker* decision, John has been the subject of retrospective articles in the *Des Moines Register* and other publications. On those occasions he has generally expressed a measure of satisfaction with his success before the Supreme Court—"I know," he has said, "that I can go to any library in the country and look up my name." But he has also voiced sadness that the "military-industrial complex" still defines so much of American life. In an interview in 1979 he lamented, "There's no such thing as personal success as long as the world is headed toward chaos."

John regularly receives letters from students interested in his case or in his thoughts about possibly analogous situations at their schools. For example, a high-school student from Indianapolis, Indiana, wrote John several years ago, noting that his class had just conducted a mock trial of *Tinker v. Des Moines*, and requested further information from

John as to what happened on December 16–17, 1965, at North High. At the end of the letter he added, "P.S. In our class, the Tinkers won 5–0." In 1991, after corresponding with John about the black-armband dispute, two Johnston, Iowa, ninth graders won a thousand dollars in the National History Day competition with their presentation on the *Tinker* case. John has also been invited to appear in several high-school and college classes to talk about his place in American constitutional law.

John's sister, Mary Beth Tinker, was living in St. Louis with her parents when the Supreme Court decision in the armband case was announced. After graduating from high school, Mary Beth apprenticed herself as a piano technician, and for several years she worked repairing and tuning pianos. Mary Beth's mother stated in a 1979 interview that the Supreme Court decision "affected both of my middle children, John and Mary Beth, so they never overcame their own rejection of advanced formal education." Mary Beth acknowledges that her mother's unhappy experience in higher education may have kept her from attending college initially. She recalls that she enjoyed having a practical skill and working with her hands: "I got kind of cynical . . . had already crossed off religion, next was education. . . . [I]t was 1970, there was this whole kind of alternative culture. I thought, I don't need to go to college and be a middle class . . . whatever." But in the mid-1970s, Mary Beth recalls, "it sort of started sinking in that another skill would be a good idea, especially when there . . . [was] a recession going on, so I went to nursing school." Ironically, given her antiwar posture, she eventually completed her nursing education at St. Louis University on a scholarship from the Veterans' Administration. Since receiving her degree as a registered nurse, Mary Beth has worked at veterans' hospitals and private hospitals. Most of her current work as a nurse involves the care of women and children.

Today Mary Beth is a soft-spoken but intense woman. Her hair, which was long and straight in the 1960s, is now shorter and curlier. She lives with her teenage son, Lenny (named after Leonard Tinker), in a spacious St. Louis brownstone. Her building is about eighty years old and is located in what she describes as "a real city neighborhood . . . racially mixed and . . . kind of international too—Vietnamese, Lebanese, Iranian, black, working-class people, middle-class people." She reaffirms how strongly she felt about the right to wear armbands in the mid-1960s but says that she "didn't realize the legal . . . implications of this case until years after it was . . . decided."

Mary Beth has been interviewed countless times about her case by reporters and legal scholars. In a 1976 interview, for example, she expressed regret that the *Tinker* case was then serving more as a precedent for students defying dress codes than as a bulwark for political expression. In the 1980s, historian Peter Irons interviewed Mary Beth for what became a flattering profile of her in a short account of the *Tinker* case in his book *The Courage of Their Convictions*. In 1991, *Life* magazine produced a special issue on the bicentennial of the Bill of Rights, which featured the *Tinker* case as one of the most important civil liberties decisions of the twentieth century. The *Life* story included a large color photograph of Mary Beth, her mother, and her son, Lenny. In spite of her smiling face in the *Life* photograph, Mary Beth has turned her back more than once on attempts to interview her for various publications. For example, when Studs Terkel, the famous interviewer and oral historian, wanted to conduct a formal interview with Mary Beth about her role in the student protest movement, she first said yes to the interview, but then, at the last minute, she stood him up.

Although Mary Beth, as a person and as a mother, does not try to parade her participation in a famous Supreme Court case, a few personnel at her son's school and some of her nursing colleagues know about her role in the historic decision involving freedom of expression. In the early 1990s Mary Beth once again attracted media attention by lobbying before the Missouri legislature to reverse a court decision that had limited the rights of high-school students to publish their opinions in campus newspapers. She has also campaigned in favor of gun control before the state legislature. Recently, when Mary Beth's son was in some minor trouble at school, he challenged his principal by asking, "Have you ever heard of *Tinker v. Des Moines?*" The principal indicated that she had. So Lenny told her, "Well, that's my mom." Later, Mary Beth, the principal, and even Lenny were able to laugh about the irony of the situation. Mary Beth encourages Lenny to talk out any problems at school with his teachers and the principal. To date he has not worn any black armbands to class.

Christopher Eckhardt has also led a full life since he wore his armband to Des Moines Roosevelt High School in December 1965. He was elected to the Roosevelt High student council during his junior year in school, but he also remained a member of his frowned-on social group, the All Center Bums. During the remainder of his high school years he had occasional disagreements with authorities. For example, he was arrested on a Des Moines sidewalk in March 1968 for throwing a snowball at a policeman. When Eckhardt gave his name to the arresting officer, the reaction was "Oh yeah, we know about you. We talk about you down at the office sometimes. You're that armband kid, you're that troublemaker."

When his parents left for Canada in 1967, Christopher stayed behind to complete his senior year at Roosevelt. Although he sought and received "landed immigrant" status in Canada following graduation, he wanted to remain in the United States for his college education. This posed a problem that many other young men of his age faced in the late 1960s: what to do about his military obligation? Given the pacifism that ran in his family and his own strong antagonism to the conduct of the Vietnam War, it is not surprising that Christopher did not want to serve in Southeast Asia. Initially, his draft classification was 1–A, but on appeal he received conscientious-objector status.

Christopher took his first college courses at Mankato State in 1968. For the next twenty-five years he attended several other colleges and held a variety of jobs. His employment resume includes selling life insurance, producing cable television programs, publishing a peace-oriented newspaper, serving as a mediator for the Department of Justice, and working for state governments in corrections and social services. In 1978 he ran unsuccessfully for the Des Moines school board — the same body that had upheld his school suspension thirteen years earlier. In 1994 he received a baccalaureate degree in political science from the University of South Florida. Christopher says that his future portends more education, either law school or graduate study in history.

As central as Christopher Eckhardt was to the 1965 Iowa armband protest, because his name is not in the title of his famous Iowa case, his role in the dispute has frequently been overlooked. Prior to 1990, Christopher was not interviewed as frequently as John or Mary Beth Tinker on anniversaries of the armband case. At times over the years

Christopher resented the fact that the Tinkers received the lion's share of the recognition. In a 1984 interview, he insisted on referring to the case as "Eckhardt v. Des Moines." He likes to point out that he was the first to wear the armband, the first to be suspended, and the one of the three litigants who faced the most antagonism—verbal as well as physical—for his actions.

In the 1990s, however, Christopher has begun to receive more attention for his place in the country's legal history. When neither John nor Mary Beth Tinker wanted to travel to Boston in 1990 to accept an invitation from the ACLU to speak to a large audience, they passed the honor on to Christopher. He remembers receiving a call from either John or Mary Beth, who said, "We've been getting all this attention for all these years, and we thought we'd . . . see if you wanted to do it." Eckhardt was happy to accept.

Two other 1990s invitations to the student litigants in the black-armband case served to further ease tensions among the three. The first took place in May 1992, when Christopher Eckhardt came back to Des Moines's Roosevelt High to participate, along with John and Mary Beth Tinker and Dan Johnston, in a "visiting scholars" forum. Arranged by Melinda Voss—a *Des Moines Register* reporter and classmate of Christopher's at Roosevelt—the forum treated the Tinkers, Dan Johnston, and Christopher like returning heroes. During their 1992 visit, the three former Des Moines students discovered that armbands had become "cool." Blue armbands, for example, were in evidence that spring, worn by students and teachers protesting the not-guilty verdicts for Los Angeles police officers in the Rodney King beating case.

The other instance of recognition that helped smooth over differences between the Tinkers and Christopher Eckhardt occurred in 1993. In September of that year, the California ACLU announced that the three plaintiffs had been selected to receive its 1993 Earl Warren Civil Liberties Award. But the organization admitted in letters to Christopher and the Tinkers that it had sufficient funds to pay the expenses of only one of the three to come to California to accept the recognition. So the Tinkers and Christopher conducted a friendly discussion by phone, eventually deciding that Christopher would be the one to journey to California in December 1993 to receive the award on behalf of himself and the other two. Previous recipients of the Earl Warren

Award include Rosa Parks, Joan Baez, Roger Baldwin, William O. Douglas, and Thurgood Marshall. Christopher Eckhardt, no longer overlooked, was clearly in good company.

---

## The Tinker Precedent: the Seventies and Eighties

Anyone passably familiar with modern American constitutional law knows that the jurisprudence of the Warren Burger–William Rehnquist Supreme Courts (1969–present) is very different from that of the Warren Court (1953–1969). In fact, what has happened to the *Tinker* precedent in the last quarter century provides a rough paradigm of the overall constitutional shift from the liberal Warren Court of the 1960s to the Supreme Court of the present moment. The *Tinker* decision is still "good law"—as law professors like to say—but Court decisions of recent years have undercut it. More than one analyst since 1970 could not resist saying that *Tinker* has been "tinkered with."

Since 1969 every one of the justices participating in the ruling in *Tinker v. Des Moines* has died or retired. Ten of the twelve justices who have served on the Supreme Court since the *Tinker* decision were appointed by Republican presidents decidedly opposed to the liberal activism of the Warren Court. As a consequence of this shift in personnel, as well as due to a societal retreat from the frantic social change of the 1960s, the constitutional decisions of the Supreme Court have swirled in directions different from those championed by Warren, Douglas, Black, Brennan, Marshall—and Fortas. Although the landmark decisions of the Warren era remain, the flow of Burger and Rehnquist Court decisions has washed away substantial supporting terrain.

Justice Fortas's ruling—that the *Tinker* decision concerned "primary First Amendment rights akin to 'pure speech,'" not "length of skirts or . . . type of clothing . . . hair style or deportment"—was used against students taking appearance-related claims to court in the 1970s. Generally those students found themselves on the losing side of such actions. The papers of the ICLU, for example, reveal that the organization handled many such cases in the decade following *Tinker*. In addition, Edward Allen's history of the ICLU, titled *Freedom in Iowa: The Role of the Iowa Civil Liberties Union,* contains an entire chapter on "clothing controversies" following its discussion of the *Tinker* decision. One of the principal attorneys handling matters involving appearance in the schools was none other than Dan Johnston. Ultimately the ICLU tired of taking on so many appearance cases and adopted a policy that students alleging a constitutional right to wear long hair or short skirts would be advised to retain their own lawyers if they wished to pursue their rights in court. The ICLU did, however, agree to supply such litigants with the arguments used in other appearance cases.

Between 1969 and the mid-1980s *Tinker* served as a precedent in literally hundreds of student rights cases in the state and federal courts. Included among these cases were those concerning hair length, student dances, demonstrations, discipline, student publications, school elections, dramatic productions, prayer meetings, textbook selection, and library censorship. The test, drawn from *Tinker* and employed by these courts, provided that student expression was to be protected under the First Amendment unless it "materially disrupts classwork or involves substantial disorder or invasion of the rights of others." These case holdings, especially those concerning hair length, were widely divergent. This is not surprising, because the *Tinker* test requires case-by-case analysis based on the facts of particular situations.

In the mid-1980s, the U.S. Supreme Court, under the leadership of Chief Justice Warren Burger, heard three student rights cases dealing with serious constitutional issues. All three resulted in decisions hostile to the position of the aggrieved students. The first decision was *New Jersey v. T.L.O.* (1985). Although not a free-expression case, this matter involved student Fourth Amendment claims and demonstrated that the Court henceforth would not extend the same Bill of Rights protections to students in public schools that were available to adults in other settings. The *T.L.O.* case involved a fourteen-year-old girl caught smoking in a school restroom. She was taken to the principal's office, where her purse was searched. School officials found a package of cigarettes, rolling papers, a small amount of marijuana, and several empty plastic bags. This evidence suggested to school officials that T.L.O. was involved in selling marijuana, for which she was duly charged. Her attorney alleged that the search of her purse was without a warrant and thus violated T.L.O.'s right under the Fourth Amendment not to be subjected to "unreasonable searches and seizures." A federal district court found in favor of T.L.O., but on appeal the Supreme Court ruled that, in a school situation, a warrant to search is not necessary if school officials have a "reasonable" suspicion that evidence of a crime may be obtained from such a search. Instead of applying the normal "probable cause" standard for searches under the Fourth Amendment, the Burger Court held that the lesser ground of the "reasonableness" of a search was sufficient for minors in a school situation "when the measures adopted are reasonably related to the objectives of the search and not excessively intrusive in light of the age and sex of the student and the nature of the infraction."

The second Burger Court case of the 1980s dealing with the rights of secondary-school students did concern freedom of expression under the First Amendment. In 1986, in *Fraser v. Bethel S.D. No. 403*, the Court held that a Tacoma, Washington, school principal was within his rights for suspending a student for employing sexual innuendos in a speech before a school assembly in which he nominated a friend for an office in student government. The nominating speech drew what the district court described as "boisterous" hooting from the student audience. In addition, the lower court record noted that faculty observed a few students "simulating the speech through gestures" and other students merely appearing "embarrassed." The lower court ruled against the school district, determining that the disruption was minimal and did not warrant suspension. On appeal, however, the Burger Court reversed and found in favor of the school district because it believed that the speech threatened order in the school. The Court distinguished this case from the facts in *Tinker* by holding that the student assembly at which the allegedly offensive remarks were uttered was voluntary and not a "public forum for student expression" and that in such a situation school authorities have the responsibility of ensuring that expression is not indecent. By contrast, the Court in *Tinker* characterized the entire school campus as a public forum; thus, under the First Amendment, the administration could impose only "time, place and manner" regulations that were "content neutral . . . serve a significant governmental interest . . . and leave open adequate alternative channels of communication."

The third 1980s student-rights decision of the Burger Court came the closest to political speech of any case since *Tinker*. In that ruling the Court gave a clear signal that the 1969 black-armband decision was no longer a shield for the rights of students. The case was *Hazelwood*

*School District v. Kuhlmeier*, and it came out of the eighth circuit, the same judicial circuit that gave rise to the *Tinker* decision almost twenty years earlier. The issue was whether a Missouri school principal had the right to delete two pages from a student newspaper because of his belief that the content of the articles might offend some of the students and other readers of the newspaper. The principal also maintained that the articles did not sufficiently mask the identity of individual students. One article dealt with the effects of divorce on families, and the other concerned birth control and teenage pregnancy. Once again a federal district court found in favor of the student interests but saw its ruling reversed on appeal to the Supreme Court. The Court held in *Hazelwood* that since the newspaper bore the imprimatur of the school, the school administration had the power to determine that forms of expression conveyed in its publications were consistent with the school's educational objectives. The Court considered the paper "school sponsored expression," in contrast to the "personal expression" permitted by the Court in the 1969 *Tinker* decision.

Approximately fifteen law reviews published essays or comments on these three cases in the 1980s and early 1990s. Most were critical of the decisions and ventured the opinion that the *Tinker* precedent was now on shaky footing. For example, in discussing the 1985 Supreme Court decision that upheld the warrantless search of a student's purse, a professor of law at Washington and Lee University wrote, "*New Jersey v. T.L.O.* . . . was remarkable in the scope of its assault on juvenile privacy." Similarly, a law-student-authored case comment in a 1987 issue of the *University of Florida Law Review* concluded that the Supreme Court decision in *Fraser v. Bethel* "ignores . . . [the Court's] own warnings of the chilling effects inherent in prohibiting speech offensive to some members of society."

Of these three 1980s decisions, the greatest criticism from the legal community was directed at Justice Byron White's Opinion of the Court in *Hazelwood v. Kuhlmeier*. For example, a case comment in *Florida State University Law Review* submitted that *Hazelwood v. Kuhlmeier* "is an unsatisfactory decision" in that it "does not make clear the limits of its application" and "does not establish a sufficiently clear standard of evaluation for school board conduct in the areas to which the decision applies." This comment went on to warn that the Missouri student newspaper decision may free school boards to employ "thought control inimical to the Constitution and to the preservation of free thought." Two lawyers writing in the *Duke Law Journal* used equally strong language to criticize the Court's upholding of the prior censorship of the Missouri student newspaper: "*Kuhlmeier* eviscerates the Supreme Court's decision in *Tinker,* overrules many lower-court decisions protective of the student press, and curtails student press rights established for well over a generation." Perhaps the most strident criticism of the 1988 decision in *Hazelwood* came from a member of the Court itself. In an acrimonious dissent, Justice William Brennan declared that the decision heralded a "classroom orthodoxy" that could transform public schools into "enclaves of totalitarianism that strangle the free mind at its source."

In early 1988, reporters contacted Dan Johnston in New York, seeking his reactions to the Supreme Court decision in *Hazelwood v. Kuhlmeier.* Johnston was not willing to concede that *Hazelwood* had effectively reversed the *Tinker* case. However, he did acknowledge that, in contrast to the Supreme Court decision in the 1969 black-armband case, the recent decision concerning student newspapers "certainly reflects a different attitude toward the Constitution and toward limited government." Quoted in a *Wall Street Journal* story a few days later, Johnston appeared even more bitter about the Supreme Court's school-newspaper decision. "All my life," he mused, "I've been saying proudly I was the lawyer in *Tinker.* I'd built a statue to myself in my mind. But the Supreme Court melted down my statue when it decided *Hazelwood.*" By contrast, Ora Niffenegger expressed pleasure in the Court decision in *Hazelwood,* stating in an interview, "This brings us back closer to the situation before *Tinker.*"

In assessing the combined impact of these three major students'-rights cases of the 1980s, an essayist in the *Depaul Law Review* concluded that "[t]he Court has essentially nullified the broad constitutional rights of students which were delineated in *Tinker.*" A corresponding sentiment was voiced by two lawyers writing in a 1989 issue of the *Yale Law and Policy Review.* They argued that the First Amendment principles forged by the Court majorities in *Fraser v. Bethel* "are inconsistent with *Tinker,* reflecting more the jurisprudence of Justice Black's dissent. While paying lip service to the free speech rights of students, *Fraser* and *Hazelwood* exhibit a sweeping deference to school officials."

The most critical reaction to the mid-1980s Burger Court decisions on student rights came from a Washington and Lee law professor, William Geimer. Writing in a 1988 issue of the *Georgia Law Review,* Geimer saw the three student rights cases as indicative of a philosophy he termed "juvenileness." In spite of "soaring rhetoric" about student rights, Geimer insisted, American courts generally adhere to two assumptions in student rights cases: they believe that children are "immature" and must be shielded by adults from problems and one another; and they accept the position that children are "incapable of making reasonable decisions" and unqualified to offer solutions to "real world problems." For Geimer, *Tinker v. Des Moines* was one of the few children's-rights cases that actually upheld the rights of minors without being transparently patronizing. Professor Geimer obtained some of the impetus for writing his article, "Juvenileness: a Single-Edged Constitutional Sword," from a chance encounter with Lorena Tinker in Nicaragua in early 1987. He struck up a conversation with her and learned about her role in the well-known Supreme Court case that had long interested him. In the course of his research for his article he interviewed Lorena, John, and Mary Beth Tinker and developed an admiration for the social activism of the Tinker family. On the publication of his article, he sent a copy to Lorena Tinker with a handwritten note on the title page: "With heartfelt thanks to you and John and Mary Beth—for your help with this article but also for your continuing work for peace and justice. [signed] Bill."

The mainstream press's reactions to the three Burger Court student rights decisions of the 1980s paralleled the legal commentators'. A *Newsweek* article in the wake of the *Hazelwood* decision, for instance, noted that "for the last few years the justices have been signaling high school students that they don't have the same constitutional rights as adults." It also pointed out that Justice White's majority opinion in *Hazelwood* did not overrule the decision in *Tinker v. Des Moines* but noted that "its spirit has undeniably been curtailed." *Newsweek* also solicited the views of two of the principal litigants in the case. Hazelwood East High principal Robert Reynolds said that he was relieved that the Supreme Court upheld the administration's "local control over the curriculum." On the other hand, Cathy Kuhlmeier, former editor the *Spectrum*—the school newspaper that was censored—reacted negatively, saying that the Supreme Court decision will "turn kids off to journalism."

A February 7, 1988, *Boston Globe* article, referred to *T.L.O.*, *Bethel*, and *Hazelwood* as clear "signals" that the "expansive spirit" of the *Tinker* decision has been curtailed. Ernest Boyer, director of the Carnegie Foundation for the Advancement of Teaching, was quoted in the *Globe* article to the effect that the three Burger Court decisions were contributing to "a growing alienation between the generations" and a climate of "suspicion, perhaps fear." One of the few articles in general-interest publications that defended the Burger Court's 1980s student rights decisions appeared in *School Safety*. Titled "Schools Should Teach Character Says U.S. Supreme Court" and written by a California attorney, this article argued that the Burger Court decisions on students rights extend to school officials the "legal duty and the judicially-authorized flexibility to reasonably define and vigorously enforce standards which encourage civility and enhance the learning environment for all students everywhere in America."

One of the most interesting reactions to the Burger Court's student rights decisions came from Michael Gartner, the editor and co-owner of the Ames, Iowa, *Daily Tribune*. Appearing in the *Wall Street Journal*'s "Viewpoint" column on February 4, 1988, Gartner's opinion essay came from the perspective of an experienced journalist and an Iowan familiar with the *Tinker* case of twenty years earlier. Gartner began his essay by setting the scene at North High School, the secondary school attended by John Tinker in the mid-1960s. He characterized North as one of Iowa's "landmarks" because of its significance to the history of civil liberties and student rights. According to Gartner, Justice White's opinion in *Kuhlmeier* "ranks a child's belief in Santa Claus higher on the scale of values to be protected than a youngster's right to utter and hear the truth." Gartner concluded his biting criticism of the school-newspaper decision by proposing that the citizens of Des Moines build a statute of Dan Johnston, Christopher Eckhardt, and the Tinkers outside of North High "as a nice remembrance of freedoms past."

----

## The Tinker Precedent: the Nineties

To understand the current place of the *Tinker* precedent in American constitutional history, a comparison to the state of the law on abortion and affirmative action may be instructive. The landmark U.S.

{ *The Struggle for Student Rights* }

Supreme Court decision of *Roe v. Wade* (1973) is still the law of the land, permitting a woman to exercise substantial choice regarding the termination of a pregnancy. But a vigorous "Right to Life" movement has spawned legislation limiting late-term abortions, government funding of abortions, and abortions to minors. In addition, a handful of state and federal court decisions have narrowed the sweep of *Roe*. Finally, in some states today it is almost impossible to find a physician or a hospital willing to perform an abortion. Similarly, the leading affirmative-action decision, *Regents of the University of California v. Bakke* (1978), is still good law. But a recent decision by the U.S. Supreme Court not to review the Fifth Circuit Court of Appeals case of *Texas v. Hopwood* (1996)—which struck down a special-admissions plan at the University of Texas law school—has placed federal and state educational initiatives intended to benefit racial minorities and women in a problematic position. In addition, the Supreme Court has been increasingly critical of affirmative-action plans in employment and in the granting of federal contracts. Thus, to say that the right to an abortion and the integrity of affirmative-action programs are still supported by American law is to tell only part of the story. In the late 1990s the legal momentum, propelled by strong public feelings, is bitterly split on the abortion question and is running against affirmative action. A change in Supreme Court personnel could tip the judicial balance back in favor of abortion and affirmative action, but that depends on justices being appointed to the Court who hold philosophies similar to Earl Warren and William Douglas, rather than William Rehnquist and Antonin Scalia.

Recently published legal treatises and casebooks recognize that the Iowa black-armband case—like *Roe v. Wade* and *Regents v. Bakke*—is still a landmark decision. Experts on school law and constitutional law emphasize that *Tinker v. Des Moines* is the place to begin to obtain an understanding of student legal rights in modern America. However, due to decisions of the 1970s and 1980s discussed above, *Tinker* does not tower in its legal neighborhood the way it once did. A few examples from current legal texts reinforce this point.

In a section on "Student Rights and Discipline" in the 1994 edition of *Law in the Schools,* a volume on school law written by William Valente, professor of law and education at Villanova University, is this statement: "Student freedom of speech must now be analyzed under three landmark Supreme Court decisions, . . . the *Tinker* case and the later *Hazelwood* and *Bethel* cases." Whereas earlier editions of Valente's text presented a substantial excerpt from *Tinker,* the current edition does not feature the case. On the other hand, it does contain excerpts from both *Hazelwood* and *Bethel.* Valente's analysis of the case law on student rights notes that *Hazelwood* and *Bethel* have cut a "broad swath," limiting the *Tinker* doctrine "to expression that is not of pedagogical concern." Similarly, a volume on teachers' and students' rights, titled *Public School Law*, published in 1992, notes that "*Tinker* now applies *only* to expression that clearly does not give the appearance of representing the school" [emphasis in original]. A 1993 text, simply titled *Education Law* and written by education professors Michael Imber and Tyll van Geel, distinguishes "independent student speech" from "school-sponsored student speech." The former "consists of communications by students that take place at school but not as part of their participation in the curriculum"; the latter "occurs as part of the school program such as articles written for the school paper." The featured case under the "independent student speech" rubric is *Tinker v. Des Moines.* The excerpted cases in the "school-sponsored speech" section are *Hazelwood v. Kuhlmeier* and *Bethel v. Fraser.* Imber and van Geel's analysis of the black-armband decision includes the notation that the "lower courts' use of the *Tinker* test has produced a set of cases with mixed results." The authors' discussion of *Hazelwood* and *Bethel* is much lengthier than that of *Tinker.*

Constitutional law and constitutional history texts still accord *Tinker* a prominent place in their discussions of symbolic speech. Melvin Urofsky's *A March of Liberty: A Constitutional History of the United States* cites *Tinker* as a leading case for the principle that "symbolic speech . . . comes under the First Amendment umbrella." Urofsky juxtaposes *Tinker* with *U.S. v. O'Brien* (1968), the draft-card-burning case. The difference in the two cases, according to Urofsky, was that in *Tinker* the symbolic speech was not disruptive of the schools, but in *O'Brien* the symbolic act resulted in the destruction of materials (draft-registration documents) in which the federal government had a legitimate interest. The 1996 edition of Craig Ducat's massive *Constitutional Interpretation* also singles out *Tinker* as a still-important precedent for symbolic speech under the First Amendment. Following his long excerpt from *Tinker,* Ducat includes a shorter excerpt from *Bethel v. Fraser.*

Back in Iowa, *Tinker v. Des Moines* is called to mind whenever a high-school or college student protest takes place. Inevitably someone involved in the dispute or a journalist reporting on the controversy suggests parallels to the black-armband case. For example, in the fall of 1992, a sixteen-year-old Davenport high-school student was told to remove a small tattoo of a cross from her hand. The school district objected to her tattoo because it was reputed to be a gang symbol. When this story appeared in the Iowa newspapers, several school officials and ACLU personnel recalled the *Tinker* decision. Civil liberties officials maintained that the *Tinker* precedent protected a student's right to display such a symbol at school. The school superintendent, on the other hand, said *Tinker* should not be controlling here because of the disruptive potential posed—even in small-town Iowa—by gang symbols. The U.S. Supreme Court has not rendered a definitive opinion as to whether gang colors or gang symbols constitute protected speech. However, lower court decisions have consistently held that a student's right to display gang symbols is not protected speech if a probability of gang-sparked violence exists in the school in question. Thus, if the Davenport superintendent was correct about the potential for gang-related trouble in his school district, he did not act illegally in demanding that the girl remove her tattoo. The student and her mother took the path of least resistance, spending $500 to have the tattoo obliterated by laser surgery. In April 1997, however, the Eighth Circuit Court of Appeals in St. Louis ruled that the Davenport school regulation on gang activity that occasioned this debate was unconstitutionally vague.

In the spring of 1994, about eighteen months after the tattoo controversy, another freedom-of-expression problem flared in Iowa schools. A small number of students at Des Moines Roosevelt High and suburban Urbandale High distributed racist and anti-Semitic literature. A few days after this literature circulated, anti-Semitic graffiti were spray-painted on the exterior of a Des Moines synagogue. These incidents aroused Des Moines students, school officials, and religious leaders to condemn the racial incidents in their city. The *Des Moines Register* editorialized several times that spring about the need to confront and denounce racism. In all the coverage that these incidents received in the press, however, there were few mentions of the need to censor racist literature. The consensus of students, teachers, and school officials seemed to be that it was better to expose and counter expressions of racism than to try to suppress it. Mary Beth Tinker, after being informed about the racist literature circulating in some central Iowa schools, told a *Register* reporter, "Personally, I don't think students should be . . . [expressing] hate messages. . . . But I guess they should be allowed to say these things. Then you just fight them in other ways."

On February 24, 1994, the twenty-fifth anniversary of the Supreme Court's decision in *Tinker v. Des Moines,* the *Register* carried a brief story recognizing the importance of the armband decision in the history of American civil liberties. Part of the legal backdrop for the story was the circulation of hate literature in Des Moines and Urbandale schools. But another free-expression controversy also provided a contemporary context for the silver anniversary of the *Tinker* decision. This dispute involved risque T-shirts—hardly as weighty an issue as that raised by Christopher Eckhardt and the Tinkers when they donned black armbands in 1965, but a potential First Amendment issue nonetheless.

The "T-shirt flap," as it was called, began when a few students at the Ames Middle School in Ames, Iowa, tired of seeing male students wearing T-shirts to school advertizing Hooters, a restaurant chain known for waitresses attired in sexually provocative outfits. These T-shirts contain a picture of an owl with eyes peering out from the o's in Hooters and bear the slogan "More than a mouthful." Apparently some male students at this school had been wearing Hooters' T-shirts for a year and a half without any objection from school administrators. The students critical of the Hooters T-shirts were offended by what they perceived as the sexist message conveyed. So they decided to fight fire with fire: they created their own satirical T-shirt design. It had the word "Cocks," a picture of a rooster, and the slogan "Nothin' to crow about!" In April 1994 a female student requested permission to wear the homemade T-shirt to school but was told by the principal that it would not be permitted. Fourteen students defied the principal and wore the "Cocks" T-shirts anyway. Four students (three of them male) were sent home when they refused to remove the T-shirts or turn them inside out. This confrontation resulted in a ban of Hooters *and* Cocks T-shirts from the school. The middle-school students who came up with idea for the rooster parody said that it was not their intention to have the Hooters T-shirts banned. Sarah Hegland, one of the students who created the satiric T-shirt design, remarked, "We wanted to make people talk and think about it. We wanted them [the Hooters T-shirts] to be socially unacceptable rather than legally unacceptable."

Shortly after the two sets of T-shirts were banished from the Ames Middle School, two of the students who had wanted to wear the Cocks T-shirts contacted the Iowa Civil Liberties Union to inquire as to their rights. But, unlike in the black-armband dispute a quarter century before, the school administration did not suspend the students, and no students decided to sue. Instead of a contentious school board meeting, the Ames Middle School held an open forum in the school auditorium to discuss issues raised by the T-shirt controversy—including freedom of expression, sexism, sexual harassment, and sexual discrimination. Instead of expressing apprehension about outside agitators, the school administration invited to the forum Ira Glasser, executive director of the ACLU, who fortuitously happened to be in Ames at the time to deliver a speech at Iowa State University. And, rather than dissolving into a shouting match like the 1965–66 Des Moines school board meetings, the Ames forum took place without rancor. The Ames Middle School principal even confessed to committing some mistakes in the handling of the T-shirt affair—a far cry from the intransigence of the Des Moines Independent Community School District's administration and the school board twenty-five years earlier. And, unlike the months of constant headlines in the Des Moines newspapers over the armband dispute, the press reports, columns, and editorials on the T-shirts played themselves out in a few days. Compared, thus, to the bitter armband controversy of 1965–69, the T-shirt flap of 1994 was a small, amusing story.

Before their own little dispute had flared, most of the students involved in the Ames T-shirt dispute had not heard of Christopher Eckhardt, John Tinker, or Mary Beth Tinker. But they know their names now. They have since learned that in December 1965 three Iowa kids, imbued with the idealism of the 1960s and their own sincere beliefs, wore black armbands to school to do their small part to try to stop a war. Although their act of conscience did not end the war in Vietnam, the right they sought—to express themselves in a symbolic, nonthreatening manner—was realized by a decision in the highest court in the land. That decision, *Tinker v. Des Moines,* will be remembered as long as students demand the right to be heard as well as seen.

Late November 1965:   Large anti–Vietnam War march on
                      Washington, D.C., takes place. At least twenty-
                      five thousand participate, including about fifty
                      Iowans.

December 11, 1965:    Several Iowans (adults and students) gather in the
                      Des Moines home of William and Margaret
                      Eckhardt to plan local demonstrations expressing
                      their feelings about the Vietnam War. One protest
                      option proposed is for students to wear black
                      armbands to school for the dual purpose of
                      mourning casualties in the war and endorsing an
                      open-ended truce in the fighting.

December 13, 1965:    Des Moines Roosevelt High School student Ross
                      Peterson's draft article for the school newspaper
                      on the armband protest is denied publication by
                      the school administration.

December 14, 1965:    Des Moines senior-high principals meet and
                      recommend the banning of black armbands from
                      their schools. This reaffirms a decision made by
                      the district central administration the previous
                      day.

December 15, 1965:    The morning *Des Moines Register* carries an article
                      reporting the district administration's decision to
                      ban armbands in the Des Moines secondary
                      schools. Announcements are made in the schools
                      that black armbands will not be permitted.

Mid-December 1965:    Christmas bombing truce in the Vietnam War
                      commences.

December 16, 1965:    Christopher Eckhardt (a sophomore at Roosevelt)
                      and Mary Beth Tinker (an eighth-grader at Des
                      Moines's Harding Junior High) wear black
                      armbands to their respective schools. Both are
                      suspended. In response to a phone call from a
                      student, school board president Ora Niffenegger
                      refuses to call a special board meeting to discuss
                      the armbands.

| December 17, 1965: | John Tinker (brother of Mary Beth and a sophomore at North High in Des Moines) wears a black armband to his school. Although not suspended, he is asked to leave school. Two other students receive suspension notices for wearing armbands in defiance of the school district prohibition. [Perhaps several dozen other Des Moines students wear black armbands to school on December 16 and 17, but are not disciplined.] |
| --- | --- |
| December 21, 1965: | Des Moines school board conducts a regular meeting, which is dominated by the armband issue. Over two hundred attend. Board votes 4–3 to postpone review of the district policy prohibiting armbands. |
| Late December 1965: | United States ends Christmas bombing truce in the Vietnam War. Approximately 170,000 American soldiers are in Vietnam. About 1000 Americans have died in the war. |
| December 31, 1965: | Des Moines school board conducts "secret" meeting with its attorney, Allan Herrick, concerning the armband controversy. |
| January 3, 1966: | Des Moines school board conducts its next regularly scheduled meeting. Once again about two hundred from the community attend. Board votes 5–2 to maintain the policy prohibiting armbands and uphold the suspension of the armband-wearing students. |
| Early January 1966: | Christopher Eckhardt, John Tinker, and Mary Beth Tinker return to their Des Moines schools, without armbands. |
| January 1966: | Dan Johnston and the Iowa Civil Liberties Union agree to represent Christopher Eckhardt and the Tinkers in a lawsuit against the Des Moines school district, asserting that the students have been deprived of their right of symbolic expression by the ban on armbands. |
| Mar.–July 1966: | Johnston files suit on behalf of Eckhardt and the Tinkers in U.S. district court. Attorney Allan Herrick files an answer for the school district. Depositions of potential witnesses taken by attorneys. Trial briefs filed. |

| | |
|---|---|
| July 25–26, 1966: | Trial of the armband case before Judge Roy Stephenson in U.S. district court in Des Moines. |
| September 1, 1966: | Judge Stephenson issues "memorandum opinion" upholding the Des Moines school district's ban on black armbands. He rules that the right of the school district to act reasonably to maintain order outweighs the students' right to symbolic expression. |
| Sept. 1966–Apr. 1967: | Johnston and Herrick prepare for an appeal of Judge Stephenson's decision to the U.S. Court of Appeals, Eighth Circuit. |
| April 26, 1967: | Three-judge panel of the eighth circuit in St. Louis, Missouri, announces that it cannot come to a decision in the armband appeal and orders a rehearing before an en banc panel of the eighth circuit. |
| May–Oct. 1967: | Johnston and Herrick prepare for en banc hearing of the eighth circuit. |
| Mid-October 1967: | En banc hearing held, again in St. Louis. |
| November 3, 1967: | An equally divided (4–4) eighth circuit court affirms the district court ruling without explanation. |
| November 17, 1967: | Eighth circuit court issues a stay of its decision pending application by Johnston for certiorari to the U.S. Supreme Court. |
| Nov. 1967–Feb. 1968: | Johnston (with David Ellenhorn and Melvin Wulf of the American Civil Liberties Union) and Herrick prepare certiorari briefs to the Supreme Court. |
| March 4, 1968: | U.S. Supreme Court grants certiorari in *Tinker v. Des Moines*. Vote later revealed to be 5–4 in favor of hearing the case. |
| Mar.–Nov. 1968: | Johnston and Herrick prepare their Supreme Court briefs. |
| March 1968: | Lyndon Johnson announces that he will not be a candidate for re-election to the U.S. presidency. |
| Spring 1968: | Anti–Vietnam War protests take place on scores of American campuses. Martin Luther King Jr. assassinated. |

| | |
|---|---|
| May 1968: | Amicus curiae brief in *Tinker v. Des Moines* filed by the U.S. National Student Association. |
| Summer 1968: | Chief Justice Earl Warren announces his retirement from the U.S. Supreme Court, effective the following summer. President Johnson nominates Associate Justice Abe Fortas for the chief justiceship. Riots occur in and around the Democratic National Convention in Chicago. Democratic Party nominates Hubert Humphrey as its presidential candidate. Richard Nixon nominated by the Republican Party. |
| October 1968: | Fortas's nomination for chief justiceship withdrawn in the face of substantial opposition. President Johnson orders bombing halt in Vietnam to rekindle stalled peace talks. |
| November 5, 1968: | Richard Nixon elected President of the United States. |
| November 12, 1968: | Oral argument before the U.S. Supreme Court in *Tinker v. Des Moines.* Johnston speaks for the students; Herrick represents the school district. |
| November 15, 1968: | U.S. Supreme Court conducts confidential conference at which *Tinker v. Des Moines* is discussed. Opinion of the Court assigned to Justice Abe Fortas. |
| Nov. 1968–Feb. 1969: | Draft opinions in *Tinker v. Des Moines* written and circulated among the Supreme Court. |
| Late December 1968: | Approximately five hundred thousand American soldiers are in Vietnam. The American death toll in the Vietnam War approaches thirty thousand. |
| February 24, 1969: | Supreme Court announces decision in *Tinker v. Des Moines.* Writing for the seven-person majority, Abe Fortas holds that public school students have the right under the First Amendment to the U.S. Constitution to wear black armbands to school to express their concerns about the war in Vietnam, provided that their actions do not substantially disrupt school activity. Justices Potter Stewart and Bryon White write concurring opinions; John Marshall Harlan and Hugo L. Black write dissenting opinions. |

| | |
|---|---|
| May 5, 1969: | Abe Fortas resigns from the U.S. Supreme Court in the face of ethical questions. |
| May–June 1969: | Warren Burger nominated by President Nixon to replace Earl Warren as chief justice. Burger confirmed by the U.S. Senate and takes seat on Supreme Court. |
| 1980s: | Decisions of the Supreme Court—*New Jersey v. T.L.O.* (1984), *Fraser v. Bethel S.D. No. 403* (1986), and *Hazelwood School District v. Kuhlmeier* (1988)— weaken the precedential value of *Tinker v. Des Moines.* |
| February 24, 1994: | Twenty-fifth anniversary of the Supreme Court decision in *Tinker v. Des Moines.* |

For reasons not altogether clear, booklength studies of historic U.S. Supreme Court cases—which were once a staple of legal and constitutional historians—have fallen out of fashion in recent years. Among the best of the "older" booklength studies are the following: Anthony Lewis, *Gideon's Trumpet* (New York: Alfred A. Knopf, Inc., 1964); C. Peter Magrath, *Yazoo, Law and Politics in the New Republic: The Case of* Fletcher v. Peck (New York: W.W. Norton & Co., 1967); Richard Kluger, *Simple Justice: The History of* Brown v. Board of Education *and Black America's Struggle for Equality* (New York: Alfred A. Knopf, Inc., 1976); Maeva Marcus, *Truman and the Steel Seizure Case: The Limits of Presidential Power* (New York: Columbia University Press, 1977); Don Fehrenbacher, *The Dred Scott Case: Its Significance in American Law and Politics* (New York: Oxford University Press, 1978); Stanley Kutler, *Privilege and Creative Destruction: The Charles River Bridge Case* (New York: W.W. Norton & Co., 1978); Joel Dreyfuss and Charles Lawrence III, *The Bakke Case: The Politics of Inequality* (New York: Harcourt Brace Jovanovich, 1979); and Bernard Schwartz, *Swann's Way: The School Busing Case and the Supreme Court* (New York: Oxford University Press, 1986). See also my own study of the Supreme Court's leading decision on nuclear power: John W. Johnson, *Insuring against Disaster: The Nuclear Industry on Trial* (Macon, GA: Mercer University Press, 1986). Two excellent recent contributions to the case-study literature deal with the same 1960s civil rights/civil liberties case, *New York Times v. Sullivan:* Anthony Lewis, *Make No Law: The Sullivan Case and the First Amendment* (New York: Random House, Inc., 1992); and Kermit L. Hall, *Heed Their Rising Voices:* New York Times v. Sullivan (New York: McGraw Hill, forthcoming). Finally, mention should be made of two recently published volumes in the "Landmark Law Cases and American Society" series, the series of which my book is a part: Melvin I. Urofsky, *Affirmative Action on Trial: Sex Discrimination in* Johnson v. Santa Clara (Lawrence: University Press of Kansas, 1997); and Harold M. Hyman, *The Reconstruction Justice of Salmon P. Chase:* In Re Turner *and* Texas v. White (Lawrence: University Press of Kansas, 1997).

Although *Tinker v. Des Moines* has not benefited from a detailed booklength study, several short popular treatments discuss the Iowa black-armband case. They include the following essays or book chapters: Nat Hentoff, "Why Students Want Their Constitutional Rights Now," *Saturday Review* (May 22, 1971): 60–63, 73–74; Hentoff, *The First Freedom: The Tumultuous History of Free Speech in America* (New York: Delacorte Press, 1980), 3–9; Peter Irons, *The Courage of Their Convictions* (New York: The Free Press, 1988), 233–52; Joseph F. Wall, "The Right of Children To Be Seen as Well as Heard," in John W. Johnson, ed., *Historic U.S. Court Cases, 1690–1990: An Encyclopedia* (New York: Garland Publishing, Inc.,

1992), 723–26; and Richard, Lord Acton and Patricia Nassif Acton, *To Go Free: A Treasury of Iowa's Legal Heritage* (Ames: Iowa State University Press, 1995), 286–92. Several authors and publishers have justifiably felt that the *Tinker* case might be interesting to young readers. Such publications include "The Black Armband Case," *Goldfinch* 8 (February 1987): 17–18; Doreen Rappaport, *Be the Judge Be the Jury:* Tinker vs. Des Moines (New York: Harper Collins Publishers, 1993); Cheryl Fusco Johnson, "Protest Heroes," *Goldfinch* 18 (Fall 1996): 18–19; and John W. Johnson, "The Forgotten Litigant," *Goldfinch* 18 (Fall 1996): 20. Two of the participants in *Tinker* have offered interesting perspectives on the case in their own publications: Mary Beth Tinker, "The Case of the Black Armbands," *Youth* 20 (April 20, 1969): 16–23; and William Eckhardt, "The Black Arm Band Story," *Journal of Human Relations* 17 (1969): 495–515. Edgar Bittle also shared with me his essay on the black-armband controversy, "The *Tinker* Case: Reflections 25 Years Later" (unpublished essay, adapted from a presentation at the School Law Seminar, College of Education, University of Iowa, 1994).

From the time that *Tinker v. Des Moines* came to the attention of the American legal community in 1968 until about two years after the Supreme Court decision, academic lawyers and law students wrote extensively about the case. Among the many law review articles focusing on the *Tinker* decision in the late 1960s and early 1970s, I found the most useful to be: Benjamin C. Sanchez, "Restrictions on Freedom of Expression By School Authorities," *Gonzaga Law Review* 3 (Spring 1968): 227–36; Jerry E. Benezra, " Freedom of Expression: *Tinker v. Des Moines Independent Community School District*," *Suffolk University Law Review* 4 (Fall 1969): 169–75; "The Supreme Court, 1968 Term," *Harvard Law Review* 83 (Fall 1969): 154–61; Peter L. Dearing, "Freedom of Expression in Student Demonstrations," *University of Florida Law Review* 22 (Summer 1969): 168–74; Theodore F. Denno, "Mary Beth Tinker Takes the Constitution to School," *Fordham Law Review* 38 (October 1969): 35–62; "Regulation Prohibiting War Protest in High School Is Unconstitutional," *Minnesota Law Review* 54 (1970): 721–29; and Sheldon H. Nahmod, "Beyond *Tinker:* The High School as an Educational Public Forum," *Harvard Civil Rights & Civil Liberties Law Review* 5 (April 1970): 278–300.

While the secondary literature described above proved valuable in understanding the issues in this constitutional dispute, the real starting place for a serious study of this case—as for any individual American court case—is in the primary documents. First and foremost are the official reports of the case, available in law school libraries and in many university and public libraries. The Supreme Court opinion in *Tinker v. Des Moines Independent Community School District, Inc.* is found in the *United States Reports* at 393 U.S. 503 (1969). An "unofficial" publication of the *Tinker* opinion, complete with various aids and cross-references, is found in the *U.S. Supreme Court Reports (Lawyers' Edition)* at 21 L.Ed.2d 731 (1969). The granting of certiorari in *Tinker* is noted in the *United States Reports* at 390 U.S. 942 (1968). The en banc decision of the Eighth Circuit

Court of Appeals in *Tinker* is found in the *Federal Reporter* at 383 F.2d 988 (1967). And the decision of the District Court of the Southern District of Iowa is found in the *Federal Supplement* at 258 F.Supp. 971 (1966).

Published case reports, however, only scratch the surface of a judicial study. Much of the really interesting legal and personal detail in a constitutional dispute can be gleaned only from the oral arguments and written briefs of the attorneys in a case. The transcribed oral argument before the U.S. Supreme Court in *Tinker v. Des Moines* was obtained from the Library of the U.S. Supreme Court. Excerpts of the oral argument in *Tinker* can also be found in Peter Irons and Stephanie Guitton, eds., *May It Please the Court: The Most Significant Oral Arguments Made before the Supreme Court Since 1955* (New York: The New Press, 1993), 122–31. The Supreme Court briefs of the lawyers for the student plaintiffs, the Des Moines school district, and the amicus curiae U.S. National Student Association can be found on microfilm in most law libraries. Appellate court materials on *Tinker*—consisting mainly of the appellate briefs of the parties—were obtained from the clerk of court for the U.S. Court of Appeals, Eighth Circuit, in St. Louis, MO. The district court materials—the trial briefs, the exhibits, and the trial transcript and other parts of the lower court "record"— were procured from the clerk of court for the Federal District Court, Southern District of Iowa (housed in the U.S. District Court Building, Des Moines, Iowa).

One disappointment in connection with the "behind the scenes" legal research on the *Tinker* case was that the working files of the lawyers on the case were either not preserved or unavailable. This disappointment was partially offset by the fact that the papers of the Iowa Civil Liberties Union (ICLU), housed in the special collections section in the University of Northern Iowa's Rod Library, contained some interesting materials on the black-armband case and student rights litigation since 1965. Also useful on the ICLU and the armband case is Louise Noun's autobiography, *Journey To Autonomy: A Memoir* (Ames: Iowa State University Press, 1990), and an "official" history of the state civil liberties organization, Edward S. Allen, *Freedom in Iowa: The Role of the Iowa Civil Liberties Union* (Ames: Iowa State University Press, 1977). General information on national civil liberties issues is available in Samuel Walker, *In Defense of American Liberties: A History of the ACLU* (New York: Oxford University Press, 1990).

Legal research on American subjects is expedited by an array of reference works, many of which are found in regular libraries as well as law school libraries. Kermit L. Hall, ed., *The Oxford Companion to the Supreme Court* (New York: Oxford University Press, 1992), is an excellent source of information on Supreme Court procedure. For definitions of legal terms, *Black's Law Dictionary*, 5th ed. (St. Paul, MN: West Publishing Co., 1979), is a staple reference work. Short but thoughtful biographical treatments of Supreme Court justices can be found in Melvin I. Urofsky, ed., *The Supreme Court Justices: A Biographical Dictionary* (New York: Garland Publishing, Inc., 1994); after each essay is a selected bibliography for further reading. For the two Supreme Court justices central to the *Tinker* case, the most helpful biographies are Gerald T. Dunne, *Hugo Black and the Judicial Revolution* (New York: Simon & Schuster, 1977); and Laura Kalman, *Abe Fortas: A Biography* (New Haven, CT: Yale University Press, 1990). The legal papers of several justices serving on the Court at the time of the *Tinker* case are available for study in the manuscript division of the Library of Congress in Washington, D.C. Particularly rich materials on *Tinker* are in the Hugo L. Black papers. Also useful on the black-armband case are the papers of Earl Warren, William O. Douglas, Thurgood Marshall, and William Brennan.

Much of the personal background and most of the impressions of persons presented in these pages could have been obtained only with the cooperation of the principal participants themselves. To obtain these invaluable perspectives, I conducted interviews in person or by telephone during the first half of 1994 with the following individuals: Edgar Bittle, Christopher Eckhardt, Margaret Eckhardt, Dan Johnston, Louise Noun, John Tinker, Lorena Jeanne Tinker, and Mary Beth Tinker. Especially helpful were the miscellaneous files and papers on the black-armband case that Christopher Eckhardt, John Tinker, and Lorena Jeanne Tinker kindly shared with me. Quoted statements in the text from deceased individuals—such as William Eckhardt and Leonard Tinker—were drawn from interviews with family members or from published sources. I also obtained background information on Iowa law, politics, and culture in the 1960s from interviews with two knowledgeable Iowans, Daniel Holm and Kenneth Lyftogt.

Countless issues of the *Des Moines Register* from 1965 to the present (along with issues of the afternoon *Des Moines Tribune* until its closing in 1982) provided a font of information and insight on the armband case and later developments in the lives of the leading participants. The *Register*—together with the *New York Times*, the *Washington Post*, the *Wall Street Journal*, and the *Christian Science Monitor*—furnished good sources for public reactions to the *Tinker* case as it worked its way through the federal courts.

The three pivotal 1980s student rights cases of the Burger Supreme Court that narrowed the *Tinker* precedent are contained in the *U.S. Reports. New Jersey v. T.L.O.* is found at 469 U.S. 325 (1985); *Bethel School District No. 403 v. Fraser* is at 478 U.S. 675 (1986); and *Hazelwood School District v. Kuhlmeier* is at 484 U.S. 260 (1988). Of the many law review articles that examine these cases and the changing character of student rights in the last generation, I found the most useful to be the following: James C. Dever III, "*Tinker* Revisited: *Fraser v. Bethel School District* and Regulation of Speech in the Public Schools," *Duke Law Journal* (December 1985): 1164–93; William S. Geimer, "Juvenileness: A Single-Edged

Constitutional Sword," *Georgia Law Review* 22 (Summer 1988): 949–73; Bruce C. Hafen, "*Hazelwood School District* and the Role of First Amendment Institutions," *Duke Law Journal* (September 1988): 685–705; J. Marc Abrams and S. Mark Goodman, "End of an Era? The Decline of Student Press Rights in the Wake of *Hazelwood School District v. Kuhlmeier*," *Duke Law Journal* (September 1988): 706–32; and Shari Golub, "*Tinker* to *Fraser* to *Hazelwood*—Supreme Court's Double Play Combination Defeats High School Students' Rally for First Amendment Rights," *DePaul Law Review* 38 (1989): 487–515.

Treatises on education law placing *Tinker v. Des Moines* in its modern context include: Martha M. McCarthy and Nelda H. Cambron-McCabe, *Public School Law: Teachers' and Students' Rights,* 3rd ed. (Boston, MA: Allyn and Bacon, 1992); Michael Imber and Tyll van Geel, *Education Law* (New York: McGraw-Hill, Inc., 1993); and William D. Valente, *Law in the Schools,* 3rd ed. (New York: Macmillan Publishing Company, 1994). Constitutional history/law treatises that place *Tinker* under the symbolic speech rubric of the First Amendment include: Melvin I. Urofsky, *A March of Liberty: A Constitutional History of the United States* (New York: Alfred A. Knopf, 1988); and Craig R. Ducat, *Constitutional Interpretation,* 6th ed. (St. Paul: West Publishing Company, 1996).

Dress code
  and Iowa Civil Liberties Union,
    197–98, 206–7
  as legally different activity from
    wearing armbands, 156, 159, 171,
    182, 187, 203
Ducat, Craig, 214–15
Duke University, 169

Earl Warren Civil Liberties Award,
    205–6
Eckhardt, Christopher P.
  attendance at Des Moines school
    board meetings concerning
    armband demonstration, 33, 46
  deposition of, 71
  in Liberal Religious Youth
    (LRY), 13
  mentioned in press reports on
    *Tinker*, 182
  mentioned at Supreme Court
    conference on *Tinker*, 165
  mentioned in Supreme Court
    decision on *Tinker*, 170
  Niffenegger's comments on, 39–
    40, 56
  as object of community attention,
    52, 55–60
  participation in armband
    demonstration in Des Moines
    schools, 16–19, 21, 23–25, 27
  preparing for appeal of district
    court ruling, 104–8, 110, 115, 117,
    119
  preparing for appeal to Supreme
    Court, 121, 123, 125–26, 129–31,
    136–38
  preparing for district court trial,
    48, 61–64, 66–68, 71–72, 74
  preparing for school board
    meetings concerning armband
    controversy, 31, 37, 44–45

profile of, 9–11
  reactions to oral argument in
    Supreme Court, 157, 161
  reactions to Supreme Court
    decision, 183
  referred to at district court trial,
    79–80, 90, 93
  referred to in oral argument
    before Supreme Court, 144,
    151–52, 154, 158–59
  role in planning armband
    demonstration, 2–3, 5, 7–8, 15,
    99, 138
  since Supreme Court ruling in
    *Tinker*, 199, 204–6, 212, 216–17
  testimony at district court trial,
    85–88, 97
  *See also* Johnston, Dan; Tinker,
    John; Tinker, Mary Beth
Eckhardt, Margaret
  agreeing to serve as plaintiffs in
    armband case, 8–9
  attendance at oral argument
    before Supreme Court, 144, 158
  characterization of by school
    district attorneys, 119, 141–42,
    158
  at district court trial, 79
  introduced, 2
  as object of community attention,
    31, 37, 40, 44, 52, 55, 58
  participation in school board
    meetings on armbands, 33, 46
  preparing for appeal of district
    court ruling, 104–6, 108, 110
  preparing for armband
    demonstration, 3–4, 85, 87–88,
    126, 137–38
  preparing for district court trial,
    56–57, 61–64, 66, 71
  preparing for school board
    meetings, 21, 27, 29

{ *The Struggle for Student Rights* }